KT-416-470

'If you're dreading a weekend car trip with small children, this book can't fail to cheer you up.'
DAILY MIRROR

04407721

ARE WE NEARLY THERE YET?

BEN HATCH

A FAMILY'S 8,000-MILE CAR JOURNEY AROUND BRITAIN

summersdale

ARE WE NEARLY THERE YET?

Copyright © Ben Hatch, 2011

All rights reserved.

No part of this book may be reproduced by any means, nor transmitted, nor translated into a machine language, without the written permission of the publishers.

The right of Ben Hatch to be identified as the author of this work has been asserted in accordance with sections 77 and 78 of the Copyright, Designs and Patents Act 1988.

Summersdale Publishers Ltd
46 West Street
Chichester
West Sussex
PO19 1RP
UK

www.summersdale.com

Printed and bound by CPI Group (UK) Ltd, Croydon, CR0 4YY

ISBN: 978-1-84953-155-9

Substantial discounts on bulk quantities of Summersdale books are available to corporations, professional associations and other organisations. For details telephone Summersdale Publishers on (+44-1243-771107), fax (+44-1243-786300) or email (nicky@summersdale.com).

To the two 'D's: my dad and wife Dinah

Ben Hatch lives in Hove, East Sussex. His first comic novel, *The Lawnmower Celebrity*, which was republished under the title *The P45 Diaries* in 2013, was based loosely on his time as a chicken sandwich station monitor at Darlington McDonald's, and was one of Radio 4's eight books of the year in 2000. His second, *The International Gooseberry*, about a hapless backpacker with a huge ungovernable toenail, was published in 2001 and described as 'hysterical and surprisingly sad' by the *Daily Express*. Ben was on the long-list of Granta's 2003 list of the most promising 20 young authors in the UK. With his wife Dinah, he has also written three guidebooks – *Frommer's: Scotland with Your Family*, *Frommer's: England with Your Family*, and *Frommer's: Britain for Free*. Ben's next big journey is recounted in all its horribly accurate detail in *Road to Rouen* (2013).

CHAPTER 1

The splurge of bags on the pavement is so huge and unruly it reminds me of news footage of a French baggage handlers' strike. It's bad enough going on a week's holiday with two under-fours. But packing for a five-month road trip – you'd struggle to get all this in a Pickfords van.

'Two more for you, love,' Dinah says brightly, shuttling from the hall to the kerb with two more suitcases I'm expected to find room for.

'Do these contain any more pairs of your boots?'

'Getting stressed, love?' says Dinah.

'No, but it's like being on the bloody *Krypton Factor*. Inside these two rectangular spaces – the boot and the roof box – there's only one way to fit all these incredibly complicated three-dimensional shapes.'

'Well, this is clothes.'

'Honestly?'

'What are you saying, Ben?'

'Dinah, are there any more shoes of any description in these two bags?'

She laughs.

'Darling, I've packed all my shoes.'

'Because I'm going to open them and check.'

'I thought we agreed no shouting this morning.'

I start undoing the zip of the first one.

'OK, OK,' says Dinah, rushing forward, delving into the case and pulling out a pair of black heels.

'I can't believe you.'

'It's just one pair, Ben.'

'That you actually wrapped in a towel to disguise!'

'You're not a girl. You don't understand.'

It takes an hour to cram it all in and when I'm done, without blowing my own trumpet, it's a piece of genius. I walk into the kitchen, arms aloft.

'And tonight's winner with a Krypton factor of forty-six is Ben Hatch, the computer programmer from Yeoooooovvvvvvil. You've got to look at this.'

Dinah follows me outside.

'You got the travel cot in, then?'

'In the roof box.'

'Very good. And the kids' clothes bag?' She peers into the car. 'Between their seats. Nice one.'

'Told you.'

'Oh dear, are you going to tell me again how only a man can pack a boot?'

'I am. We have a natural feel for space. That's why we load dishwashers. And how many professional female snooker players are there?'

'What?'

'How many pro snooker players are women? I'll tell you: none.'

'You know that, do you?'

'Yep. Angles, you see. We know about angles. We know how many bumper packets of Pampers size five nappies will fit behind a wheel arch. You see?'

'Three,' she says.

'Exactly. And come round here. We know just how far you can squidge down a cool box containing breakable bottles of Dolmio Original Bolognese Sauce. We know to hold back padded items such as jumpers to stuff down the sides of a Halfords 250-litre roof box to reduce suitcase shunt.'

I open the roof box again.

'Very good,' she says.

'Shall I tell you how we do it? What we do is carefully hold a mental picture in our heads of everything that must be packed, the size and dimensions of the whole as well as how each packed item reduces this overall.'

'That's what you do, is it?'

'That's how we do it.'

'And everything's in?'

'Everything's in.'

'You sure?'

'Absolutely.'

'Including the double buggy that was down the side return about two minutes ago that I told you you'd forget?'

'Oh!'

'And the big green suitcase that was upstairs on our bed that I reminded you this morning was too heavy for me to bring downstairs?'

'I thought you brought that down.'

'And, by the way,' Dinah says turning to go. 'That Dolmio sauce *is* leaking.'

She holds up an orange-stained fingertip.

'WE ARE NEVER GOING TO LEAVE HERE!'

We've rented out the house through a holiday letting agency that has such strange kitchen inventory stipulations (butter dishes, tea cosies, a gravy boat) I can only assume they're lining us up as a Saga short break destination. There are landlord rules on the number of matching side plates and the precise ratio of egg cups to guest (0.75 to 1, for some reason). We should have tackled these requirements much, much earlier.

'OK, let's not panic, love. Now, where do we get a tea cosy from? Do they even still exist?'

'Dunelm Mill,' says Dinah.

'Where's that?'

'Worthing.'

'You want to go all the way to Worthing for a tea cosy! Where do you plan to go for the baking tray – Stoke-on-Trent? We need a department store type place.'

'Bert's Homestores on George Street?'

'OK, good, what else from there?'

'Maybe jelly moulds and the gravy boat.'

'We need jelly moulds?'

'That's what it says.'

'Who the hell comes to Brighton to make jelly? OK, it doesn't matter. Let's go. I'll drive. You nip in.'

We visit home-ware stores in an ever increasing frenzy, me mounting the kerb outside, say, Robert Dyas, putting the blinkers on while Dinah dashes inside volleying off enquiries like: 'Please help me, we need a Lancashire potato peeler' or 'Bath mats, non-slip – which aisle?'

Just to increase the pressure we carry out the 'professional clean' ourselves as well. We vacuum and make beds as the kids do their best to undo our good work. Every personal item – pictures, clothes, toys – must be locked away in the downstairs study. We drop off multiple sets of keys to the agency, photocopy gas safety certificates and accomplish a hundred and one jobs ten times harder to achieve when you've got two bored under-fours fed up with the colouring-in books you bought them specifically for this day, and who are at your knees demanding you 'spin me round really, really fast and then I climb on your back and be a nasty lion. I WANT TO BE A NASTY LION, DADDY.'

Finally, we're all in the car outside the house.

'And you definitely got the buggy in this time?'

'I definitely got the buggy in.'

'And the green suitcase?'

'And the green suitcase. And you've smuggled in all the footwear you need?'

'I have.'

'Good. We're ready then. OK, radio on.'

Dinah presses the button.

'A little higher.'

She turns it up.

The first song that comes on is 'Leaving On A Jet Plane' by John Denver.

'Very appropriate.'

I put my hand out. Dinah slaps me a high five. I put my hand round the back seats accepting low fives from Charlie and Phoebe. And although technically speaking we aren't leaving on a jet plane but inside a very cramped Vauxhall Astra diesel 1.1 hatchback so heavily laden I can't do over 35 miles per hour on the Kingsway without beginning to fishtail, it still feels perfect.

We pass Hove lawns and the blackened, burned-out skeleton of the West Pier. At the roundabout next to the Palace Pier, I shout over the music, 'Say goodbye to Brighton guys.'

'Goodbye, Brighton,' Phoebe and Charlie shout.

And as they continue shouting out up the Old Steine – 'Goodbye, lady at the bus stop, goodbye bus, goodbye tree, goodbye building' – what's seemed abstract for the months it's been in the planning suddenly becomes real. We are *actually* going.

'Can you believe it?' I ask Dinah.

'I can't really.'

'Are you scared?'

'A bit.'

'Me too.'

We're researching a guidebook on family-friendly attractions in Britain, have never done it before and it's something everyone's tried to talk us out of.

'Eight thousand miles in a small car with two under-fours. You're mad,' friends have told me.

'You'll get divorced,' Dinah's sister Lindsey warned.

My brother Buster's even predicted we'll end up murdering each other. 'A different hotel each night – packing up, moving on every morning, seeing four or five different attractions a day! For FIVE MONTHS! One of you is coming home in that roof box! Chopped up in a bin bag! You've gone loopy.'

But on this balmy spring afternoon, looking back at the Brighton sea, arranged in three perfect strips of colour – blue, green and turquoise – the sun warming my forearm through the open window, the music vibrating through me, watching the kids laughing in the back seat as they shout goodbye at more and more inanimate objects ('Goodbye building next to the other building' … 'Goodbye windows in the building of the building next door to the other building'… 'Goodbye person's face in the window of the building next to the other building), I know in my heart it's going to be magnificent.

CHAPTER 2

Draft Copy for Guidebook:
If its famous residents (Robbie Williams, Heston Blumenthal and Steve Redgrave, to name but a few) have earned Marlow the nickname England's Beverly Hills, then the North Bucks town's Beverly Hills Hotel is surely The Compleat Angler. The Georgian inn, nestling in the shadow of All Saint's Church, has beautiful views from its garden terrace to the cast-iron Tierney Clark suspension bridge and is where the Queen ate her first public meal outside London in 1999 and where many celebrities have dined including Princess Diana (pork), Sir Paul McCartney (fish), Clint Eastwood (ribs) and Naomi Campbell (OK, we admit – we have no idea what they ate). Set against the swan-clustered banks of the River Thames, a rowing seven glided silkily past as we climbed out of the car, creating such a quintessentially old English ambience we half expected to bump into Miss Marple enjoying an Eccles cake with her spinster pal Dolly Bantry in the hotel's Aubergine restaurant, which we walked through to get to reception.

Named after Izaak Walton's famous angling guidebook, The Compleat Angler's bedrooms are all themed after fly-

fishing terms. We stayed in Dibbling, complete with under-floor heating, Molton Brown accessories and a widescreen TV on which our bemused kids, whose only previous exposure to men on horses was a cartoon western, watched Channel 4 Racing ('Daddy, those cowboys are wearing funny clothes!').

As we fill out guest registration at The Compleat Angler, and Charlie keeps doubling back to stroke/dirty the paintwork of the sprinkling of super cars in the car park, a liveried porter passes behind us, according our three already-starting-to-split plastic Tesco carrier bags an embarrassing degree of reverence.

'Bless him. Look! He's trying to pretend it's normal luggage. That makes us look so chavvy, Ben. We must buy another bag.'

In our interconnecting rooms, clearly usually reserved for the disabled, Charlie has fun pulling all four red alarm cords in the bathroom and bedroom. Meanwhile Phoebe, obsessed with rabbits since I inadvertently let her watch *Watership Down* while we packed, methodically draws bunnies with ripped ears on hotel notepads, handing each one to me and demanding I put it in my pocket, as if to say, 'Look, I have no control over this. You exposed me to The General and this is the result.'

We'd planned to wander to Albion House in the centre of Marlow and pose a family snap of us all pulling scary monster faces outside our first attraction, the building where Mary Shelley finished writing Frankenstein in 1818. But with the restaurant not serving food until 7 p.m., Dinah bathes the kids while I go out alone.

Mary Shelley, aged nineteen when she lived here with her famous poet husband, wrote of Marlow, 'All your fears and sorrows shall fly when you behold the blue skies and bright sun of Marlow – and feel its gentle breezes on your face.' And although not all my fears have flown – it took me almost as long to find what we needed from the boot as it did to pack the entire car earlier – I do feel pretty good. It's a warm summer evening. The Thames slides past me. And, for the first time in years it seems, at 6.30 p.m. I'm not knelt on a sopping wet bath mat holding a teddy bear towel out, shouting over noisy splashing: 'For the last time – no more evil dolphins. If you want stories tonight, you must get out NOW!'

Marlow Historical Society describes Mary Shelley's house as 'the home of the monster'. It conjures up an image of a creepy, gothic-looking property beset by lightning flashes and thunder claps not quite drowning out the blood curdling wails of, 'IT LIVES!' Renamed Shelley Cottages, the house is now split into three twee, whitewashed homes. There's a blue plaque on the wall and the only mildly frightening thing is a man in a cable-knit cardy outside it recounting to a neighbour in terrific detail his delayed train journey from Maidenhead. I was going to persuade a passer-by to take a humorous snap of me outside the address looking cross-eyed, my arms outstretched, with two Molton Brown bottle tops I took from the hotel ablution basket pressed into each side of my neck. But unwilling to risk embroilment in the points failure discussion, I just take an establishing photo of the house and return.

The hotel's second restaurant, Bowaters, has views over the Thames, which is raised and fast flowing after a fortnight of rain. We feed the kids here, read them stories back in the room and rig up the Bébétel baby monitor, before returning to the restaurant ourselves. Our table is surrounded by well-fed city boys discussing the Bank of England's latest rate move with mobiles hanging like sunglasses from the middle buttons of their shirts. Dinah spots someone who looks like Nick Hewer, Lord Sugar's right-hand man from the BBC series *The Apprentice*. Although she's based this solely on the greying back of his head and four overheard words,

'The wine list, please', it's enough to fuel another discussion about Dinah's brainwave for a buggy with a special sleep compartment in it for an adult ('So the parent can hop in and catch up on sleep when their baby sleeps').

'Are you talking more loudly than normal, love, because you're a bit drunk or because you're hoping Hewer overhears and reports the idea to Lord Sugar as a business opportunity?'

She laughs. 'Let's imagine that.'

'OK. What would you do if Lord Sugar suddenly landed behind the hotel in his private helicopter and offered you £250,000 a year to develop the prototype for Amstrad? I'll be Sugar. You be you.'

'OK.'

''Ello there. I'm Lord Sugar, Britain's toughest boss. My eyes and ears Nick 'ere says you've 'ad a great idea. It sounds pretty 'air-brained to me, but I am willing to invest two 'undred and fifty grand in you because I like the way you weren't fazed bringin' them placcy bags into this 'ere posh 'otel owned by a good friend of mine.'

'I'm afraid my husband and I are currently writing a guidebook about travelling around England reviewing baby-changing facilities and kids' menus. Would it be possible to give you a ring in September?'

'You wouldn't say that.'

'I know.'

'Have another go?'

'Go and check on the kids first. It's your turn.'

Standing at the bedroom door I watch Charlie fast asleep in his travel cot. His face is pressed into the mattress and he has his bum in the air like he's praying to Mecca. Phoebe has arranged her limbs into almost exactly the shape of the emblem for the Isle of Man.

'Bum still in the air?' Dinah asks back at the table.

'About a foot off the ground.'

She laughs.

And, as the restaurant empties, and the city boys roar home to barn conversions in their Porsches and BMWs, and we learn that Nick Hewer turns out to be an innocent Mr Watson enjoying a birthday meal with his wife, we drink a toast.

'To the trip.'

'To the trip.'

We clink glasses. And, for some reason, looking at Dinah I feel quite emotional. About what? I'm not quite sure. That Dinah agreed to all this when initially she hadn't wanted to. That the kids are both safely asleep. And, of course, there's my dad.

Dad and my step-mum Mary had driven down to Brighton with a picnic hamper and a bottle of champagne to celebrate my birthday a couple of weeks ago.

'I won't kiss you. I've got a bit of jaundice. It might be a virus,' Dad said on the doorstep.

'He's gone a bit yellow,' said Mary.

'You look yellow,' I said.

'I'm yellow,' said Dad.

He walked inside and, in the kitchen, I'd lifted his sunglasses. The whites of Dad's eyes were yellow.

'Yellow,' said Dad.

We ate the picnic outside. Dad had ordered it from the deli in Chalfont St Giles. Salami, chorizo, olives, Roquefort, pumpkin and cream cheese delicacies. We said how lovely it was. Dad gave me my birthday present – a Rand McNally road map of Britain and a cheque for £100: 'To get the car serviced with.' On this map we showed Dad and Mary our proposed route around the country. They gave the kids a present each. Then back at the table we chatted – about Dinah's job, about Pen, my sister, and Buster, but Dad wasn't quite there. He read an article in *The Times*, his head held low. On the doorstep, leaving, he said he'd call after seeing the doctor. His hug was no stronger nor weaker than the one he'd given me when he arrived. I kissed Mary goodbye but, in her eyes, as they walked down the path, I saw something – a communication of fear.

Two days later Mary answered the phone. I asked for news. Mary said, 'It's bad.' There was a catch in her voice. 'I'll pass you to your dad.'

'My darling,' Dad said. 'I have written this down because it's too difficult to say.'

He started to read a letter he'd prepared. He'd seen the doctor, who'd referred him to a specialist. He'd had a scan. The results were not good. The specialist told him he had a massive tumour in his liver. There was evidence it had spread to his lungs and his abdomen. It was inoperable. Chemo would be useless. He'd asked for a prognosis and been told months, months in single figures. He realised this was a shock. It was a shock to him too.

'From looking slightly yellow to this in three days,' he said.

Mary and he would spend the night working out what to do next. He'd have a biopsy. We'd speak then. He talked about quality of life, decisions to be taken, but my head felt too tight to take in any more.

I was in Hove Park with the kids. I called Dinah.

'Oh, love. Where are you? I'll come and get you.'

I called my sister, Pen. 'It's not good,' I said.

'Tell me.'

I told her.

She cried.

I called Buster. The phone was engaged. Pen was telling Buster. I called Pen again. She'd spoken to Dad, was angry, didn't want to see him suffer like Mum, couldn't bear all that false hope.

She's getting better.

No, she isn't.

I leant on the metal fence surrounding the play park and I remembered standing by the stone wall outside the Chiltern Hospital talking to Dad about Mum when she was dying. 'Pace yourself,' he'd told me. 'Don't come home every weekend. I'll need you more towards the end. Pace yourself, my son.'

I tried Buster again. He sounded numb. We wondered how Dad would play it, couldn't imagine him dying, couldn't imagine saying goodbye. I called Dad back. He was drinking a twenty-five-year-old bottle of red wine. 'This is how I'll play it. Nothing will change. I will carry on as before and hope the momentum takes me over the line.'

And in the play park afterwards I couldn't stop hugging the kids. It was a strange genetic love chain. Dad was dying so I hugged my children, his grandchildren.

CHAPTER 3

*D*raft Copy for Guidebook:

Stratford-upon-Avon puts you in the forsoothing home of the world's most celebrated playwright, William Shakespeare. Sitting on the River Avon, the town is a pretty, time-capsuled monument to the Bard where you're never more than a codpiece away from an Elizabethan pub he supped in or a thatched cottage he gadzooked at. There are five properties owned by the Shakespeare Birthplace Trust that it is imperative you visit. Do not skimp and only go to Shakespeare's Birthplace. Do not think you can whip around Ann Hathaway's Cottage, poke your nose in Mary Arden's Farm, and then tell everyone you've done Stratford-upon-Avon. Get in there, do it properly and go to all the attractions, even Hall's Croft, owned by a friend of a friend of Shakespeare's uncle who wasn't really even his uncle but a family friend who once bought a glove from his dad or something we can't quite remember. Up to your neck ruff with the quill-scratching fiend? Take a family outing to nearby Warwick Castle, where admission includes a host of activities including archery and falconry demonstrations, as well as the firing of a colossal mediaeval trebuchet, all of which are perfectly timed so, if you rush madly between them,

alternately bribing and scolding your children to hurry up, you
can still just about miss every single one. For an extra £2.75 in
the Ghosts Alive Exhibition actors in period garb will jump out
at you when you least (most) expect it shouting chilling words
like 'murder' and 'killed' and 'Sir, can you move your bag – we
need to keep the thoroughfare clear.'

The first town we're blitzing is Stratford-upon-Avon. We picked it for
no other reason than Ettington Park Hotel on its outskirts was the first
hotel we blagged. Or rather that Dinah blagged, because she's been
blagger-in-chief. Whereas I have tended to cave in on the phone, and
lose my bottle, listening to Dinah, a seasoned travel journalist, over the
last few weeks knocking off the 150 free nights we've needed for this
trip, sweet-talking hotel chains, coaxing PR companies, and talking
us up to publicity departments, it's been like observing a slightly less
glamorous long con on an episode of *Hustle*. I say blagged, although,
of course, it's more complicated than that. Because our Frommer's
contract stipulates we aren't allowed to promise reviews in return
for freebies, something that could compromise the impartiality of the
guidebook, we've only been allowed to promise that a hotel offering
a free room will be *considered* for a review. Also, a complimentary
stay we've had to make clear doesn't guarantee a favourable review.
It's made Dinah's efforts even more sterling. We had a calendar on
the wall and every time she scooped a free room Dinah would raise
a hand mid call for me to slap her a silent high five. I'd cross out
the day and, if it was a particularly good hotel with grounds, twin
rooms, a parking pass, maybe an evening meal minus drinks thrown
in, when she came off the line, we'd conga into the garden to do a
victory circuit round the clothes line prop.

'She's blagged it, she's blagged it,' I'd sing holding her arm aloft.
'She's only gone and blagged it.'

'I've blagged it, I've blagged it,' she'd sing, as we kicked our legs out, 'I've only gone and blagged it.'

It was only later, blasé, spoilt and bloated on her success, I began to churlishly ask, after these celebrations, things like, 'But you did ask about a complimentary meal?' Or, 'Oh, so the rooms aren't interconnecting, then? That's a shame.'

Ettington Park is the former home of the illustrious Shirley family, whose ancestors fought with Henry IV and include the last nobleman to be executed for a felony in England. The house, with 40 acres of grounds, is also where the recipe for toad-in-the-hole was apparently invented, and helped inspire Shakespeare, a regular hunting visitor, to write his balcony scene for *Romeo and Juliet*. We have a two-bedroom suite with dinner and are about 10 miles away from the country house hotel, approaching the twenty-four-hour Tesco in Wroxton, when it suddenly comes upon me.

'You'll have to pull over,' I tell Dinah, 'I don't feel well.'

Now, my wife, Dinah, is lovely. She's understanding, patient, and innately kind. She's clever and has a great sense of humour. She's also my best friend and has been for the eighteen years we've been together. But if she has one flaw, it's her bedside manner.

'What?'

'I think it's that pan-fried duck last night. I feel terrible. You need to pull over.'

'Really? We're nearly there.'

Thick beads of sweat break out on my forehead. I'm going intermittently hot then cold. My stomach's pulsating like an electric current is passing through it.

'Please, don't make me spell out what's about to happen.'

'OK, OK,' she says. 'But we'll be late for the butterfly farm. And if you're going to be sick, open the window. We're going to be spending a lot of time in the car.'

She swings into the Tesco car park, finds a space and raises an eyebrow as I hurriedly undo my seat belt and make an unseemly dash for it.

'I told you,' she shouts, after me. 'We didn't need that extra carafe. Honestly, Ben! On our first night.'

After a sorry episode in the disabled toilet, Dinah upgrades my condition.

'Perhaps you've got a bit of food poisoning,' she says, when I return to the car, ashen-faced. 'Although I'm fine and we had the same thing. Have you got that window open? You stink.'

We planned to drop the bags off at the hotel and drive to the Stratford Butterfly Farm and then visit the various Shakespeare attractions, but a few miles further on, I take a turn for the worse and I'm forced to ring ahead for an early check-in at Ettington Park while Dinah keeps the children abreast of developments.

'Guys, I'm afraid Daddy's not feeling well.'

They're busy watching *Finding Nemo* on our new cheapo Argos DVD player that disconnects from the cigarette lighter socket and sends the film back to the beginning every time the person in the passenger seat so much as scratches their leg.

There's no response. Dinah leans over me and pauses the movie.

'Guys, listen to me. Dad's got a poorly tummy, so there's a problem with the butterfly farm, OK?'

A big 'Awwwwwwww' from the back now.

'But if you like we'll drop Daddy off at the hotel where he can carry on being sick and *I'll* take you.'

'HOORAY!'

There's still a slim chance I'll make it in time until Dinah takes a wrong turn a mile from the hotel, confusing the A3400 with the A429. 'Oh, that's strange – there's supposed to be a right turn here.'

'DINAH! PLEASE!'

As she pulls into a lay-by, rings Ettington Park for directions and becomes frustratingly embroiled in a conversation about the precise timing for high tea, I cannot even swear at her. Incapable of full sentences, my entire being is focused on maintaining control of what I'm fast losing control over. Instead I punch my upper thigh in the passenger seat rhythmically with a clenched fist and, like a heavily pregnant woman whose waters are breaking on her way to hospital, implore her, 'Faster, faster, faster!'

Dinah finds the driveway to the sixteenth-century mansion, but just 200 yards from the sweeping gravel entrance I'm compelled to spring from the still-moving car and dash for the trees, scrambling up a steep grassy bank to relieve my front and back ends ignominiously behind an oak tree like a sick animal.

As I climb back into the car, Dinah says 'Oh, Ben!', as if I've just done something on the same incorrigible par as maybe neglecting to recycle a wine bottle.

In the room I run a deep bath and am left mercifully alone to equalise my blood sugars with pints of Coca-Cola whilst half-heartedly reading about experimental new jams in *Cotswold Life* magazine. It's in here that I overhear Phoebe telling room service staff arriving with more Coca-Cola, 'My daddy ate some meat that wasn't cooked properly and did a poo in the grass. I'm making him feel better by stroking his head.' Although actually what she's doing is just wandering into the bathroom occasionally to stare at me and ask with curious detachment, 'When are we going to the butterfly farm, Dad?'

When Dinah leaves for Stratford-upon-Avon I discover the staff are mostly slightly po-faced East Europeans. Sample conversation:

'Sorry, do you have any more blankets – I'm cold.'

'No.'

'Could I get some sent up?'

'No.'

'Maybe I should ring the manager.'

'That is up to you. This is my first day.'

But eventually I fall asleep. When I do I dream about my dad.

CHAPTER 4

As a kid when I couldn't sleep my dad would lie next to my bed. When I cried he'd dab my eyes with his hanky and make me laugh. I loved the smell of his aftershave when he kissed me on the forehead in the dark early mornings before he left the house. My dad was a ball of competitive energy and good humour, who did everything 10 per cent more noisily, better, and 10 per cent more showily than anybody else. He'd slap imaginary dust from his legs like a cowboy when he walked. Choosing a wine from the drinks cabinet he would cuddle the bottle like a baby and stroke the label like it was a beautiful face. He performed imaginary rowing strokes with his arms and shoulders when pleased with himself. He was always immaculately groomed but always in incredibly bright, ill-matching clothes, the more garish the better – multicoloured jumpers, green suit jackets, yellow trousers, pink sweaters, socks with Dennis the Menace on them. He wore Dr Who scarves, novelty ties and braces and spoke like he was reading the news; great pauses for emphasis, like Brian Perkins. He also had the best laugh in the world. When my dad laughed he'd lean so far forward he'd nearly fall over and have to grab your arm to stop himself. He'd throw his whole head back and roar like a bear.

28

'Ben, what are you doing?' says Dinah.

I'm sitting on a chair at the end of the bed doing my laces up.

'Going on a run.'

'What?'

'And to take pictures.'

'It's six in the morning!'

'We missed a day yesterday.'

'And what are you wearing?'

'You forgot to pack my trainers.'

'*I* forgot!'

'One of us forgot. I've got nothing else.'

'They're suede, you'll ruin them.'

She bangs her head back down on the pillow.

'No, Dinah,' she says to herself. 'Don't get involved. OK. Just go, then. Go on. But please don't wake the kids slamming the door.'

I drive into Stratford-upon-Avon. I park, and run round photographing as many attractions as possible, while casing the town for later. I run up Henley Street and snap the thatched Shakespeare's Birthplace museum. I snap Thomas Nash's half-timbered house. I snap almshouses, swans on the River Avon. I snap anything that looks vaguely historical and wind up on the banks of the River Avon at Holy Trinity Church, where Shakespeare was buried. It's 8 a.m. and a Sunday holy communion service is in full swing. I want to look at the bard's tomb and photograph it to tick it off my list, but something tells me it might be disrespectful to wander past the reverend mid prayer to snap it. Instead I sit at the back of the church. There are about thirteen pensioners in here and I start to feel conspicuous. Since Dinah forgot to pack my trainers and also my running shorts (whilst remembering ALL her shoes) I'm in suede brogues, nylon swimming shorts and, because I didn't want to wake the kids rifling through bags, the T-shirt I slept in.

Sweating lightly from my run, I start to feel a great whirr inside me. It's like a great turbine starting up.

My dad always used to tell me – whatever it is you do for a living, be the best you can at it. 'That's all you can do. Talent will out, my son.' At the time I was the McChicken Sandwich station monitor at Chesham McDonalds in charge of ensuring the correct proportion of shredded lettuce and mayonnaise was added to the breaded chicken meat patty, so it didn't mean that much. I was dismissive of him. But he carried on telling me the same thing throughout the years I struggled to make it as a novelist. It helped me carry on believing. I picture my dad now, the yellow whites of his eyes, Mary's look of fear on the doorstep, and, as I listen to the creed, I feel a sort of epiphany. My dad's father, Raymond, was a vicar. My Uncle Dick was one too. Maybe it's something to do with these connections. And churches always make me think of Dad. I close my eyes and try to feel the spirit of Shakespeare within me, to be moved by the Lord, communicated with in some way, but all I sense is the sweat running down my back. Instead, I make a pledge in the church where Shakespeare lies buried – this is how I'll compensate for not being with Dad for the next few months. What I'll do is write the best guidebook I can. I'll write the best guidebook that's ever been written. I'll revolutionise guidebook writing. I'll turn guidebook writing into an art form. The guidebook won't only contain practical advice about admission prices, it will include personal stories about what happened to us. It will tell a subtle, truthful yet inspiring story, between the reviews and the plonky detail about ticket admission prices and the availability of baby-changing mats.

Back at the hotel I bully everyone up. Dinah protests.

'I haven't got my lenses in yet. Slow down. What's the matter with you?' But I brook no opposition. We must see things and record their child-friendliness right now. After a frustratingly slow breakfast ('He's two – he can't eat scrambled egg any faster without choking, Ben. And that tablespoon's far too big for his mouth.') we check out. I drive us to our next hotel, Alveston Manor, in the centre of Stratford-upon-Avon and frog-march us to Shakespeare's Birthplace, where we hear an impromptu Shakespeare Aloud soliloquy from *Macbeth* in the courtyard, tarnished only slightly by Charlie wiping an eggy hand down a pair of MacDuff's pristine white tights. We move to Nash's House, where Phoebe develops a kleptomaniac tendency to snatch information leaflets on other attractions featuring anything in cartoon form or showing an animal from every display case we pass. She carries them in her Dora the Explorer rucksack that, finally too heavy for her by the time we reach The Shakespeare Experience, she hands to me.

'You carry Dora bag.'

Already with a camera, a notebook, my iPhone, a mini computer to write my notes up on and a wallet, I can do without more baggage, but when I try to put the bag in the buggy basket I'm reprimanded, 'No, YOU carry it, Daddy. YOU do it.'

After visiting Mary Arden's Farm we board the City Sightseeing bus. Phoebe and Charlie want us all to sit on the top deck, where they stand on the seats, dodging the overhanging branches that threaten to decapitate them on the way to Anne Hathaway's Cottage. They charge around the deck ricocheting, as the bus rounds corners, off seats and people like giant pinballs. The on-board commentary is drowned by Phoebe's rival tour.

'Listen to my talk, Daddy. That's a car,' she says, pointing. 'That's a tree. That's another tree and that is a house, Daddy. Daddy, do you like my talking?' Shouting now, 'I SAID DADDY DO YOU LIKE MY TALKING?' We're forced from the bus not by this, but by Charlie, who, anxious to be walking about, protests at his confinement in Dinah's arms by emptying her purse, that she's given him for some peace and quiet, on the floor of the bus; which, as it's navigating a roundabout at the time, spreads the purse's contents to the four corners of upstairs, forcing Dinah and me to crawl on our hands and knees under the seats of Japanese tourists to pick it all up. 'Sorry, these are my wife's keys... If you could just lift your *As You Like It* goody bag...'

After the tour I marshal the family to the riverbank, where we board a Bancroft boat cruise. On a pootle up the River Avon we see rowing boats and mini flotillas of ducks. Swans and Canada geese line the banks. Dinah trails her hand in the cool water. Charlie shouts and points at passing wildlife: 'A DUCK. A SWAN. ANUDDER DUCK. ANUDDER SWAN.' Phoebe draws more injured rabbits in my notebook.

'That's lovely, Phoebe. But where's the other leg?'

'Bitten off.'

'What are the red lines for, pops?'

'Blood. Mummy, do you want a scratched one with one leg, or one with an eye missing?'

'Phoebe, you know that film that Daddy let you watch with the rabbits in it? It was just pretend, you know that, don't you?'

'Of course, I know that.'

We're in the hotel's oak-panelled restaurant listening to a cartoonish Lancashire couple and their ten-year-old son, who for the last twenty minutes have been boastfully debating their knowledge of where it's safe to drink tap water ('Now, Tunisia, you must never have ice in your drink...') while also chronicling their outrage that on their side plates they've been given tomato bread ('Tomato in bread! That's messing bread about!'). They've now moved on to the concept of baggage handling at hotels.

'Now at the Imperial,' he's saying, 'they park yer car for yer, someone takes yer bags. Then when yer get to yer room... they're there! Tha's class.'

'It's weird,' says Dinah. 'You say these things to me, I don't know, like we're going to buy a house, or we're going to write a guidebook, and I never think they'll come off but in the end they almost always do. I think I'm going to start listening more closely to what you say to me.'

'So how's it going so far?'

'Shitty start.'

'Literally. But overall?'

'Good. Although don't take this the wrong way...'

'You think we did too much today.'

She smiles. 'A bit.'

I tell her some of what I was feeling in the church. When my mum died thirteen years ago it knocked me sideways, sent me off the rails. A bit of me feels guilty this hasn't happened yet with my dad. Maybe I'm more grown up, or it's easier because Dad's older or the second parent. Whatever it is, while half of me wants to be by my dad's side living every cough and spit, every new drug, every scan, every appointment with the consultant – the way I did when Mum got sick, the way Penny and Mary are now – the other half of me wants to be as far away as possible to protect myself. I don't want to see him fade away and I don't want to risk going too deeply into the black hole of bereavement in case I come out somewhere different and jeopardise everything I have now, like my family.

'OK, why would you lose your family?' asks Dinah.

'I don't know. What happened before.'

Dinah and I split up for a while after my mum died.

'That was different, Ben.'

'Was it?'

'You were a bit of a twat then,' she says.

'Thank you.'

'You're not any more.'

'Such praise.'

'You know what I meant, Ben.'

'I have ceased to be a twat. That's good news. Should I make an announcement? Put an ad in *The Times*. Ben Hatch would like it to be known he is no longer a twat. Births, deaths, marriages and people who are longer twats.'

'Have you exhausted that one?'

'I think so.'

'Good.'

I ask for more wine. It comes. I top up our glasses.

'You never know what will happen when someone you love dies. That's all I'm saying.'

'I see. And this is why we had to go to Nash's House even though it wasn't child friendly? And is that why you were cross with me for having shortbread cake in the cafe? Because it's what your dad would have done – got stroppy because everyone wasn't marching to his orders. That's your way of feeling close to him, acting like him?'

I think about this.

'I do feel my dad growing inside me.'

'You're nothing like your dad. You always say that.'

'I think I'd like to be now.'

'Oh dear,' says Dinah.

'The good bits. The nice bits.'

'Please don't get up at six tomorrow.'

'I don't think I'd be able to.'

The waiter comes over. We sign for the bill and, as we get up to go, from the neighbouring table we hear him moving on to underwear. 'It's not lazy – it's common sense because I can go fifty-seven days wi'out a change of underwear. I've got a hundred and two pairs of boxers and fifty-seven pairs of socks. Now, if I had more socks...'

CHAPTER 5

*D*raft *Copy for Guidebook:*
On May 14 1796, Edward Jenner performed the first
successful vaccination for smallpox, the cancer of its time,
a disease accounting then for one in ten deaths worldwide.
Smallpox, around since ancient Egyptian times, had wiped
out the Aztec civilisation, and by the eighteenth century
was responsible for the deaths of 400,000 Europeans each
year. The disease attacked lungs and the blood, covering
sufferers in hideous blisters, making beauty spots and
women's veils must-have eighteenth-century fashion
accessories.

Jenner (1749–1823), a country GP, noticed, like many
others had before him, that milkmaids rarely contracted the
disease. He wondered if it was the less virulent cowpox they
caught from cattle which protected them. To test his theory
he infected his gardener's eight-year-old son, James Phipps,
with cowpox and once he'd recovered, with smallpox. The
boy survived, a mass government-led immunisation followed,
and by 1980 smallpox was eradicated from earth save a small
sample kept in an Atlanta lab. It's estimated Jenner's work
saved half a billion lives.

We're at Edward Jenner's former home, a grade II listed Queen Anne mansion in Berkeley, Gloucestershire. The kids are tearing around Jenner's recreated study wearing the stick-on smallpox blisters we bought them from the gift shop while Dinah and I are marvelling that, despite saving more lives than anyone in human history, Jenner still found time to be the first person to notice that a) hedgehogs hibernate and b) birds migrate south for the winter. Not only that, it was Jenner who revealed the precise way cuckoo chicks use a hollow in their backs to hoof rival eggs from their host's nest, while also laying claim to being the first man to fly in a hydrogen balloon.

We're walking from Jenner's study to the Temple of Vaccinia, a small thatched outhouse next to the house, where Jenner inoculated the village poor for free.

'Wow,' says Dinah. 'I think I love Jenner. What an incredible achievement.'

'I know. Can you imagine what half a billion people looks like? What's that, five thousand Wembley stadiums full of people? And think of all these people's children and the generations of their children. Half the world's population is probably down to Jenner.'

'Actually, I meant the hedgehog thing,' says Dinah.

'You are joking!'

She pulls a face.

'Of course I am, you dozy twat.'

We pass a gallery of pictures of smallpox victims that a couple of Jenner volunteers are gathered round. The faces of the sufferers are so raised and distorted with blisters and welts they look barely human.

'Look at my face, Dad,' says Phoebe.

'Oh no, Phoebe,' I say. 'What's the matter with your face? Look at Phoebe's face, Mummy.'

One of the Jenner volunteers looks round just as Phoebe whips it off. 'Only joking, Dad! It's just pretend. I haven't *really* got smallpox. LOOK! It's just the sticker you bought me.'

'Phew-weee. That's lucky, Phoebe.'

Staring at the volunteer, who's looking pityingly now at the children for having parents like us, I add, 'Because I thought for a moment, Phoebe, the raised lesion was a precursor to sub-conjunctival bleeding, fever and respiratory failure. Time to move on, kids.'

I smile at the volunteer.

'Bring your smallpox pustules with you, guys.'

Outside Jenner's house, Dinah says: 'OK. Two choices. Berkeley Castle, which you have to go on a guided tour of, and this is bearing in mind the kids are knackered and will go mad, that there are probably loads of steps, and one of us will end up carrying Charlie the whole way round and it's also already 4.30 p.m. so they'll be late for bath and bed. Or we could go back to the hotel to watch telly?'

'HOTEL,' shout the kids.

'Can't you give me more of a clue what you prefer, love?'

Dinah laughs.

'Actually, though, I still prefer the castle.'

The kids groan.

'Only kidding! The hotel FOR TELLY!'

A belt up the M5 later, we're lying in a line on a double bed, munching complimentary ginger biscuits and watching CBeebies at the Cheltenham Chase, a business-orientated hotel within sight of the famous Cooper's Hill, where around forty foolhardy thrill-seekers are annually stretchered to hospital after chasing a wheel of Double Gloucester cheese down a vertiginous 2 in 1 gradient.

We watch *Chuggington*, *SpongeBob SquarePants* and *Underground Ernie*, after which in the bath before dinner Phoebe tells me a little more about Mr Nobody, a tiny invented character only she can see, who at home lives in an empty wine bottle in our recycling basket in the kitchen, but who sneaked into the boot, to come away with us on the trip.

'He found some space in the boot, did he? Did Mummy smuggle him in with her shoes?'

Dinah smiles.

'Yes, and do you know what else, Dad?'

'What, pops?'

'He brought his whole family with him.'

'Did he?'

'Yeah.' She nods vigorously. 'Brother Nobody, Sister Nobody and Mummy Nobody. He did.'

'I thought they had jobs. How did they get the time off?'

Back home Phoebe's already told me Mr Nobody and Mrs Nobody both have mini computers and tiny chairs and work in the study beside me and Dinah on our desktop.

'They're on holiday. Of course, they're on holiday. Why wouldn't they be on holiday? AND do you know something else about Mr Nobody?'

'What's that, pops?'

'He's writing a guidebook for Frommick's. He is.'

I laugh.

'Not Frommer's?' asks Dinah, smiling.

'No, Frommick's. It's like Frommer's. But it's Frommick's. He's writing a guidebook and he has to take loads of pictures of Sister Nobody and Brother Nobody and visit museums and castles and drive for miles and miles every day.'

I look at Dinah.

'And is that fun for them?'

'They get biscuits, of course it is.'

Dinah takes the kids downstairs to satiate whatever appetite they have remaining after the two packets of ginger biscuits, while I edit the photos and write up my notes. An hour later, after we've put them to bed, alone in the restaurant, Dinah and I go through our highlights so far.

'I think we can be nostalgic already, don't you?'

'I think so.'

'OK, funniest moment?'

'Definitely the look on that volunteer's face today when Phoebe whipped that smallpox blister off.'

'That was great. The sanctimonious little shit. OK, most interesting place?'

After Stratford-upon-Avon we'd backtracked through the Cotswolds. We came through Oxfordshire, did a little bit of the Chilterns and then bombed down into Gloucester on the Welsh border. Highlights have included an afternoon at Blenheim Palace, Winston Churchill's former home, the acrobats at the middle-class Gifford's Circus in Stroud (no lions, and dried fruit handed out while queuing to get in) and an Oxford college tour. So far we've only had one argument, at the Ashmolean Museum, which happened after I accused Dinah of following an Italian man from the Arthur Evans Prototype gallery into Dynastic Egypt.

'Love, I didn't follow anyone.'

'The good-looking guy with the man-bag. You followed him.'

'Ben, I'd never follow a man with a man-bag. I hate man-bags.'

'Well, you followed him into Dynastic Egypt. I saw you.'

'I went into Dynastic to look at some ancient cursive script, my love.'

'Then you followed him to the sandstone shrine of Taharqa. You tagged him all the way to the Renaissance. You stared at him through that violin case exhibit. You spent ages at the Adoration of the Shepherds because he was there. Then you followed him into the Malley Gallery.'

'I was following Charlie. I was worried about the stairs.'

'God knows what you were up to in Treasuries when I had to double back for Phoebe. Why are you laughing?'

'Sorry. This is so funny,' she'd said. And even the argument had ended well. 'You think I was following a man with a man-bag. In a way it's really sweet. Come here, you jealous fool.'

'I bet I know what your most interesting one was,' says Dinah.

'What?'

'Blenheim Palace. Standing in the room Churchill was born in.'

'That was amazing.'

'Do you want to know what mine is?' Dinah pastes some cheese onto a cracker. 'It's not an attraction. Is that allowed?'

'It's allowed.'

'Aylesbury.'

'Ahhh. Being back in The Ship?'

She nods.

'Me too, actually. And seeing the house.'

I met Dinah on *The Bucks Herald* newspaper almost twenty years ago. We'd just finished our training and sat opposite each other at a desk overlooking Exchange Street just off Aylesbury High Street. We shared a phone – ext. 233 – and became friends over lunches in The Ship discussing the parish council meetings she'd skived off, and the quotes I'd embellished. She covered the satellite village of Princes Risborough. I was the main man in Wendover. All the reporters went out Thursday nights when the paper went to bed – drinks in The Ship Inn, Yung Ying chips and curry sauce under the John Hampden statue and a taxi home. Often Dinah took a cab back to the house I shared with Buster to watch one of his 'helicopter movies', as she called them, where she'd regale us over the action shots of Jean-Claude Van Damme about the celebrities she didn't think deserved their fame like Emma Bunton from the Spice Girls ('Just because she's got horse teeth. And she doesn't even look like a baby – I look more like a baby and I'm bubblier.'). When we kissed for the first time in The Ship Inn, 'Blackbird' by The Beatles played on the jukebox.

A few weeks later – sooner than I'd probably have chosen – she moved in. Buster had just landed a job presenting for the forces radio station, BFBS, and was relocating to Germany so I needed 'someone to cover the rent', as, Dinah joked, I put it so romantically. She slept in my brother's old room for a week until one morning after another night in The Ship, this time deploring The Corrs ('Silly Irish sisters dancing on tiptoes.' 'You're thinking of Michael Flatley's *Riverdance*. That's line dancing.' 'I know what I'm talking about – they spend too long on tiptoes.') she woke up under my duvet. Dinah was the first girlfriend I'd lived with and there was a thrill to the novelty of this dynamic: deciding which side of the bed to sleep on, who should put the bins out. We enjoyed apportioning responsibilities. I was Head of Security – locked the doors and closed windows at night and remembered to leave lights on when we went out. She cooked and cleaned, and seemed to relish this, dressed in rubber gloves and an apron with a picture of a teapot on the front. We competed at game shows – *Fifteen to One*, *University Challenge*, *The Krypton Factor* – and I came to realise something; that you didn't always need to go to the pub with your mates to have a good time. You could have just as much fun ringing programmes in *TV Quick* magazine with your girlfriend, working through a bottle of red wine, looking forward to a packet of Maltesers cooling to marble hardness in the fridge ready for the post 9 p.m. watershed movie, hopefully about the outbreak of a deadly disease threatening mankind.

'Tring Road,' I say.

She breathes in and sighs. 'It knocked me for six a bit.'

'Did it?'

'Even thinking about it now...'

'I know what you mean.'

I take a sip of wine and, when I look up, Dinah's curling a tear from her eye with an index finger.

'You all right?'

'Yes,' she says, laughing at herself.

I squeeze her hand. She pulls it away. It shoots back up to her eye to catch another tear.

'What's up?'

'It's just remembering,' she says. She half laughs. 'How happy we were.'

The waiter tops up our glasses.

'It was the little things I fell in love with,' I tell her later. 'Your hot red thighs when you came back from the gym.'

She laughs. 'My big fat thighs you mean.'

'No. I liked them. I still like them. The way you'd cook a saucepan of chilli, leave it out and live off it for a week sometimes. Heating the congealed slop up each night and eating a new square of it without ever contracting food poisoning. Your iron stomach, I suppose!'

She laughs.

I remember how Dinah began to treat me like a small boy within a few weeks of living under the same roof. 'You are *not* wearing those boxer shorts again. Give them here!' The habit she developed of sniffing me to see if I needed a bath. 'Get in there *now*, smelly boy.' The way she stared at my hands after a chicken fajita to check there was nothing on them I could wipe down the sofa arm. Her habit of placing kitchen mess – a dirty knife or an unwashed plate – under my nose like she was litter-training a pup: 'And I found it on the sideboard!' The delight on her face when she saw me in the bath. The pleasure it gave her to wash my hair. Her passion for buying scatter cushions, chunky candles and wooden tea trays. The love she showed for a perfume when she screwed the lid back on the bottle. The VAT-free children's T-shirts from Mothercare she squeezed into, which were, 'Good on one hand – they're cheap. But also bad, as many do actually have Care Bears on the front.' The way her green eyes turned a paler grape colour when she cried. Her stomp of a walk when cross. The quizzes we gave each other: 'My ex-boyfriend, who crushed the can of baked beans into his forehead in frustration at where our lives were going?'

'Pete.'

'No, Jeremy!'

'OK. Why did I resign from Copenhagen Reinsurance? I've told you twice.'

'Because you worked out the wrong insurance cover for a supertanker and got worried it would sink. My turn. OK, my mum's sister – what is the strange thing about her and margarine?'

Then there was the way we read the customer comments book in our local Tesco, those wonderful outpourings of bilious frustration we loved so much: 'Andrex £1.09 for four. They're 85p in Kwik Save. Rip off!!'... 'I do wish you'd remember to restock haricot beans!'... 'I'm not satisfied! Where is your ham roll?'

Dinah wipes away another tear.

'The waiters will think I'm being a bastard. Stop it.'

I stretch my arm out across the table, put my hand up her sleeve and grip her wrist.

'It also reminds me how old and grumpy we've got,' she says.

'You're not grumpy.'

'I am, and I'm fat.'

'No, you're not.'

'I am. It's thinking of Phoebe too,' she says. 'I don't know why, I have this image of her in my head, of driving to Little Dippers when she was a few months old, her face in the car seat next to me. That's the face I think about when she says something serious now.'

'I remember her birth,' I say. 'The way she plopped out. That birthmark on her back.'

'Those first six months,' she says, tilting her head. 'We'd go into her room sometimes just to stare at her.'

'I know.'

'I was so happy then,' says Dinah.

'Me too. But I'm happy now too. I want to freeze time, though. Stop everything where it is.'

'I know you do,' she says. 'Why are we sad tonight, Ben?'

'We're being reflective. It's the end of our first week.'

'Shall we go to bed?'

'I think we'd better.'

But we don't. We drink more wine and talk. I end up telling Dinah what I'd really like to do is convert our cellar into a laboratory so I could carry out experiments like a Victorian eccentric.

'Are you a bit drunk now, love?'

'Yes.'

Dinah laughs.

'I'd investigate the whole world. Everything. I'd be like Edward Jenner.'

'Would you, love,' she says, patting my hand.

'Yes, I would. I'd observe things like Jenner, carry out experiments. Dissect animals, birds, dead bodies, brains. I bet there are loads of other animals that hibernate or birds that fly places that nobody knows about.'

'Do you want to find things out about hedgehogs?'

'I do. I'd have loads of test tubes and conical flasks and Bunsen burners down there. Can you imagine it?'

'I can imagine smells wafting up into the kitchen from the cellar.'

'And there'd be explosions.'

She laughs.

'You wandering back upstairs looking a bit dazed.'

'My hair singed. My clothes in tattered rags.' I put on a German accent. 'Just a little less potassium pomegranate!'

She laughs. 'Come round here and give me a cuddle, you fool.'

I do what she says. I walk round the table and drape myself over her shoulders like a scarf.

'We're all right, aren't we?' I ask.

'Of course we are.'

We hold hands in the lift. In the room, just like at home, I fill two glasses with water. I leave one by her side of the bed and another by my own. I double check the door's locked.

'Head of Security,' she says, from under the covers.

'What I'd also like to do down in the cellar…' I start to say.

'Bedtime now, Mr Jenner,' she says.

CHAPTER 6

In the evenings Dad, home late, changed into the kaftan he preferred to pyjamas. He'd come downstairs, pour himself a drink and eat the dinner Mum cooked him on a little pine table in front of the telly sat on the floor, his legs threaded through the table legs. 'He, he, he,' he'd say, rubbing his hands together if it was yellow fish. His meals ended with a peanut butter and Marmite sandwich that he'd fold into his mouth in one go like he was stuffing a hanky in a breast pocket. Afterwards he'd haul himself back into his armchair where he'd watch telly until he eventually fell asleep and snored like a foghorn, his head tipped back like a lid.

Saturday morning was family time. We'd fly kites on Winchmore Hill, visit Whipsnade Zoo. Or we'd frequent garden centres and gift shops in Wendover and Weston Turville, tutting at the windmill memorabilia Dad was into. Because we lived in one, he couldn't get enough of things shaped like windmills or with windmills on them. Windmill tea towels, windmill plates, mugs, thimbles, a brass windmill bell, a miniature wooden windmill for the garden. Sometimes we'd visit other windmills, where Dad introduced himself as 'David Hatch, Cholesbury Windmill' as if it was some select club he belonged to that allowed us to have biscuits in any home shaped like ours.

'Come on, Dinah!' I shout at the closed door. I'm sitting on the giant green suitcase trying to close the zip. Dinah's on the dreaded tour with the hotel manager being led around their conference facilities, informed of their occupancy rates and other details we'll have no room for in our review. Meanwhile, Charlie, cleverly taking advantage of my preoccupation with packing, is quietly ripping up the *A Guide to Guest Services* handbook. At the same time Phoebe's putting her hand into a tub of her aqueous eczema cream and is smearing it all over the bedcovers. On the overhead telly *Survival with Ray Mears* is playing extraordinarily loudly because Charlie sat on the volume button of the remote. I finally close the case and then chase Charlie into the bathroom and yank the remains of the handbook from him like he's some kind of gun dog giving up a dead partridge.

'Please, guys, behave for Daddy.'

He throws his head back in a rage, bumping it on the toilet seat just as Phoebe knocks over an open bottle of shampoo on the bath rim that spills onto the tiled floor that Charlie then slips over in. Phoebe joins him and they writhe about in the VO5, laughing as the last of their clean clothes bite the dust, before Charlie scuttles away to indulge his new love – rifling through and tugging at potentially hazardous wires, this time on the internet set-up box behind the writing desk. Unsure where to begin clearing up after them, I stare at Ray Mears. Ray's thirsty in the outback, and has rigged up a transpiration bag to obtain water from the leaves of a eucalyptus tree. He's hungry and hot because he has no shelter. And I want to shout, 'Oi, Ray. Never mind your transpiration bag, bollocks to your lean-to shelter. Survive driving round England with two under-fours, staying at a different hotel each night and visiting four or five attractions a day. Sleep all in the same room then wake up at seven in the morning and do it all again the next day with the prospect of another one hundred and forty nights of the same – then come and tell me about survival in your khaki fucking shorts.'

I think you only really realise how bad a time you're having when you tell someone else about it. And sometimes your crap time can only get better once you've truly acknowledged it. We're in the gigantic Coventry Transport Museum. It's the largest museum of its kind in the world and I'm on my way back to the Maudsley Tea Rooms with Charlie's baby food, which I've returned to the car for, when I stumble accidentally into the Spirit of Speed Gallery. Thrust2, the former holder of the land speed record is here, along with ThrustSSC, the current holder, and there's also a ThrustSSC simulator. My simulated experience of Andy Green's 763-mile-per-hour record-breaking drive is made, if anything, marginally more exhilarating by Dinah texting every few seconds 'What are you doing?' then 'Hurry up, he's starving' and finally, 'If you're in that bloody simulator…'

We finally leave the museum after Phoebe almost falls off a nineteenth-century hay-fork tricycle in the Cyclopedia exhibition and Charlie throws a Jelly Tot at the Humber staff car driven continuously by Montgomery from the D-Day landings to the German surrender in 1945. Afterwards we're supposed to be visiting the Northampton shoe museum (or the Northampton Museum and Art Gallery, as it's officially known), but coming hot on the heels of my supersonic pelt across Nevada's Black Rock Desert, it doesn't seem quite right to charge around the M45 and back down the M1 just to stare at some East Midlands footwear, so instead I reinstate the Santa Pod Raceway Summer Nationals near Wellingborough onto our itinerary. Dinah previously vetoed the dragster event because, 'Oily men talking about Castrol GTX! Is that going to be fun for the kids?' On the way, Dinah first tries to re-interest me in the shoe museum ('I think there's a model of Emma Bunton in high heels') and, when this fails, infers the simulator and the prospect of seeing dragsters is making me drive too fast through the village of Podington.

'Slow down, Andy Green.'

'What?'

'You're veering all over the road. What's the matter with you?'

'I want to get there.'

'So do I. In one piece.'

And finally she sulks. 'Why are you railroading me? This is going to be awful. I thought we were going to make today fun.'

Whenever friends cautioned against this trip we countered smugly that in later years, when Phoebe and Charlie were broad-minded, implausibly well-rounded adults, they'd end up thanking us. This sense of a higher purpose ended a couple of days ago when Phoebe wet herself on a walking tour of Ledbury and the same day I lost the key to the roof box containing Charlie's nappy stuff – meaning we were forced to change him on a bench outside the Knight's Maze of Eastnor Castle using nothing but three tiny KFC lemon fresh wipes Dinah found at the bottom of her handbag. Tucked up in bed at 7 p.m. that night as the hotel had no listening service and the Bébétel baby monitor didn't work, the honeymoon period of this trip well and truly over, we'd held hands across the mattress, telling each other we just needed a routine. We got one. Phoebe wet herself the next day too, at the Elgar Birthplace Museum in Worcester, and, meanwhile, Charlie's new debilitating dread of wax mannequins meant he fixed himself to my leg like a shin pad the whole way through the Soldiers of Gloucestershire Museum ('Daddy, I want a cuddle.'). Crossing the Welsh border, we hit a new low when we realised after it rained in Cardiff that not only had Dinah forgotten to pack my trainers, she'd also forgotten to pack all our coats.

From not arguing, suddenly we were at each other's throats. At the Kington Small Breeds Farm Park Dinah and I even managed to have a dispute about which type of owl was best – tawny or barn ('Fuck off, you're just saying the opposite to annoy me – the tawny owl has much better directional hearing') – which led to Dinah storming off and calling me childish.

Dinah seems to have forgotten how to map read, too. Tired from Charlie's dawn feeds, she keeps failing to notice tiny things such as road numbers changing, keeps refusing to accept that bypassing cities is quicker than going through their centres ('It looked small, Swansea, on the map') and can't remember she's map reading at all if she's, say, reading an article about Gwyneth Paltrow's children in *OK!* magazine.

Our clothes, too. We can't afford to wash them in hotels, there's no time for a launderette and we've yet to stay in a serviced apartment. It's something Dinah's been blaming for her bad mood. 'I'm sorry, Ben. I struggle to enjoy myself when I actually smell.'

At the Santa Pod Raceway we stop at a booth to pick up our press passes. Each pass includes a passport-sized photo of one of us set against a chequered flag style background. Hung around our necks on lanyards they make us look like we maybe work for the McLaren team. And it's all looking up slightly, until I open the driver's door a few hundred yards from the track. The noise is incredible. It's so loud it's like a dozen jet engines all taking off at once.

In the stands, surrounded by men in Santa Pod caps and pro-drag hoodies eating chip cobs, it's even more deafening. Here it's like actually being *inside* a jet engine.

'We'll get used to it,' I shout across to Dinah, as she holds her hands over Charlie's ears and I do the same with Phoebe's.

We watch a series of races, which each last about eight seconds, and are categorised meaninglessly (for us) as things like: Super

Modified, Street Eliminator, Pro Stock Cars. After the VWs-with-modified-engines class race I risk a joke.

'Shame there isn't one for Vauxhall Astra diesels. I could buy some nitrous fuel and enter us.'

Dinah doesn't laugh. 'Do you see any other under-fours here, Ben? I'm going to buy some ear muffs. They'll get tinnitus.'

After buying the kids ear muffs at the Motor Shack, which they both refuse to wear, Dinah leaves to find the kids' caravan while I grimly stay on for Super Twin Top Fuel and the Outlawed Flat Four. The trouble is I don't know the drivers, or what the Summer Nationals even are exactly. I listen to overalled racers rueing earlier mistakes on the track ('I shouldn't have lent it so far over, John') as 'Ace of Spades' blares out of giant-sized speakers and begin to realise Dinah's right. The children's area, when I find it, is a static caravan, containing two other bored children colouring in pictures of super-bikes. Dinah's furious. 'Can we go now, please?'

In a last-ditch show of defiance on the way out I buy a chip cob and a 'Throttle in a Bottle' T-shirt for Charlie. And, to compensate Phoebe for maybe never again being able to hear properly in the presence of background noise, I treat her to the pod-racer dodgems next to the car park, where, after I'm told off for going the wrong way round the track, Dinah refuses to let me drive back through Podington again.

Inside Birmingham's National Sea Life Centre, our next attraction, Dinah won't talk to me even when I pass on an interesting fact about the shore crab having its nose under its armpit. She's up to some old tricks. She slows down her walk so if I continue at my normal pace it looks like I've stormed off. Her voice is quieter too, so whatever I say seems somehow louder, enabling her to accuse me of 'shouting' as well. An aquarium, however, is a dangerous place to fall out with your husband if you have chelonaphobia.

My wife, I must tell you, is scared – not just scared, terrified more like – of all tortoises and all creatures that look like tortoises including turtles. When she was seven and living in South Africa, so the story goes, she was confronted at a bunny park in Benoni by a giant tortoise she describes as being 'the size of a Fiat Uno'. Her dad had asked her to come and look 'round this corner, Dine' at something he'd found. After bursting into tears at the sight of the giant tortoise, and wetting herself, the fear was born. At home, if I show her a tortoise picture Dinah will irrationally attack me with whatever is in her hand. We cannot watch *One Foot in the Grave* because of the tortoise in the title sequence. Freelancing on travel technology stories in the study, her chelonaphobia isn't an inconvenience, but seeing as though virtually every day on this trip we're at some wildlife park, it's become one. Normally I rove ahead at risky attractions – aquaria, zoos (butterfly farms are particularly dangerous) – guiding Dinah through them by the hand like she's some geriatric pensioner with a shattered hip, as she holds up a brochure to her face on whichever side I've deemed 'the tortoisey one'. But there have been accidents, screams, a little bit of hyperventilation, and a few accusations (the Kington Small Breeds Farm: 'You bastard. You said they were hibernating.').

Today she has lost me. Today she's on her own. I sit on a bench outside the Atlantic Mirror Maze and guiltily watch her walk obliviously into the turtle sanctuary. I count to ten and sure enough, I hear a muffled scream and a few seconds later Dinah, red-faced and furious, scurries out. Ahead of the kids.

'You arsehole!'

I try to look shocked.

'What?'

'Why didn't you say something?'

'About what?'

'You know what.'

'What?'

'You must have seen those red-bellied turtles in there?'

'I didn't see anything.'

'They were right at the surface, Ben. They could have got out of their tanks.'

'Sorry, I was just sat here.'

'The kids drove me towards them.'

'Kids, you mustn't drive Mummy towards the turtles.'

In the cafe, before setting off, the kids busy sharing an Under the Seas kids' lunch box, we make up when I help Dinah complete a Sea Life Visitor Centre Survey. Under statement five: Queuing spoilt my experience? I cross out the word 'queuing' and replace it with the word 'turtles' and after this she ticks the box: I Strongly Agree. Thrusting it into the customer comments box, as we head for the car park, she says, 'I mean it. Someone should warn you how close they are to the surface. That was horrid. Horrid.'

On our last drive of the day the kids usually fall asleep. It's when Dinah and I tend to chat. We're staying in the Rotunda, an iconic cylindrical building next to the Bull Ring shopping centre that's been refurbished into luxury apartments. We have a penthouse on the twentieth floor and although I know she's been looking forward to it, Dinah's uncharacteristically quiet.

'Tomorrow will be better. Come on.'

'It's not just that,' she sighs.

'What's up?'

'You'll think I'm being silly.'

'I won't.'

'You will.'

'Try me.'

'I've been thinking about Sarah Smith again.'

Every journalist has someone they trained or worked with who, despite possessing more or less the same level of ability as oneself, goes on to have such a stellar media career, it can't help but prompt reflection on how you yourself went so wrong with yours. For Dinah it's Sarah Smith from her NCTJ journalism course in Preston. The story of Sarah Smith, now a high-flying national BBC news reporter, is more poignant as her sister Jacqui Smith was, until the last election, the Labour Home Secretary. Passing by the Smiths' house in Great Malvern the day before, Dinah had remembered sharing a baked potato there with Sarah Smith and Jacqui Smith and hadn't quite been the same since.

'Tell me you're not actually jealous that you're not the Home Secretary?'

Dinah laughs.

'No, but it does make you think. We're in our forties, Ben. It's a week day. Everyone else is finishing work now, coming home. We've seen a clown fish and a few Daimlers in Coventry.'

'What's your point?'

'These are economically supposed to be our most productive years. People are forging ahead.'

'Who's forging ahead?'

'Everyone we know.'

'Like who?'

She goes through a list of friends.

'You'd like us to forge more?'

'I don't know. I'm worried. Jacqui Smith's the same age as me.'

'So?'

'She's already been in charge of the country's entire national security. What am I in charge of? Remembering to pack Charlie's lunchtime pot in the emergency bag.'

'Which you forgot today.'

'Thank you, sensitive husband, for that.'

I try to persuade her to look at it another way – we're spending more time with our kids than anyone else gets to do. That's surely a bonus. But Dinah's unconvinced.

'But are they even enjoying themselves?' she asks.

'Not every minute. But they'd still misbehave at home. Of course they're enjoying themselves. They were cracking up in that mirror maze.'

'I know, I know. I'm just venting my spleen. Don't listen to me.'

'Anyway, imagine how shit you'd be in charge of national security. You crapped yourself about a turtle back there. Imagine a real threat. You'd lock down the country, call a state of emergency just because some pancake tortoise escaped from its hibernation box, never mind al-Qaeda.'

'And I'd definitely go to war with the Galapagos Islands.'

'Yeah, they'd be in big shit.'

The penthouse has an open-plan living area with designer furniture, Eames chairs and two 5-foot-high tripod standard lamps that within five minutes Charlie's knocked over. The views over the city are amazing, however, with floor-to-ceiling windows giving on to a wide glass-fronted balcony overlooking Digbeth and New Street train station.

Before bath and bed we watch *Charlie and Lola* on the widescreen TV. Charlie's on Dinah's lap, Phoebe's on mine. The episode is about Lola breaking Charlie's cardboard space rocket from the 'high shelf' in their shared bedroom. At the end of the programme as Lola says sorry, hugging Charlie, her eyes closing with pleasure as she clasps his neck, Phoebe says, 'That bit makes me want to cry.'

A tear rolls down her face.

'Ah, pops!'

'She's not crying, is she?' says Dinah.

'Yes. That's so sweet.'

I stroke the back of Phoebe's head.

'To stop myself I do this.' She widens her eyes and boggles them at me. 'I do it really hard and the tears go away.'

She pops her thumb back in. I give her a cuddle.

It's my turn to read Charlie and Phoebe a story tonight. Charlie bounces on my stomach laughing, Phoebe lies beside me with her thumb in. My heart sometimes feels like it will burst for them both. The love has a strange fleeting intangibility about it and seems always to disappear and be converted into the past even before I have properly grasped it.

After they're asleep, in the oak-floored living room sipping wine, making my notes, I say to Dinah: 'I think we're going to have to be more circumspect around Phoebe.'

Dinah looks up.

'I think there has to be no shouting in front of her. I'm not saying this has anything to do with it but she's very sensitive. You saw her tonight.'

'I know.'

'And her eczema's flared up again. Maybe it's stress.'

'Don't put that on me.'

'I'm not.'

'That's really unfair.'

'I'm not saying it's you. I'm saying *us* and it might not even be anything to do with it.'

'Point taken.'

I change into my pyjamas, and put on one of the fluffy dressing gowns left for us in the bathroom. Dinah does the same. But we can't relax. There are trendy designer books lying around about architecture and modern living like *The Phaidon Atlas* and a book called *21 Stories* (the number of floors in the Rotunda) containing sentences such as this: 'The rotunda has become a constant, sometimes subliminal presence in my life. It lives in the psyche of the city and its innate congenital knowledge…' Yeah, we want to say, but the curtains are too thin in Charlie's bedroom so he keeps waking up, the trendy chrome tap fell off in the bathroom just now, and when the washing machine's on it shakes the apartment so much it feels like we're in a rocket on the launch pad at Cape Canaveral.

'You're right about the shouting,' says Dinah, later.

'We'll argue in note form.'

'Rip out pages from notepads and pass them to each other,' she says.

We watch an episode of *Mock the Week*. Dinah says to me when it ends, 'We still love each other, don't we? We're not one of those couples who get divorced after the kids leave home. I know we argue but it means nothing.'

'No, we hate each other,' I say.

She smiles.

'Don't worry, we'll still be travelling when they've left home. We'll have plenty to do.'

'Of course we will,' she says.

We move on to the balcony. There's a distant squeal of train wheels from New Street station. The city stretched before us is a mass of orange lights. Dinah puts her arm round me.

'This is nice.'

'There's something satisfying about being this high up.'

'It must be a throwback to Neanderthal times – some dormant gene, being able to see your enemies approaching,' I say.

'The prey you're stalking. It makes you feel safe.'

'Tomorrow will be better,' I tell Dinah.

'Remind me again why we're doing this?' she asks.

Dinah was approached by Frommer's after her name was mentioned to the UK commissioning editor who was looking for potential guidebook writers prepared to travel with young families. We were broke. My novels had dried up, and in the economic downturn Dinah's freelancing had taken a battering. It was also the last summer before Phoebe started school. We wanted to make it special. Almost three and a half years ago, after Dinah's maternity leave ended, it made financial sense for me to stay at home and look after Phoebe while Dinah returned to work full-time. Mistakenly believing I could carry on writing 'because babies sleep most of the time', I was Phoebe's main carer for over a year before Dinah went freelance. It was me who saw her crawl the first time. I witnessed her first steps, her first smile. I was bitten by her first tooth. I remember once explaining this experience to a friend with a career that meant he spent weeks away from his kids. He assumed I felt marginalised, emasculated somehow or at the very least cheated by the way things had worked out. And in truth in the early days I had sometimes felt like this. But in many ways, although looking after Phoebe and later Charlie has been difficult, it's also been the most rewarding experience I've ever had, and one I was still not quite ready to surrender to anyone else. That's ultimately why we took on the guidebook. No tag-team parenting for a summer. All of us together for five months.

'Still think that way?' laughs Dinah.

'No way. Boarding school for her when we get back... Course I do.'

'Poor Charlie's ears in that stand.'

'I know, and Phoebe was cute on that huge bike.'

A glass of wine later, we admit we quite like the apartment after all. Half a bottle down we're flicking through *The Phaidon Atlas*, talking about the gaping-mouth style living rooms of the Netherlands' Sound Houses and the playful design of Peckham Library. We're using phrases like 'innate congenital knowledge of the design', and arguing about the 'clean lines' of the new EDF tower in Paris.

At midnight we turn in but I wake shortly afterwards feeling like someone has pressed charged heart paddles to my chest. I'm sweating, out of breath, gasping for air. The covers are stuck to my back. There's still an image from my dream burned into my mind like a date stamp. The yellowness of Dad's skin.

Dinah's looking at me holding her heart.

'Ben, you frightened the life out of me!'

'Sorry.'

'What's the matter? A nightmare?'

I nod. I sip some water. My heart's still pounding.

'I thought you were having a heart attack.'

'Me too.'

'You're sweating. You all right?'

'Yeah.'

'Come here. Two nights in a row.'

'I know.'

'I think you need to see your dad.'

CHAPTER 7

*D*raft Copy for Guidebook:
Springing to prominence during the Industrial Revolution, Birmingham – the former city of a thousand trades – now prefers to remind visitors it has more canal miles than Venice, more trees than Paris and is home to the brand new science museum Thinktank, which includes an IMAX cinema and planetarium, as well as a wildlife room where you can hear the various calls of the urban fox including hunger, fear and 'yippee I just found a whole Zinger Burger in the bin outside Moor Street Station'. At Cadbury World, meanwhile, you'll learn that tens of thousands of Aztecs died at the hands of brutal Spanish conquistadors in the sixteenth century, but that on the upside their defeat and extinction as a people led ultimately to the Curly Wurly. At this working chocolate factory you'll be rained on by Cadbury chocolate, see a giant Cadbury egg larger than a house, get to write your name in Cadbury chocolate, and in fact become so brainwashed by Cadbury chocolate that, opening a Nestlé manufactured KitKat for lunch, you might become as seriously scared as we were that a factory hooter will sound, and that you'll be suddenly swooped on by a team of purple and white uniformed Oompa-Loompas and maybe dunked in a tempering vat.

That's not to say, of course, that the whole bashing out of rivets side of things isn't well catered for in the Midlands. It is. In Ironbridge Gorge, Telford, there are ten separate attractions dedicated in such detail to the Industrial Revolution there's an actual museum of tar, the Tar Tunnel. If you visit one of these make it Blists Hill Victorian Town, a recreated industrial town, where we got to hang out in a Victorian pub and also saw unruly schoolgirls being rebuked for wolf whistling through a gap in the hoardings at Balfour Beatty builders working on yet another Industrial Revolution themed museum (the Museum of Rivets, The Museum About A Machine That Makes A Massive Clanking Noise – who knows?).

We're supposed to be visiting the Mappa Mundi in Hereford Cathedral but on the way, stopping to buy bottled water in Bromyard, Worcestershire, we see the sign: the Bromyard Museum, Time Machine and Coffee Shop.

'A museum, a time machine AND a coffee shop!'

We google it and are now faced with a tricky choice: Mappa Mundi, the thirteenth-century map of the world and treasure of medieval England, or The Bromyard Museum Time Machine and Coffee Shop, which has original *Thunderbird* and *Stingray* puppets in realistic studio settings *and* a jumper belonging to Sylvester McCoy.

Entering the museum through mocked-up Tardis double doors we descend into a labyrinth of underground rooms. Modern museums, bitten by minimalism, tend to be chrome, smoked glass, and interactive computer screens aimed at relaying the minimum amount of stupid-proof facts that attention-deficient visitors can absorb. Here displays are pleasingly handwritten, lengthy and personal and some of them are about Troy Tempest. 'This was the first colour TV series ever. It was fantastic,' one sign reads. There's a full-size David Tennant model next to a 6-foot Cyberman and, of course, the 'rare Sylvester McCoy pullover worn during *Remembrance of the Daleks*'.

'Does it actually say rare?'

'Yep.'

'Like there are other less collectible cardigans belonging to Sylvester McCoy?'

'I know.'

'That's brilliant.'

On another wall I show Dinah a picture taken in 1969 of the two owner brothers we met upstairs in the cafe, posing with their boyhood Action Men.

'And you haven't even seen Billie Piper's pyjamas yet?'

The giddiness increases when we come across a rare 'sexed doll' (it has genitalia) from 1860, and a scary-looking Armand Marseille bride doll with four even-sized fangs.

'A dolly with fangs. It's just so random here.'

'And earnest.'

'Earnest and random – the best combination.'

'Do you know what, I think if we actually came across Jon Pertwee gaffer-taped to a chair I wouldn't be surprised.'

We find a citation on the wall discussing how one of the two brothers met fictional astronaut Captain Paul Travers, the commander of the spacecraft *Zero-X* in the 1966 film *Thunderbirds Are Go*, in Coventry. But in 'Miscellaneous Toys', hysteria taking a grip, I have a disturbing thought.

There's been a spate of world news stories about creepy imprisonments in cellars. Nobody's been down to these rooms since we arrived. The museum's not on our itinerary so nobody knows we're here and there's no mobile reception.

'Stop it, Ben,' says Dinah, laughing.

'Why are you laughing, Mummy?' says Phoebe.

'Because Daddy said something funny.'

'Stop laughing, Mummy.'

But we can't because now it makes sense, the seemingly innocent 'everyone guaranteed to be exterminated' line we read upstairs. The fact the brothers didn't seem interested in our Frommer's credentials.

'We've been lured here.'

'Shut up.'

'They're probably dressing up as cyborgs right now. They'll come down the stone steps any minute to torture us when we fail to answer trivia questions about *Captain Scarlet and the Mysterons* correctly. "Please, let me go. I told you, I don't know who became a target for the Mysterons' powers of retro-metabolism in the 'Fire at Rig 15' episode of 1985."'

'Ben, stop it! They'll hear you.'

'When they tire of our inability to find merit in *Joe 90* we'll be killed, papier-mâchéd over and turned into Dick Tracy or a life-sized model of someone from *Blake's 7.*'

'Mummy, stop laughing.'

'I'm sorry, sweetheart. Come on, love. I think they've had enough.'

'Inkberrow,' says Dinah, reading from the blue folder. The blue folder is our bible. It's ring-bound and contains sixty typed pages in date order detailing everything we're doing over the five months, from attractions to meals out and hotel stays. The blue folder's so vital, and would be so devastating to lose, we have two copies, which like the US president and his vice president, never travel together. While the first blue folder (Blue Folder One) goes everywhere with us, the second (Blue Folder Two) stays permanently in the roof box.

'Inkberrow. That might be fun. That's the village where *The Archers* is based, isn't it?' Dinah asks.

'It is.'

'Ahhhh, did you put this on the itinerary for me?'

'I did.'

'Thank you, love.'

'It'll make some box copy, won't it?'

Dinah's such a fan of the Radio 4 farming drama, it's not unusual for her map reading to be punctuated during the show's broadcast with intermittent cries from the passenger seat of things like this: 'It's a Northumberland pig, what does he expect?' Or, 'Chris, for God's sake, you've your farrier exams to think of.'

Whereas I'm bruised from smug farmers' sons in the countrified Buckinghamshire village of Cholesbury making fun of my childhood inability to distinguish haylage from silage and because 'Ha ha ha, he doesn't even know the reversible plough counteracts downhill soil slippage', Dinah, brought up in the industrial town of Widnes, sees it all more idyllically.

The focal point of Inkberrow turns out to be The Forge Shop, where we stop to buy our lunch and a *Barney* magazine for Phoebe.

'If this really were Ambridge she'd be Susan Carter from the village shop,' Dinah informs me in the bread aisle about the woman behind the till.

'What was her name?' I say taking my notebook out.

'Susan Carter.'

I write it down.

The shopkeeper doesn't take credit cards but kindly lets me off a few pence when I haven't enough change for our ham rolls and outside, Dinah says, 'That's weird – I don't think Susan Carter takes Visa either.'

I take my notebook out and write this down too.

'This box copy,' says Dinah. 'Are you planning to take the piss out of me in it by any chance?'

Back in the car we follow the woman's directions to The Old Bull pub, where the show's stars gather sometimes for *Archers* reunions. The timber-framed pub doesn't open until lunchtime, but staring in through the windows Dinah starts to recount the heart-warming episode when Nelson lied about his age so he could take Mrs Perkins to an over-sixties tea dance, 'even though he was only fifty-seven'.

'You can't stop yourself, can you?' I say, taking my notebook out again. And soon she's spotting them everywhere. The faint sound of a woman's voice inside the pub – probably the cleaner's – reminds her of Pat Archer's. Whilst in the car park, a young guy doing a U-turn in his Citroën Xantia is, 'just like Ed Grundy. He was saved from crack addiction after Oliver Sterling entrusted him with his herd of Guernseys. That enough to make fun of me?'

'Plenty.'

Rejoining the A422, moving on now, reality and fiction begin to merge because *The Archers* comes on the air.

'Whoa!' we both say together.

Never mind that it's 10 a.m., the time *The Archers* omnibus has been broadcast since about 1821; we stare at each other in wonderment as if it's somehow our presence here that's sparked the show into life. Dinah cocks her ear and leans forward, as we half expect the plot to swerve into one about two guidebook writers driving around Ambridge with not enough money for a *Barney* mag. (The actual show cliffhanger an hour later about some Brookfield cheese with a lower than average fat content is, of course, only marginally more exciting.)

And as we leave the village and head towards Kidderminster, exhilarated by the sunshine, the views of the Welsh Black Mountains in the distance and the fact that we've already got two attractions under our belts by 10.30 a.m., we wind the windows down and shout Archerisms at passers-by through my open window.

'THINKS HE CAN TELL ME HOW TO RUN MY FARM!'...
'I 'EAR WILLOW FARM'S UP FOR SALE'... 'WHEN YOU'VE
GOT TB IN YOUR HERD YOU'RE VIRTUALLY POWERLESS.'
'Thank you, that was great,' says Dinah.
'Because the kids didn't get out of the car.'
'It's the secret of the family-friendly attraction.'
'Keep the kids in the car.'

Mostly we're welcomed at attractions – most want to be in our
guidebook. But occasionally the message hasn't got through to
the entrance gate, or the person I arranged free entry with is at
lunch or away, or in some cases the regional tourist board PR has
forgotten to clear it with the attraction. When this happens we flip
them our Frommer's business cards. Although, to be honest, we
might as well show off our Blockbuster memberships. Although
Frommer's is big in America and still growing fast everywhere,
it's still relatively new here and we're writing one of their first UK
guidebooks. It means this is usually how it goes:
'Hi, we're from Frommer's.'
'Frommer's?'
'The guidebook people. They're the equivalent of TimeOut in
America. I rang a few weeks ago.'
The person behind the desk usually then makes a phone
call. 'Duncan. We've got two journalists from... [looking at us
suspiciously] Where was it again? Flounder's?'
'No, a flounder is a type of flat fish best grilled and served with
lemon and sage. We're from Frommer's. FROMMER'S.'
At the entrance to the West Midlands Safari and Leisure Park in
Kidderminster today it's a slight variation. 'Sorry, did you say Frodo's?'
I look at Dinah.
'No, Frodo was the hobbit of the shire, who inherited Sauron's
ring from Bilbo Baggins and undertook the quest to destroy it in

the fires of Mount Doom. We're from Frommer's. FROMMER'S.'

The woman blinks once slowly, as if absorbing what I've said through her eyelids.

'If either of us were Frodo, we'd be much shorter, have pointed ears and probably be talking to you in an elfish language.'

The woman, still staring at me, reaches for her phone. Dinah looks admonishingly my way.

'Ben!'

'Weeell, I'm tired of it.'

When Frodo woman comes off the phone she asks us to back out and wait by a grass verge. The manager's coming down to see us.

'That temper of yours!'

'It'll be fine.'

I park up. Dinah laughs nervously. 'They won't call Frommer's, will they?'

'I haven't done anything wrong.'

The manager arrives in a jeep. He talks to Frodo woman at the kiosk and occasionally looks across at us.

We brace ourselves as he strides over. I wind the window down, but instead of being angry the manager has two glossy brochures, which he leans into the Astra to pass to me. I see him take in the unidentifiable smell as he does so. The unidentifiable smell has been around a few days. Is it the rotting banana in the driver's side pouch? Maybe. Is it coming from the stain on the middle of the back seat that might or might not be Dairylea Dunkers related? Could be. Or perhaps it's the Tupperware container of spaghetti sauce between the front seats that's crusted like dried paint? Another good guess. I watch the manager take in the empty sweet wrappers, the empty crisp packets and the filthy back-seat footwells knee-deep in toys, books and hardened bread crusts as I pass the brochures back to the kids.

'Guys, can you thank the man?'

'Thank you,' they chime but, immune to these after three weeks on the road, they're dropped unceremoniously to the floor with the rest of the rubbish.

'They'll probably look at them later.'

The manager withdraws his head and drinks in some fresh air. Embarrassed now, to change the subject, Dinah indicates the 'Animal food for sale' sign on the kiosk window and asks the manager what the food is, maybe expecting a bloodied side of impala to be tossed into our boot for £3.

'One second,' says the manager.

He returns to the kiosk. We watch Frodo woman hand him a bag of pellets for the llamas and giraffes that you can hand-feed through your car window.

'See,' I tell Dinah. 'There's nothing wrong.'

Back at the car, the manager, who doesn't put his head through the window this time, I notice, hands me the pellets and, as he begins the spiel about conservation and breeding programmes that all zoos and safari parks nowadays trot out to assuage the guilt of locking up wild animals, in between nodding occasionally, I pour half the pellets into a different Tupperware pot for Phoebe and give Charlie what's left in the bag.

'Sorry about this,' I say to the manager, as I pass them back to the kids. 'Now you're not to,' and before I can say 'eat them, Charlie. They're for the animals,' he's popped one in his mouth.

The manager carries on talking about the snow leopard.

'Grass and vitamins, probably. It's not going to kill him, is it?'

The manager starts to reply.

'Can *I* have one?' says Phoebe.

'They're not sweets, guys. They're for the animals.'

'Just one. *Please*, Dad.'

'Just one then.'

'Ben!' says Dinah.

'I think we'd better go in now,' I tell the manager.

He waves at Frodo woman, who opens the barrier and he's still staring after us as we drive in, Dinah now madly knocking pellets from the children's mouths.

'Why on earth did you do that?'

'He saw the mess in here and thought we were terrible parents. It was a joke about his preconceptions.'

'Which you just reinforced by letting the kids eat llama pellets, Ben.'

'They didn't swallow any.'

'Well, that's OK then.'

'We got in, didn't we?'

In my day, winding car windows down in a safari park meant moustachioed rangers in stripy Land Rovers all over you with tranquiliser guns. Here we watch a 7-foot llama put its head so casually into the driver's window of a Ford Focus to nibble food pellets from their dashboard, it actually looks from behind like it might be giving the family directions to The Discovery Trail.

We find a spot in the Big Cat Enclosure to make up our lunch – made slightly more difficult because, although we have sliced bread and ham, we forgot to pack a knife so have to spread the butter with the sharpened end of a carrot. It's the sort of mishap we're accustomed to now. It's such a rush getting on the road each morning things get overlooked. In various hotel rooms so far we've already left behind Dinah's Lancôme make-up remover, her hairdryer, an iPod charger, a telephone charger and my swimming trunks. The only advantage is it's making the car progressively easier to pack.

Inverting the conventional safari concept, the lions wander over to observe *us* eating and we're enjoying assigning them Brummie accents ('Somewhere 'otter would 'ave been noyse, but act-shull-eee it's roit bostin 'ere') when one lion pats the rear bumper of the safari jeep beside us. It's probably feeding time, but as the rest of the pride lollops over, Dinah panics that it's the smell of our ham rolls (every lion's favourite snack) that's excited them. She locks all the doors, keeps the car in gear and starts issuing erroneous voice-wavering advice to Phoebe along the lines of, 'Now Phoebe, lions are very dangerous so if ever you see one, you must *never* go up to it.' Maybe useful if you're born into a sub-Saharan African tribe. Sort of irrelevant when you live in East Sussex.

Dinah once read an article about how many deaths in plane crashes are caused by people's brains freezing so that they forget simple things like how to take off safety belts and open doors. The crucial thing is to have a plan and execute it in an emergency, so now, and throughout White Tiger Ridge, she goes through what-if drills. What if Charlie choked on a Walkers Square crisp in the back seat? Would we get out and administer the Heimlich manoeuvre or summon a ranger by blasting our horn? What if Phoebe jumped out of the car – who would run after her and would that person remember to shut their door after them to protect the remaining family members inside? Phoebe, who for over a year was scared of, among other things, the moon, flies and kettle steam, and is still frightened of anything alive over the size of a one-pence piece, starts to freak out.

'Phoebe, you will not get eaten. Mummy didn't mean that about the ham, did you, Mummy?'

'I'm just trying to keep everyone safe, my love.'

'But we don't want to scare anyone, do we?' I say.

'I didn't mean to scare anyone.'

'Can we go now, Daddy? I don't like it.'

'Yes, I think we've seen enough animals. Dinah? Shall we do the steam train now?'

'So long as you're not blaming me, Ben.'

'Not at all. You were just passing on safety tips.'

The Severn Valley Railway is so tangibly not as exciting as the West Midlands Safari and Leisure Park; its highlight is a fleeting glimpse through the steam train window of a camel *from* the safari park. On the journey Phoebe gets pins and needles sitting cross-legged colouring in pictures from her *Barney* mag (or 'my newspaper' as she calls it) and Charlie, in search of entertainment, bangs his head hoofing up the narrow passageway between the seats to find children of a similar age to scratch in the face. And *Steam Days* magazine, the only reading matter for sale on the platform, isn't even ironically amusing.

Outside Bewdley the kids wave at old ladies eating gammon in the passing dining train but that only quells the boredom for so long. The Engine House in Highley, further up the line, is a brand new museum that tells the story of the Severn Valley Railway. Here the kids get to dress up on the mail train, and Dinah and I have fun competing to overhear the most boring railway question asked of a SVR volunteer (the winner: 'So tell me about the vacuum brake system').

Normally I'm at the wheel because when Dinah drives she presses her face up against the windscreen like Mr Magoo and cannot look round when you talk to her – or else she gets lost, swerves into somebody else's lane or, most scary of all, pulls at her hair while nervously chanting, 'Concentrate, Dinah. Concentrate.' But this afternoon she's driving because I'm in the passenger seat writing up my notes, meaning it's she who has to merge from the M5 onto the M42. Dinah will not mind me saying this but merging panics her. Her merging also panics me. In fact, if we'd known there was a merge, I'd have driven. But now there's nothing for it. I put down my computer and pump her up.

'OK. Be brave.'

She breathes in.

'Just go for it.'

She breathes out.

'Go for it,' copies Phoebe, laughing in the back.

'Phoebe, Mummy's merging so...'

And as I once, controversially, taught her, Phoebe crosses herself once and puts the palms of her hands together.

'Please, don't make fun of me, Ben,' says Dinah.

'Phoebe! Stop that!'

After several minutes stationary near the end of the slip road being hooted at by other drivers, who swerve around us staring into our vehicle to see who can be this incompetent, Dinah begins her mantra, 'You can do it, Dinah. You can do it.'

I offer more encouragement. 'Remember, traffic coming towards you doesn't want to smash into you just as much as you don't want to smash into it. Just be brave.'

Dinah revs repeatedly in readiness for her launch into the motorway, yanks off the handbrake and then edges forward but each time stops herself after a shoulder check because of some speck on the horizon coming towards us. I try to remain calm, but finally, when she begins to reverse, 'because I need more of a run-up', I pull on the handbrake and get out of the car. I walk round to her side and wrest control of the vehicle. I shunt her back into the passenger seat and climb in. Dinah's furious. It's the fault of the M42 and 'lorry drivers who don't give a shit'. 'They wouldn't let me in, Ben. You saw them. *Nobody* would let me in.' It's also my fault for never letting her drive at home. It means she's rusty and anyway this sort of thing only ever happens when she's with me. I make her nervous. If she hadn't been nervous, she'd have merged no problem.

It's early evening when we finally arrive at the train station. The street lights are coming on as we enter Birmingham city centre.

'I feel sad now,' says Dinah.

It's something we haven't spoken about all day.

'Me too. Shall I say something?'

'Guys?' says Dinah looking in the rear-view mirror.

'I have something to tell you,' I say.

'Daddy,' Phoebe says. 'Can you carry on talking to Mummy? I do like talking to you, but we're watching the film.'

Dinah pauses the movie.

'Guys, Mummy's dropping me off at the station in a few minutes, OK? I'm going to see Granddad for a couple of days.'

'Now?' says Phoebe. 'This night?'

'When we get to the station, yes.'

'Awwww. You won't be able to read us a story.'

'Will you be back in the morning?' asks Phoebe.

'No, sweetheart.'

'What about the other morning? The one after that.'

'Not the next morning either. But the one after that I will.'

Phoebe stares at her hand and pulls up one finger then another. She holds them up. 'So two nights.'

'Yes.'

'Is Mummy staying with us?' asks Charlie.

'Of course,' says Dinah.

'Good,' he says.

'Now guys, when I'm gone I want you to be good for Mummy, OK?'

'OK,' says Phoebe, sounding disappointed.

'When she merges what aren't you going to do?'

Phoebe puts her hands together in prayer and we all laugh.

'And Charlie? No running off, OK?'

'OK,' Charlie says equally sadly.

'And guys, if you're really good guess what – I'll bring you back a present.'

Dinah turns into New Street and drives up to the loading and unloading bay and parks.

'Got everything?' she asks.

'Yeah. Now you know what you're doing?'

'Yes,' says Dinah.

'Don't try to do too much. Anything you manage by yourself is a bonus. And remember to take the camera off the landscape setting if you take any pictures.'

'Phoebe?' Dinah says.

'What? Oh yes,' says Phoebe.

She scrambles for her Dora bag, opens various pockets.

'Phoebe has something, Daddy. It's to give to Granddad.'

'What do you mean? Something for Granddad?'

'Don't tell him, Mummy,' says Phoebe, stiffening with frustration, still rooting. 'It's a 'prise.'

A few seconds later she smiles shyly as she passes me a card.

'What's this, Phoebe?'

She bites her lip.

On the front of the envelope it says 'Granddad'.

'Is that a card for Granddad?'

She nods.

'And did you write "Granddad" by yourself?'

'Mummy helped me.'

'Phoebe, that's so kind.'

'It's a picture of a rabbit,' says Phoebe. She looks at Dinah. 'And it's got all its legs, Daddy.'

'All of them?'

'Count them if you like.'

'Thank you, Phoebe.'

'And *I* drew on it,' says Charlie.

Phoebe leans forward. 'He actually scribbled,' she says with one hand over her mouth in the semblance of a whisper. 'But we're calling it drawing.'

'Thank you, Charlie. And thank you, Phoebe. That's lovely. Granddad will be very pleased.'

'We did it while you were in the shower.'

'Did you?'

'We were very secretly.'

'You must have been *very* secretly. And Granddad will be very pleased.'

A taxi behind hoots. I step out of the car. Dinah gets out to hug me. I open the kids' doors in turn and kiss Charlie in his seat and then Phoebe in hers.

The sinking feeling starts in the queue for my ticket.

CHAPTER 8

'Daddeeeee!' Phoebe's Dora bag bounces on her back as she runs full pelt along the platform towards me. I bend to one knee, drop my bag and take the force of her in my arms. I hug her head and pick her up. She squashes my cheeks together. It's been three days but already she somehow looks indefinably different.

'Guess what?' she says.

'What?'

'Mummy stood in my poo.'

Charlie toddles over, beaming from ear to ear, waving a Thomas the Tank Engine toy. I scoop him up too.

'As hard as you can,' I tell him.

He squeezes.

'That's very hard.'

'I a big boy.'

'You are a big boy.'

'Thomas,' he says.

'Wow. Is that yours?'

Charlie grits his teeth and pats my cheeks matily between his palms like Eric Morecambe. I carry them towards Dinah as Phoebe informs me the car stinks 'to high heaven'.

'To high heaven. Really? Hi, love.'

I hug Dinah.

'How was it?' she asks.

I rock my hand back and forth.

We're at Leicester train station. The car's parked on Conduit Street round the corner. We head there.

'Why does the car stink to high heaven?'

'Phoebe! Daddy doesn't want to hear that.'

'He does,' I say.

Dinah starts to say something but Phoebe squirms in my arms. 'Let me tell him. Daddy, we were in the car heading for the first attraction.'

I laugh at how the word attraction has entered her vocabulary and Dinah smiles.

'DADDDEEEE,' she twists my face away from Dinah's.

'I'm listening, pops.'

'Right.' Phoebe wriggles contently. 'We were heading for an attraction and I needed a wee. Well, I thought it was a wee anyway.' She laughs, putting her hand in front of her mouth. 'But it was *actually* a poo...' She squeezes my cheeks together again. '... as well as a wee so then...' Phoebe boggles her eyes '... so then Mummy stopped the car and I had a nature wee. You don't know what a nature wee is.'

'One outside that's unplanned.'

'You're *cor-rect*. But the poo sort of slipped out. Oh my goodness me. And then Charlie ran off. And Mummy was cross because we were near a big, big road and the cars were going whooosh really, really fast. And Charlie was crying and...'

'I'm so pleased to be here,' I say.

'Daddddeeee!'

Dinah kisses me.

'Daddddeeee!'

'I've missed you all so much.'

'Daddddddeeee, you're not listenin' to me.'

'Phoebe, let Daddy talk to Mummy as well.'

'But I'm telling my story.'

'OK pops, carry on.'

'So the cars were going whoosh and Mummy was running after Charlie and that's when she trod in my poo. And got it all over her 'spensive shoes,' says Phoebe.

'Been a bit like that has it, love?'

Dinah closes her eyes and nods.

'Daddy, listen!'

'I am, pops.'

'And because Charlie was running away Mummy didn't notice what she'd done. It was very foolish, Daddy, because she didn't notice the poo on her 'spensive shoes so she got it all over the petals in the car.'

'Pedals, Phoebe.'

'Mummyyyyy! *I'm* telling the story.'

'All over the pedals what you press with your foots when you drive and so the whole car stinks to high heaven.'

She sighs.

'Can I have my present now, Dad?'

The train was late into King's Cross and Dad was in bed when I arrived. The next morning he was reading *The Times* when I came downstairs. His eyes looked more yellow, or maybe I'd forgotten how yellow they were before. Over the kitchen table I watched him eat two boiled eggs.

'Two! That's excellent, Dad.'

'It is good,' said Mary.

'Fuel,' said Dad.

'You don't enjoy it at all?'

'He feels full all the time, don't you darling?'

'My tum,' said Dad.

That morning we watched telly together. Dad had stopped talking. I'd heard it from Buster who'd heard it from Mary. Dad was retreating into himself, spending long hours watching snooker on TV. Before I came down, I thought to myself that I'd open him up, be the one to make him talk, make him feel less lonely. But in the telly room that day beside Dad on the adjacent sofa, watching old war films, occasionally getting up to adjust the cushions under his head or to answer his phone ('Hello, David and Mary's phone') and having my questions stifled by reluctant replies, I realised this wasn't going to happen. Dad seemed slowly to exhaust himself, gradually winding down, becoming slower in his responses like the second hand of a failing watch, so that by 11 a.m. he'd fallen asleep.

I tried to help but there was nothing to do. They had a housekeeper, a gardener. Meals from Pen and Mary's mum, Kathleen, dropped over in foil containers. Buster, visiting from Cyprus, had already changed the two down-lighter spots that had gone and mended the leaky sink. It became a small joke. 'I want his lights to fail, his plumbing to cause a flood, then I can tidy up his shoddy work. What can I do, Mary?'

'Just watch television with your father.'

That afternoon Mary went out for walk so I heated up Dad's fish pie for him. But every time I did anything I made a mistake.

'Less than half, and can you put some ketchup on it?'

'Thank you, but can I have the dessert on a *tray*, my son?'

'Whipped cream *please* on the strawberries...'

'Can you put that down for a few more minutes?'

'No, my son, no Roquefort salad. NO. OK?' said sternly after I bought the ingredients to surprise him.

After lunch we watched more telly. *The Guns of Navarone*. We watched Gloucester versus Leicester Tigers.

'It's a thrashing,' I said, when Leicester reached twenty-one points.

Dad made a noise.

'Good game,' I said, at the end.

Dad made another noise.

People rang and I answered the phone, handed it to Dad if he nodded and replaced it on the receiver when he finished. These were the moments he came alive, talking to showbiz or actor pals from his comedy days at the BBC. He'd laugh, manage a joke – 'I ain't going anywhere just yet' – but then afterwards, his wrist flaccid, he'd hand me the phone to replace, a small piece of him used up, it seemed.

The next day was the same. I watched more telly with Dad – Wolves v WBA, Man U v West Ham. Buster came over.

'I'm going back Thursday,' he said. 'I said I'd come back every ten days. Too soon, Dad said. So I'll come back in a couple of weeks.'

'Me too,' I said. 'What do you reckon?'

'Mary spoke to the GP. He'll sleep more and more. Eventually he'll slip into a coma, but nobody knows when.'

'Is that what she said?'

'Yeah.'

'Jesus!'

'I know.'

'And there's nothing they can do?'

'They might fit a stent. There might be some targeted chemo. It's all long shots.'

When Dad fell asleep after Buster left I sought out Mary in the living room of the barn conversion.

'He's pleased you came,' she told me. 'He said he'd had a lovely time.'

'Did he?'

Her face shifted. Her eyes filled. I had to look away.

'It isn't the worse thing,' she said. 'He's in no pain, his mind hasn't gone.'

'Small mercies.'

'Your dad doesn't complain. Nor should we. I've had a good life, that's what he says.'

'Although that's changed slightly.'

'I know,' said Mary. 'He's very sad now. He doesn't talk to me.'

'I thought he'd talk to me.'

'He doesn't talk to anyone.'

She held up her book, *How Can I Help?* Mary read me a section called 'Towards The End'.

'Cancer sufferers retreat from the world. First they stop going out of the house, then they stop answering the phone. Eventually,' said Mary, 'they end up in one room. It's a common response.'

She looked away.

I stared into the front garden.

'Your dad loves you all,' she said, looking back at me. 'He's seen you all married. All your children. He was terribly pleased when you married, Ben. He was worried you wouldn't settle down. Your mum never saw that. Or your children.'

'Small mercies.'

Mary laughed. Her face crumpled again. 'We'd be opening a bottle of wine normally now. I try to think of positives but it's hard. Just six weeks ago he was in the doctor's surgery in his multicoloured jumper bouncing around. Doctor, I look yellow. Then bang.'

'I know.'

'It's the nights. I keep thinking he's going to die beside me, which in one way would be good.'

'Nice way to go.'

'Exactly.'

'But…'

Mary looked away.

'There's no nice way to go,' I said.

'Exactly,' said Mary, recovering. 'And at least he knows we love him and we know he loves us. Every day he tells me. You must do the same because you never know, you know.'

'You're right.'

'Although you tried hard not to like your dad.'

'I think I realised I couldn't be like him so I rebelled and went the other way.'

'Yes,' said Mary. 'And he was a rebel in his day. For the first ten years at the BBC.'

'I know. He carried a letter of resignation around with him permanently.'

'Anything he wasn't happy with.'

'Wallop.' I slapped the table.

'I know,' said Mary. 'He was only later absorbed by the establishment. And I bet his father was none too pleased when he took up the stage. That wouldn't have gone down well.'

'I'm going to be more like him,' I said. 'I'm going to try to be.'

Dad was awake in the TV room when I went in to say goodbye. I gave him a hug. He pointed to the table. There was £40 there. I said no.

'Towards the fare,' he said.

'It's free. I'm writing a box about the Midlands main line.'

He became angry. 'Take it.'

I folded it into my pocket. I knelt down and hugged Dad. I kissed his stubbly cheek. I closed my eyes and he rubbed my back.

'I'm going to become more like you,' I said. 'That's my strategy.'

'Please don't,' he said.

'Not completely. Only the best bits.'

'We're a close family,' he said.

'We're lucky.'

'I love you, my son.'

'I love you, Dad.'

I packed my bag, left out cards for both of them in the kitchen that I bought in the village and wrote the night before because it was what my dad would have done. But when it was time for Mary to take me to Gerrards Cross station I felt an explosion inside me as I hugged my dad one more time. I stroked his thinning grey hair and the tears flooded into my eyes. It was like a spring breaking free. My stomach compacted, expanded like a sponge in water. I had to breathe heavily. I looked at Dad. He seemed serene, to be feeding, gaining strength from this. I blew him a kiss at the door. And in Mary's car I slumped back. I said to her, 'It's hard to say...' and I went on the word goodbye. Mary went too. I felt sick and exhausted. We drove though the rain to the station. I bought my ticket at the machine after hugging Mary goodbye. She waited in the car for the £20 note to take in the slot. I waved my ticket at her. And she looked so lost in the driver's seat behind the rain-flecked windscreen I thought about her words, 'You tried hard not to like your dad.'

'OK, have a guess where we're going now, guys?' I ask the kids on the Leicester ring road.

'To another museum?'

'Yes, but this is a special museum,' I say. 'Phoebe, this is a museum that tells you... WHAT HAPPENS TO POO!'

'In real life!'

'In real life, Phoebe.'

'As if they haven't obsessed enough about poo already today,' says Dinah.

'I know.'

'CHARLIE!' shouts Phoebe. 'Did you not hear that? We're going to a POO MUSEUM!'

'Hooray!' shouts Charlie.

Dinah and I lived in Leicester for two years after our *Bucks Herald* days. She worked on the features desk at the *Northampton Chronicle & Echo*. I was a general news reporter on the *Leicester Mercury*. We lived together in a rented terraced house off Victoria Park, drank in the Clarendon and communicated sometimes in headlines, pretending our lives themselves were newspapers.

'What's your front page?' I'd ask.

'That nice letter from my mum. What are you splashing on? Is it still the EDF refund?'

'That's page three now. I'm going with what Gus told me about Jacey's tattoo.'

We had another running joke about Dinah's impressionability. She was very easily influenced. If she met a marine biologist, for example, I could guarantee within days there'd be an announcement. 'Ben, I've applied to do a post-grad oceanography course at University of Plymouth. Please don't try to stop me. I've longed to study plankton for years.' There was her human rights lawyer moment after watching *Erin Brockovich*. Not to mention the time she wanted to be an MP's researcher after speaking to one for ten minutes on a plane. 'You must know that about me! I've had a fascination with Westminster all my life.' It's strange, but when she started talking about wanting children so soon after her sister Lindsey gave birth, I actually thought it was part of the same thing. I didn't take her seriously. I assumed it would blow over. She was suddenly making a beeline for any under-two in a room, stroking baby pictures in magazines. She was teasing me, I assumed. It was a joke. Then my mum got sick and six months later she died and the next thing I knew Dinah, tired of waiting around for us to get married, have kids, move on to that next stage, had slept with some guy who worked in a record shop and she'd left me. Cue a year of misery and chaos before we eventfully got back together.

Now here we are back in Leicester with the kids I said I wasn't ready for in the back of the car, albeit several years later than Dinah would've preferred, heading for the Abbey Pumping Station.

The pumping station opened in 1891 and was responsible for piping Leicester sewage to the treatment works in Beaumont Leys. The grand Victorian building, now the Leicester Museum of Science and Technology, houses the largest operating beam engines in the country, although it's not these we've come for.

'Where's the poo?' whispers Dinah, a few minutes into our visit. The poo is what we both remember about the place. It's why we thought Phoebe would love it.

'I don't know.'

'Ask someone,' says Dinah.

'What, you mean, "Excuse me, where's the poo?" You ask.'

'I'm not asking,' she says.

'Daddy, you said there'd be poo.'

'I know, we're looking for it, pops.'

Dinah tries to divert Phoebe with the children's trail. It's a quiz sheet asking under-fives to find small cuddly teddy bears hidden amongst the beam engines. They're balanced on large iron wheels and inside various piston mechanisms.

'Daddy, that is *not* poo. That's teddies and engines.'

'Yes, it is. I'm sorry.'

'Oh Daddy, you said there'd be poo. Why did you say there'd be poo?'

I tell Phoebe I thought there was poo, but I was wrong and I'm sorry, and it threatens to turn ugly until Dinah, who's moved ahead with Charlie, returns triumphantly.

'Phoebe! Look!' She squats down, pointing ahead. 'Over there!'

'A toilet?' says Phoebe, sceptically.

'Yes, and what goes in toilets?'

'POO!' shouts Phoebe, her eyes widening.

She breaks into a run. 'Charlie, over here! Poo!'

There's something about the preponderance of poo, the amount of times we've uttered the word today and sheer joy of shouting out things like: 'Phoebe! Over there! Look! *Another* toilet!' that changes the mood of the day.

Phoebe follows the progress of poo via a see-through pipe from a Leicester toilet to the Wanlip sewage works ('Look, Daddy – there it goes'). Charlie can, for the first time in his young life without being lectured about germs, actually put his hand *down* a toilet. There are teenagers around laughing at the dummy feet sticking out of the bottom of a mocked-up toilet cubicle. And how can anybody not fall in love with a museum informing you in a matronly fashion that 'the escaping spray from a toilet flush will spread germs over four cubic metres'? Then there's the least likely museum exhibit in England: 'Stand or crouch? How posture assists bowel movement.'

'Excellent choice, Daddy,' says Dinah, outside.

'Thank you.'

Next door's £52 million National Space Centre has the only Soyuz spacecraft in the UK, a planetarium and six galleries of exhibits telling the story of the solar system, manned space flight and the creation of the universe. Charlie crawls through a black hole. Phoebe drives a Martian rover. Both stare in amazement at a 40-foot Thor-Able space rocket and, in slight confusion, at teenage schoolchildren pinching each other's bums in the darkness of the stellarium. Yet all Phoebe talks about on the way to our next attraction, the Jain Centre, is 'the poo-poo place'.

Dinah isn't very keen on the Jain Centre a) because it's liable to be non-child-friendly and b) because we have a prearranged guided tour, something that's been so problematic with the kids in the past that a blue badge guide on a walking tour round the guildhall in Worcester actually made a joke about 'using chloroform'. The centre is off the Leicester gyratory system on Oxford Street and, entering the lobby area of the former nineteenth-century congregational church, we're met by Dr Ramesh Mehta. Dr Mehta shakes my hand and informs us shoes and food are not allowed in the more holy upstairs section. Charlie and Phoebe hand Dinah the Quavers they were bribed with to come here and take their shoes off while Dr Mehta tells us there are 1,000 Jains in Leicester, 30,000 in the UK and 10 million in India. He explains the three main tenets of Jainism. The first is non-violence in the physical realm; i.e. you're not allowed to harm another living thing (Jains wear gauze masks so they don't accidentally swallow insects). There's also non-violence in the verbal realm (don't say bad things) and in the realm of thought (or think them).

The second tenet of Jainism is limiting possessions.

'You set parameters,' says Dr Mehta. 'I will only have eighteen shirts, so if my son gives me another for my birthday, I will not reject it. Instead I give away a shirt. As you get more spiritual your parameters become smaller. Do you see?'

I nod. I do see. I look at Dinah nodding. She looks at me looking at her nodding and smiles. We nod at each other. Dr Mehta has rather hypnotic eyes. They seem to make you want to nod. There's a liquidity about them, a gentle softness, an openness I suppose that I have only ever seen in one face before. The face of the woman who recruited me to be a Samaritan volunteer in Ealing.

Dr Mehta disappears to check it's OK to go upstairs.

'What do you think?' I ask.

'I think he's great.'

'Me too.'

'Have you seen his eyes?'

'I love his eyes,' says Dinah.

'They're like Khan the snake's in *The Jungle Book*.'

'Only in a good way,' says Dinah.

'That makes you nod.'

Dr Mehta returns.

'One moment,' he says.

While we wait for upstairs to be readied he explains that the third tenet of Jainism is multiplicity of viewpoint. He holds up his index finger.

'Do you see my finger?'

I nod. I do see his finger. Dinah nods. She sees it too.

'You see the nail and from my angle I see the pulp. We're both right.'

I nod again. What a good point. Dinah clearly agrees, judging from her nodding. What a novel way of expressing a difference of opinion, I think.

'Conduct is also important,' says Dr Mehta. 'To have a small ego and be humble. I used to get annoyed when someone left off the doctor in front of my name. Now I don't care.'

I look at Dinah. I left it off. I called him Mr Mehta when we shook hands. Dinah doesn't look back. She's staring into Dr Mehta's eyes. He tells a story about turning up at a function and there being no place set for him on the top table. In the old days he might have been angry.

'I am president of the largest Jain temple in Europe. Why haven't I got a seat? Now, I sit on the floor. I don't mind. They see me on the floor and invite me to the top table. I have been humble. Now, if the children are ready.'

We follow Dr Mehta. The temple, from the outside, looks like a slightly fancier than usual Methodist chapel. Inside, with over forty-four hand-carved sandstone pillars weighing 250 tons that took 100,000 man hours to complete, it looks like a forest. The altar is its clearing. Here incense burns. There's an amazing, light feeling of peace. The images at the centre are of the sixteenth tirthankar, while stained glass windows tell the story of the twenty-fourth and final tirthankar, Mahavir's journey from birth to nirvana.

As Charlie puts the devotees off by attempting to dismantle the statue to the sixteenth tirthankar, Dr Mehta, seemingly oblivious to this, informs us anyone can become a Jain. It doesn't need a ceremony. To be a Jain all you do is act Jain.

'Charlie!' I shout.

Dr Mehta flaps his hand. 'It's OK,' he says, and Dinah and I exchange a look of wonder. Dr Mehta is the nicest man we have met in Britain. We go back downstairs. It's been a very enjoyable hour and now I don't want to go. I want to nod at more things Dr Mehta has to say. I shake his hand by the shoe rack. He holds both of mine this time, a symbol of how we've connected, I like to think. It's now clear he came in today especially to show us his temple and now he's going home. And suddenly it all makes sense. Everything he says. Dr Mehta is right – everyone should be a Jain. It would make the world a better place for everyone. Well, except those working at Thomas Pink, maybe. As he prepares to leave, Dr Mehta doesn't ask when the guidebook's coming out. He doesn't want to know how many words we'll write, isn't interested in copy approval or what pictures we're planning to use. All he wanted to do was tell us about Jainism. I thank Dr Mehta once more and before he goes I shake his hand one final time and stare into his liquid eyes half hoping, somehow, he sees into my soul, reaches out, and calls me to his faith with some simple instantly understood words of spirituality. He says something I don't quite catch because the kids are shouting. I ask him to repeat himself and lean forward expectantly to hear his wise words.

'I said they can finish their Quavers now,' he says.

I laugh and Dr Mehta smiles.

'Wow,' says Dinah outside.

'Wow,' I repeat.

We steer the kids across the road and Dinah says, 'I think my neck's a bit sore.'

She waggles her head about.

'The nodding?'

'Yeah.'

The *Leicester Mercury* building has been upgraded, I notice walking down Charles Street. The outside sparkles with a new blue plate-glass skin. We separated in The Shires shopping centre – Dinah to buy general bits and pieces with the kids, while I'm seeing an old colleague from the newspaper. The lobby also has a different layout. White and modern. The receptionist rings the newsroom and I wait for Jeremy flicking through that day's city edition. A few minutes later he steps out of the lift looking as scruffy as ever in a string tie with his white-collared shirt untucked. I haven't seen Jeremy for fifteen years. Apart from a few grey hairs, he looks the same. On my last day at the newspaper in 1997 I asked Jeremy if he'd swap ties with me. I wanted it to be like the Pele and Bobby Moore shirt swap in the 1970 World Cup. A mark of mutual respect for each other's reporting. Jeremy refused, or didn't take my request seriously. 'Yours has a cheese on toast stain on it,' he'd said. I'd been slightly insulted at the time.

Jeremy laughs when he sees me, I'm not sure why. I laugh too. He wants to know where the kids are. I tell him and all he keeps saying is, 'Well, well, Ben Hatch. *Ben Hatch.*' The canteen's now on the ground floor. It's new, Starbucks-like. We have tea here and talk about old characters. Jim McPheator, the recently deceased no-necked news editor we all loved, respected and enjoyed writing for ('Sprinkle some magic dust on that for us'). Rookie reporter Chris Benjamin, who on the 6 a.m. shift covered a fire at a hosiery factory in a pair of new trousers he couldn't work the fly on. He interviewed the chief fire officer, a detective inspector and the factory owner before he realised the reason the workers lined up outside the plant were laughing and pointing at him was that his flies were down and his boxers shorts wide open and everyone could see his cock. He hadn't noticed before because the 'heat of the fire was so intense'.

'All gone,' Jeremy says, laughing. 'Just me left – too fucking old and jaded to leave.'

He laughs like Mozart in the film *Amadeus*. It's high-pitched and I laugh too. And a memory returns. It's of giving Jeremy a lift somewhere, and telling him that he was the best writer on the paper and that he should be working for the nationals. Jeremy's deputy features editor now and I wonder whether he remembers this. He's got three children in city schools, his friends live here. He supports Leicester City, has written a book about them. Why would he leave? I wouldn't. At the same time it makes me wonder what would have happened if I'd stayed.

As if reading my mind Jeremy asks, 'I can't remember now. Did you leave under a cloud?' He laughs. 'They usually do.'

My mum had died three weeks before. I was back in the newsroom after my compassionate leave ended and I remember standing by a pillar next to the table where the news diary was kept and reading in it I was down for the next weekend shift. The news editor, Simon Orrell, fancied himself as a heavy metal fan, although actually had his hair cut at Toni & Guy. I asked him if I could swap shifts with someone else. My dad was drinking a lot. He'd been talking about Kenneth Williams' autobiography. 'Nobody knew whether he killed himself or not,' that sort of vague hint. I didn't want to leave Dad on his own. Only I couldn't say this to Orrell. He wasn't that sort of boss.

'You've been off a fortnight.'

I remember my flash of anger.

'I'd love to smack you in the face,' I said, squaring up to someone for the first time in my life. His marriage was breaking down. He had stuff he needed to work out himself. I think this explained his response. He didn't even look shocked.

'Do you want to go outside?' he said.

We walked to the lift, waited patiently for it to descend. On the ground floor Orrell, shorter than me, although in better shape, must have decided it was probably unwise to scrap a recently bereaved member of his news team in front of readers entering the newspaper's office, which was also right opposite Charles Street police station. He suggested we fight in the canteen. So we rode the lift to the fourth floor. The canteen was empty. It was 10 a.m. There was a clatter of trays being cleared away. My anger dissipated, I had to do something, so I pressed my index finger into his goatee and called him a twat. I said everyone on the paper thought he was twat as well, which wasn't strictly true. He smiled knowingly, sympathetically almost.

'That it?' he said.

He smiled. I smiled too now and we rode back down to the newsroom occasionally smiling again at each other. At my desk I was shaking. I expected to be sacked any minute. Instead, when Orrell wandered over with the editor it was to give me a story. He had his favourites and I wasn't one of them. But he gave me the chance for the front page lead. We'd behaved like old-fashioned newsmen – come close to brawling – maybe he liked that, that idea of himself. Perhaps it was an apology. Maybe he knew what would happen next. I had to door-knock the family of a man who'd fallen to his death inside a grain silo. Two hundred and fifty words and a pic. Most reporters shied away from death knocks. Sometimes they'd knock on the bereaved relative's door hoping nobody was in. Sometimes they wouldn't knock at all. I liked death knocks. It was a bit sick and I kept quiet about it, but I liked them. 'I'm from the *Mercury* – we're here to do a tribute piece.' A tribute piece. Not a news story, always a tribute piece. I'd sit in their front room. They'd make tea, I'd flip through their family photo albums. 'Ah, this is a lovely one.'

'Do you want to take it?'

'Thank you, yes.'

They'd tell me how much their father, mother, son or daughter was loved. Stories about them. They'd tell me how they died, how they heard the news, how they felt. Sometimes I'd want to stop them. I'd want to say: shut up, don't tell me that. But I'd write it all down. Sometimes I'd be moved, close to tears. I'd feel tremendous empathy. I'd want to protect them. Be a part of their grief. But then in the pool car, returning to the office, the words would form and back at my desk I'd make the story as sensational as I could within the bounds of accuracy to ensure I was bylined on the front page, feeling not a shred of guilt.

It was a terraced house behind the rugby ground. I went up to the front door and I didn't realise until my finger was right over the bell that I wasn't going to be able to ring it. I told Orrell they weren't in and somebody else went back later and got the story. Not straightaway but soon after, I quit the paper and journalism altogether after more than ten years. I don't tell Jeremy this. I cut the tale off at the aborted fight with Orrell. It's funnier that way.

'But you wrote a fucking novel,' he says. 'Two fucking novels.'

'That are out of print,' I remind him.

We finish our tea. Jeremy asks if I want to come upstairs.

'Say hello to Carter. He's still here, of course. He'll die in his fucking chair.'

I don't fancy it, though. Too many memories.

Before the lift doors close, he shouts back for me to send him a copy of the guidebook. He'll review it. 'As long as you promise to say what a shithole it really is here,' he jokes. He laughs his infectious laugh and I promise I will.

Dinah's fraught when I meet her. The kids have been acting up, running off in shops. She hasn't found a Currys so hasn't been able to replace the lead for the Bébétel we realised this morning we'd left at the last hotel.

'Basically I've failed. How was it?'

'Strange.'

'Did you miss it?' she asks.

'A bit.'

'The newsroom buzz?'

'Having work colleagues. It was nice seeing Jezzer. What are we going to do about the lead?'

'We can brave it for a night.'

But can we?

The Bébétel is a French device that allows us to go to dinner. It works like this: I enter my mobile phone number into the box, which is plugged into the room's phone socket in the kids' room. There are three noise settings that we joke are: sensitive (my phone's rung at the slightest sound in the room), medium (I'm rung if the noise is slightly louder) and NEGLECT (if a bomb went off it wouldn't trip the device). When I answer my ringing phone I can talk to the kids through a loudspeaker on the box ('It's all right – we're here'... Or if it's the fifth time it's happened and there's nothing the matter: 'Mummy and Daddy are drinking Pinot. Go to sleep.').

The Belmont Hotel is between the *Mercury* building and Victoria Park. We have two bedrooms: one large with a widescreen TV and a second with bunk beds so small it's not wide enough to put Charlie's travel cot up in. We have bitter experience of sleeping in the same room as Charlie so the only alternative arrangement is that we sleep in the bunk beds and give the kids the widescreen telly room.

Without the Bébétel, we must all have dinner together. We order wine and, over fillet of scotch beef with apricot, mint and chorizo, Dinah and I have fun competing to see who's the most Jain. Dinah's in the lead when I send a stale bread roll back.

'I think that's violence in the verbal realm, Ben.'

But I swiftly counter that I didn't want to acquire the roll. I'd set my parameters for bread rolls, and having now advanced spiritually since my asparagus salad, I'd decided to give it away.

But we're soon reminded why we usually come down alone to eat when Charlie stands up in his high chair like a pearl diver preparing to plunge from a cliff face and Phoebe starts massaging her ham omelette with her hand like a surgeon trying to restart a heart.

In the tiny bunk bed room it's also a little depressing at 8 p.m. There's no telly as it's in the kids' room, and nowhere even to sit comfortably upright. I lie on the bottom bunk, Dinah's on the top one. She calls her mum. I try Dad but nobody answers, Pen switches her phone off after 7 p.m. and in the end I call Buster.

'Hi, I'm in a bunk bed in Leicester about to go to sleep.'

'Really? It's eight o'clock. Where are Phoebe and Charlie?'

'In the much larger room next door with the widescreen TV. Probably watching a paid-for movie and eating a tube of Pringles from the minibar.'

'How's that happened?'

'Too boring to explain. What's the latest on Dad?'

He tells me Dad has an appointment with Gorhard his surgeon next week about the stent. The stent might relieve some of the pressure on his bile duct. It's this that's making him yellow.

'And how are you?'

'I'm good.'

He tells me about his summer holiday plans, a presenting award he's up for. The contact's nice but at the same time it seems so alien and out of keeping with our new life on the road he might as well be telling me about conditions inside the service module of the Mir space station.

'How is it generally, then?' he asks.

'OK, except we came away without coats.'

'You're driving around England for five months *without coats*.'

'I know, it's like going to the moon without oxygen.'

'So what's the worst place?'

'Your old city, Swansea.'

'You went to Swansea!'

Buster used to run a bar in Swansea.

'The National Waterfront Museum, the Dylan Thomas Centre and the Swansea Museum. Guess what the most interesting thing is in the Swansea Museum? A 1754 Georgian half brick.'

'Not even a whole brick.'

'Exactly. Half a brick. We couldn't believe how drunk everyone was at bus stops in the middle of the day.'

'That's Swansea.'

'And that drive in!'

'You came in via Port Talbot, then?' says Buster. 'Where else have you been?'

'Cardiff. That was as bad.'

'There are some good museums there,' says Buster, defensive now of Wales. 'The National Museum.'

'We were due to go but then we heard about a Dr Who exhibition but when we got there it wasn't on. So we went on a free tour of the next door Welsh National Assembly instead.'

'You made up an attraction?'

'We made up an attraction. We heard there was a great viewing gallery. We thought it meant views over Cardiff Bay. It was of the debating chamber.'

Buster laughs.

'And there wasn't even a debate going on. We saw a few laptops.'

'Nothing for the kids, then?'

When he hangs up, Dinah's still on the phone so I climb off the bed and check on the kids. Phoebe's curled up like a comma across the double bed. Charlie's lying with his arms outstretched and his legs apart like he's waiting to be patted down by the cops. Tomorrow we're heading to Nottingham. Back on my bunk, Dinah chattering away, I get the Rand McNally map out and work out our route.

CHAPTER 9

Buster always had my dad's shoulders back temerity. Confident, fun to be around, upbeat, trusting, generous spirited, he shared my dad's swarthy looks and athletic prowess. Pen was bossy like Dad, bright, innately kind, very organised and talked like a Hatch woman, Dad said – very fast and a little too often. A good-natured chatterbox, skinny, full of energy, she inherited Dad's artistic talents, played the piano and won school debates. She cartwheeled around the windmill like a tumbler, rode horses to Buckland Common, acted in plays and sang in choirs.

I unmistakably looked like my mother, had her temperament. Her pale skin, ginger hair. Shy, reserved, I was timid and fearful. My dad despaired of me. As a kid I slept facing the door to give me time to parry an attacker with my double-scoop Gray-Nicolls cricket bat I kept down the side of the bed. 'You're a funny boy,' Dad would say after I turned down a trip to a farm and the opportunity to stroke a dirty pig because I'd rather add another cardboard extension to my teddy bear cardboard box warren. 'You're a funny boy,' he'd say because I hated going to other children's houses as they might have a bitey dog or a brand of Bejam jelly I wouldn't like. My dad had a cricket blue from Cambridge, had played rugby for his house. Yet I couldn't work the swing in our back garden. 'Stretch your legs out. Now pull them in. I said pull them in, pull them in, in, in, in!' And without a word he'd stalk back into the house his head held back, appealing to the heavens for the patience deserting him. In the camper van I made sure the lock poppers were down. 'Safe,' I'd say. 'Safe,' I'd make Buster repeat. I hated bonfire night more than our cat Boots and watched, through the kitchen window, as Dad let the fireworks off, wincing at every bang, only coming out for my sparkler at the end, which I pretended to enjoy but really was scared of, fearing spark-related blindness. Any fair ride above the adrenalin level of the dodgems was a no-no. The waltzer seemed like Russian roulette, the big wheel was asking for it, and the ghost train might get stuck in the tunnel leading to a panic-stricken stampede for the exits and trample deaths. For years I was convinced I'd be the Yorkshire Ripper's next victim, that he was working his way towards me. I dreaded the *Ten O'clock News* bongs. Bong. Ripper Strikes Again. Bong. Another step nearer to me. Bong. Another sleepless night.

I was stubborn. Food was a battleground. 'Get it eaten!' I can hear Dad shouting. A faint but pig-headed voice, the words said quickly with lips ready to jam shut at the approach of a spoon: 'I don't like puddings with a biscuit base'... 'It's the tomato'... 'It's touching the mayonnaise'. In bed I'd hear my mum (my 'great protector', Dad called her) through the floorboards over the drone of the telly. 'He didn't mean to break it/drop it/bite it/steal it/ smash it/eat it/say this/do that/not do this. It's just that he's... he's sensitive.' At some point I think I must have decided if I couldn't be like my dad I'd become the opposite of him. He was hard-working so I chose laziness. He was extrovert; I became shy. He was trusting; I cultivated cynicism. He looked for good in people; I searched for the bad. Whatever he said I doubted. Whatever he did, I questioned. It's really no wonder I entered journalism, the one profession he despised.

The best moments of this trip are the same: checking into a new hotel (What facilities have they got? Do they have CBeebies? Have they got us down for a free meal? Will the manager gift us a bottle of Prosecco?) and checking out, moving on – turning the radio on full blast ('Whack it up, Dinah') to get a family sing-song going as we pull away to see and do something else none of us knew anything about until I read the itinerary at breakfast. We always sing loudly, we always open the windows ('Roll 'em down, Dinah!').

Leaving Leicester it's 'Total Eclipse of the Heart' by Bonnie Tyler. And we give it all we've got. Every one of us. Charlie claps and smiles his little head off, his dimples sucked in. Phoebe, with a cheeky shoulder twist, sings back the words she doesn't understand but knows we want to hear, 'Total slips of the heart.'

'Again, Phoebe.'

'Total slips of the heart.'

'One more time.'

'Total slips of the heart.'

It's a sunny day, we all slept well, there's a clean shirt on my back as Dinah caned the laundrette yesterday, and today it feels great to be on the trip. Wonderful to be alive. Nobody needs formula, a nappy change or to be led gibbering with fear away from a tortoise enclosure. Nobody's scared of a wax mannequin of Queen Victoria. Today we won't get lost. Today we'll have fun, we'll see amazing things. Today will be the best day of the trip so far.

It makes me feel giddy with joy, this singing. It's like we're the greatest family, like there's no family in the world better and I want everyone to know it. We're touring Britain. We're fitting together the fragmented jigsaw of all our memories of this country of our birth and we're doing it with the people we love the most in the world. What could be better? We all sing now at the very top of our voices: 'Total slips of the heart.'

'Again, Phoebe!'
'Total slips of the heart!'

I was twenty-four when my dad kicked me out of home, after the NatWest accidentally credited me £2,000 and I bought a Ford Transit camper van with the money. For the three years since leaving university I'd been getting periodically sacked from mundane jobs whilst spending most nine to five hours in a dressing gown working through a list of the 200 greatest works of literature. ('I'll clear away my lunch things when I've finished this Maupassant chapter, Mum.')

'What a wanker you were,' Dinah never tires of pointing out and she's right. I was a wanker. The accidental £2,000 largesse I saw not as thieving (my dad's verdict) but as an opportunity. Emulating John Steinbeck, the idea was I'd tour the country in my camper van, take its pulse, and write a great novel like *The Grapes of Wrath*. In fact, I visited The Tales of Robin Hood in Nottingham, my ex girlfriend Julie in Melton Mowbray, who thought my cooking facilities were 'dinky' but still wouldn't sleep with me in the banquette bed, and Chester Zoo. It was outside here, while I was settling down for the night with a book on the history of the Labour movement, that the van was set upon by louts. They rocked it, forced ketchup-covered chips in through a slit in the passenger window and threatened to come back when I was asleep to block my heater vent. The following day my windscreen wipers packed up and I not long after this I developed a wisdom tooth infection that spread down my neck to my jaw muscles clamping them shut, meaning I could only consume soup and food no wider or harder than Dairylea triangles. Back home in disgrace, recovering on antibiotics, I received two letters – one from the NatWest demanding immediate repayment of the £2,000 (something that eventually took seven years) and another from my dad, explaining why all my things were out in the front garden covered in dew.

Seventeen years later here I am back in Nottingham outside The Tales of Robin Hood. In 1991 when I came with my pompous literary aspirations the attraction was state of the art. Listening to a costumed Maid Marian chewing gum discussing with Robin Hood a night out at the Oceana Club later, it seems tired now. And with Dinah uninterested in my camper van reminiscences ('Sorry, but they're not exactly Che Guevera's *The Motorcycle Diaries*, Ben') I give Phoebe some context.

'Now Phoebe, that man dressed up there is Robin Hood.'

'Red Riding Hood?'

'No, *Robin* Hood. He takes from people with lots of things and gives to people with few things.'

'Is he going to give us something, Daddy?'

'Er, no…'

On the fifteen-minute monorail pod ride through a fibre glass Sherwood Forest we see skeletons hanging from trees, stuffed wolves with shiny, cruel eyes, creepy faces amongst tree branches, lightning flashes, torture victims and animal skulls, while a voice softly insinuates, 'Remember – the forest isn't always your friend.' Charlie cries and Phoebe's so scared I have to haul her back into the pod when she tries to escape. Holding her down, my hands over her ears, she cries until I promise her favourite treat – an ice cream with a flake.

Her appetite for lunch ruined by 11 a.m., we roll on to Nottingham Castle. Built in the eleventh century, it's where the final showdown took place between the evil Sheriff of Nottingham and Robin Hood. It's also where, in the Sherwood Foresters Regimental Museum, we discover the Robin Hood Rifles, the 1st Nottinghamshire Volunteer Rifle Corps, disappointingly didn't actually use bows and arrows at all. We read a few stoic citations in the gallantry award gallery while Charlie ogles the guns.

'Listen to this one. Private Bernard McQuirt won a VC on 6 January 1858 at the capture of Rowa during the Indian mutiny when he was seriously and dangerously wounded in a hand-to-hand fight with three men, of whom he killed one and wounded another. He received five sabre cuts and a musket wound, making, I quote, "an awful mess of his head and face".'

The cafe has sweeping views from Castle Rock over the city, which is blighted from almost every vantage point by hideous buildings like the Eastcroft incinerator, or the Clifton housing estate built in the 1950s and the largest of its kind in Europe at one time.

It's here the day's meltdown occurs. When Charlie gets hungry, rather than ask for his dinner, what he does is scratch other children about the same height as himself in the face. He's like a spirited Zorro but with fingernails instead of a rapier sword and an empty stomach in place of a keen moral sense of injustice. We're by the cutlery tray table queuing for our brie and cranberry paninis when we hear a wail of pain from across the room. Charlie toddles away from the scene of the crime, leaving a small boy from Wolverhampton with our son's initials practically scored in blood across his face. His Black Country parents are understanding but Dinah's so mortified she decides we must cut Charlie's nails straightaway.

'Before he's had lunch?'

'I wanted to do it this morning, Ben, but you wouldn't let me. We're doing it now.'

'OK, get the chocolate buttons out.'

'We haven't got any.'

'What!'

'We've run out.'

'You want to attempt this *without* chocolate buttons?'

An MI5 maxim holds that a city is only four meals from anarchy. On this trip we're only ever four chocolate buttons away from a tantrum.

'At least let him eat first.'

'No. I'll chase him towards you.'

After a five-minute Benny Hill-style caper round the terrace I have Charlie pinned down by a picnic table. It's like a messy citizen's arrest.

'OK, I've got his hands. Where are the nail scissors, love?'

'In my handbag.'

'I thought you had them.'

'No. Ouch! Charlie! That hurt.'

'Stop kicking Mummy, Charlie. Can you get them, then?'

'He was kicking me, Ben.'

'OK, but can you get them now. I can't hold him much longer.'

'Please, don't shout at me, I'm doing my best.'

'I'm not shouting, love. But this is actually quite tiring.'

Dinah returns with the scissors but the closer she gets to his nails the more superhuman strength Charlie somehow manages to summon.

'You have to keep him still.'

'I can't keep him any stiller.'

She has another go. The same thing happens.

'No, I give up,' she says. 'He's wriggling too much. You do it.'

'You'll have to hold him down, then.'

'I'm not strong enough, my love.'

'I can't cut them *and* hold him down.'

'Daddy, he's got a hand free,' says Phoebe.

'Thank you, Phoebe. We can manage.'

'Everyone's watching, Ben. This is so embarrassing...'

'I did say do it later.'

Afterwards, with so many cuts and welts over our faces and

arms from his flailing talons that we deserve our own citations in the gallantry award gallery, we rejoin the queue in the cafe. But to add insult to our actual injuries staff refuse to heat up Charlie's macaroni cheese in their microwave, citing health and safety rules.

'Are you really saying you can't heat his food up?'

'I'm sorry.'

'You saw him earlier, right? That was over *one* chocolate button. This is his *whole* lunch.'

'I'm sorry.'

We stay the night at an old eye hospital in the city centre. It's just off Maid Marian Way, a road which sounds quaint and olde worlde like it might just be wide enough for a horse and cart to get down, but is actually a four-lane dual carriageway jammed with beeping motorists trying to filter onto the A60. The eye hospital's been converted into serviced apartments and ours comes complete with cable TV (which means CBeebies), two bedrooms, one with an en suite shower, a small balcony and two coffee tables whose glass tops are removable, thus enabling our children to toboggan dangerously off the sofa on them. The American-style kitchen has a dishwasher, a washing machine, a microwave which doubles as an oven and a low-level cutlery drawer that, opened without shoes on, almost shaves a centimetre from the top of my left foot. There are tea bags, UHT milk cartons and washing-up liquid, but no rubber gloves, which means that while making chicken fajitas for dinner, Dinah almost winds up in the NHS walk-in centre when she accidentally scratches her bum after she's been chopping red chillies.

Once the kids are in bed and Dinah's bathed her bottom in the bidet, we're sitting on the balcony drinking wine when she says, 'When we get to Nottingham Center Parcs tomorrow I think we need to chill for a couple of days, Ben.'

A sheen of sweat shines her face. Her hair is a mess because all her shampoo spilt in the bathroom bag yesterday and she hasn't been able to wash it.

'And there's lots for the kids there.'

She looks at me beseechingly.

'Make it sort of a holiday, you mean?'

'We need a break. We don't even have weekends. I was on my own when you saw your dad. I'm not saying it was easier for you but today's been really hard.'

'Even before you burnt your bum?'

'Even before.'

She manages a laugh.

'How's it now?'

'Honestly, it's so painful.'

'OK,' I say. 'Because of the bum.'

The apartments are arranged around a central courtyard. In the apartment opposite us, I can see a couple in silhouette arguing. You can tell they're arguing from their hand gestures and sudden movements. We watch the shape of the man walk off and return. From his stance, bent forward, pleading, it appears he's the one losing the dispute. The woman rises from the sofa. Their bodies merge for a moment and we wonder if they're embracing but instead she walks away.

'It's like watching a thriller,' Dinah says. 'She'll probably come back with an axe and we'll be the only murder witnesses.'

We wait for the woman to return with an axe but she doesn't. I pour us each another glass of wine.

'Today reminded me of when I worked at the *Evening Post*,' says Dinah. 'Being in that square. I used to go there for my sad little lunch. I didn't want to go to the canteen because I didn't know anybody.'

'I forgot about your time there.'

After Dinah and I split up, I moved to London to be closer to my family and school friends while she found a job on the *Nottingham Evening Post*.

'I didn't have a portfolio. It was awful. I just wrote picture captions and news in briefs. And I got all the six o'clock shifts because I was new. One day I left the newsroom after my shift and I was called to the phone on the reception desk downstairs. It was the news desk. Where are you going? Home. No, you're not – come back here. They made me sit at my desk for ten minutes doing nothing until they said I could go.'

'Arseholes.'

'And I was seeing that Relate counsellor, who practically said what an idiot I was for leaving you. It's what I thought about in the square. I never thought you'd forgive me.'

'Tell me more about your unhappiness.'

'You like my unhappiness?'

'In the context of not being with me I do.'

She tells me how miserable she was when she heard I'd moved to London.

'And do you know what I never told you about at the time?' I ask her.

'What?'

And I'm not sure what makes me say it. 'Before you slept with that record shop guy, around the time my mum was sick I almost had a thing with a work experience girl at the *Mercury*.'

Dinah looks at me.

'Nothing happened but it nearly did.'

'That's strange you never told me that.'

'It seemed important at the time but after my mum died it didn't seem important any more.'

'Was she pretty?'

'Yes.'

'Did I know her?'

'No.'

'And nothing happened?'

'I kissed her in a taxi. She wanted us to go for dinner. I wrote her a letter explaining I was in love with you. My letter was pompous and tragic in tone. I think I invoked the film *Casablanca*.'

'Why didn't you tell me?'

'At the time? At the time I thought I was changing. Growing apart from you. She'd been in a battered wives hostel. She was a very serious person. Her hero was Nelson Mandela. I felt I could talk to her about sad things in a way I couldn't with anyone else.'

'With me, you mean.'

I don't say anything.

'So how come nothing happened?'

'I think I knew deep down it wasn't real.'

'Well, well, well,' Dinah says.

She sips her drink.

'I don't know why I'm telling you this now.'

'Why are you telling me this now?'

'Maybe because looking back on it I'm thinking it might not have happened with you and the record shop guy if it hadn't been for this.'

We stare at the apartment across the courtyard.

'I got back in touch with her after you left me too. After I moved to London. When I was writing my book. We went for dinner. She was horrible to me. Very dismissive. I was embarrassed about that. That's another reason I didn't tell you.'

'How old was she?'

'In her twenties.'

'And you were what then?'

'In my thirties.'

'You idiot,' she says.

'I know.'

'What was her name?'

'Smith.'

'Smith!'

'After some Canadian writer her dad liked.'

'I don't remember her.'

'It was a long time ago.'

Dinah sips her drink. Her face is rigid, the way it goes when she's upset with me.

'Are you upset?'

'I don't know.'

'Shall I pull the nets round so we can argue in silhouette?'

She doesn't laugh. I picture Smith. Her frizzy black hair. The tight red round-necked jumpers she wore. The childish clumsy way she juggled things in her hands – a pen, a box of matches – whenever I was talking to her. How I'd catch her eye in the newsroom. The sight of her legs walking past my desk.

'I'm going to bed,' says Dinah.

'Shall I stay here?'

'Do what you want.'

I look across the courtyard wondering how the argument is going in their flat. I walk to the fridge to fetch another bottle of wine, taking flat-footed steps, my feet slightly splayed. It's Dad's walk.

In bed Dinah's reading. I lean over for a kiss. Her eyes are red. I wonder if she's been crying.

'You all right?'

'I'm fine.'

'Fine fine? Or just fine?'

'Fine fine. Come here,' she says.

I hug her tightly and now she is crying.

'We were both such fools,' she says.

'I know.'

'To think what might have happened. That we might not have had...'

She looks towards the kids' bedroom.

'But it didn't happen.'

CHAPTER 10

Draft Copy for Guidebook:
Noddingham, as Kevin Costner pronounced it so convincingly in *Robin Hood: Prince of Thieves*, is principally known for one thing: its connection to the evil sheriff of Robin Hood fame. Many city attractions are geared around him and the thigh-slapping outlaws in Lincoln green he hunted down with his blunt spoon, including The Tales of Robin Hood and Nottingham Castle. The city has been dubbed the gun crime capital of Britain, and so we fully expected to be ducking volleys of machine gun fire every few seconds as we shopped in the Old Market Square, the largest of its kind in Britain, and can only assume these tales have been exaggerated or else it all happens at night when parents with small children are safely inside drinking wine and watching HBO box sets. Other highlights include the city's lace market, the world's oldest pub, Ye Olde Trip to Jerusalem, and, a little further out, the Sherwood Forest Country Park where you'll find the Major Oak, the tree beneath which Robin Hood plighted his troth to Maid Marian, and a visitor centre where you'll be exposed to semi-boring detail about preserving heathland and managing forests that really needn't concern you unless you are either a) John Craven or b) a vole.

At Sherwood Forest Center Parcs we're allotted a villa in the Red Maple section. A grocery hamper awaits us – milk, sausages, Kettle Chips and two bottles of locally brewed beer. The villa has three bedrooms, a lounge and plate glass doors giving on to a BBQ area, and on one whole wall of the lounge is a restful colour photo of dappled woodland. Free bike hire has been arranged and Phoebe's been gifted a make-a-teddy session. The sense of comfort and order is palpable, yet there's something disquieting I can't put my finger on. It might be the amount of people with jumpers tied round their waists. It might be the number of bikes with children's seats and tag-alongs. Or it might be us.

As we follow our map to the cycle centre, it's like being on a cheery orienteering course. People with kids in tow stop to look at signs to the village square or the information centre, or Robin Hood's Adventure Golf, then back at their maps again. Their politeness is a sharp contrast to being buffeted by passers-by outside the Gala Bingo hall on Maid Marian Way. I no longer feel I must conceal my bumbag under my jumper. Instead of litter we see squirrels, swans, rabbits and moorhens. Changing the timing for the teddy-bear-making session is fine; we don't have to argue. At bike hire we forget our docket. No problem. All we do is give our villa number and it's sorted. It's easy, effortless. We should be relaxing but like Vietnam vets on home leave, we feel alienated.

'What is it?'

'I don't know,' says Dinah.

But we do know. It's like this is no longer our world but someone else's. Our normality is getting lost on ring roads. Our world is fighting to get toddler food heated up.

As we ride our bikes to Café Rouge in the village square for dinner I start to recognise toddler faces. It reminds me of the movie *The Truman Show*. Are they the same toddlers we saw earlier looking for the village square with their parents? And are they *really* still lost, or is our whole visit being choreographed by TV producers filming in secret our every waking moment for some ultimate reality show we've stumbled into unawares? And what happens at the edge of Sherwood Forest? Are we even allowed to leave Center Parcs before turnaround day?

In Café Rouge the kids' fishcakes arrive speedily and the waiter doesn't bat an eyelid bringing our enormous glasses of Pinot Grigio, but the kids are finding the adjustment hard as well. Charlie, his face admittedly pinched earlier by the straps of his cycle helmet, is tired and cries continually, while Phoebe, brutalised by us/the East Midlands/ the drunk on Maid Marian Way yesterday afternoon muttering obscenities, wets herself and runs off shouting, 'Fuck, fuck, fuck.'

'Fluff,' we shout after her. 'It's fluff, Phoebe.'

We have trouble sleeping. The kids, used to being in together, cry out alone in their beds. Charlie demands more and more milk and Phoebe has nightmares about the skulls she saw on the pod ride at The Tales of Robin Hood.

The next morning we try to enjoy the facilities but can't relax. Cars are banned except on change-over days. You leave them at the entrance car park and use bikes. But, for some reason, we cannot bear to be without our car. We've lived in it for a month. It's our home, it's our lifeline. The one constant in our lives. Driving illegally to the Jardin des Sports, dodging bikes and walkers, for Phoebe's make-a-teddy session, I'm contemptuously stared at by parents as if I'm stood bolt upright staring out of the gun turret of a Challenger tank.

'They hate us, Ben.'

'I know.'

'What should we do?'

'Drive slowly and pretend we're lost.'

'How do I do that?'

'Shrug a lot, gesticulate.'

But emerging from the make-a-bear session there's a stroppy note on the windscreen: 'Move it.' We turn up for 'swimming with baby dolphins' at the Subtropical Swimming Paradise and find another. 'Move it immediately,' this one says, in red ink.

'What'll they do next?'

'Capital letters?'

That afternoon we try the Time Out Club for kids in the Jardin des Sports. The idea is that Dinah and I will have a little time on our own. We've not had any in daylight hours since Brighton more than six weeks ago. We're excited.

'I'll buy *Heat* magazine and read it in the bath,' says Dinah. 'What about you?'

'I'll go back to bed. I'll snooze, wake up, read, snooze again, wake up and read. I love doing that.'

'I don't feel bad. Do you?'

'Not at all. They must be sick of the sight of us.'

'We'll probably have to drag them out.'

Within minutes of dropping them off we get a call from the nursery. Phoebe won't be separated from Charlie, and is standing at the door between the two rooms stamping her feet.

'Can't they go in together?'

'What age are they?'

I tell her.

'Sorry, we don't put children that age together.'

'But they're brother and sister?'

'If I made an exception for you…'

'What shall we do?' I ask Dinah.

'Give them a few more minutes.'

A few minutes later there's another call – this time I'm told Charlie's not settling. He's crying, inconsolable. He wants Phoebe and is calling for Mum and Dad.

'What do we do?'

'This is so typical. *So* typical,' says Dinah. 'One hour. They won't give us ONE hour. I haven't even got to This Week In Pictures.'

'Do you want me to go?'

'Thank you.'

Extracting the kids, I'm caught red-handed when I come back out.

'That's your car, isn't it?' says the security man. 'I've been monitoring you.'

'Have you?'

'Yes,' he says.

'I see. I didn't know I was being monitored.'

'You're in Red Maple, aren't you?'

I nod.

The security guard asks me to move the car and, I'm not sure what gives me the boldness, but I find I'm asking what'll happen if I don't. He's clearly stumped, has probably never been asked the question before.

'Erm, I will... tell you off,' he says, 'and...' and I wait for the next bit. Will he sling us off the park? Contact Frommer's? Impound the car? Rescind the complimentary breakfast hamper with the locally brewed ales? '... and that isn't very nice, is it?' he concludes, sounding like me feebly rebuking Phoebe.

Back at Red Maple, when Dinah emerges from the bath, full of gossip about Dougie Poynter from McFly and Hayden Panettiere, we leave the park for the afternoon 'to take the heat off', we joke. At the gates we half expect to hear *The Truman Show* producer shouting to us from giant speakers to return. We joke the gates will be mysteriously broken, that choreographed traffic jams will prevent us leaving.

Our nearest attraction is the Vina Cooke Museum of Dolls & Bygone Childhood, thirty minutes up the A1. The kids fall asleep, are still flat out when we arrive.

'What shall we do?' asks Dinah.

'We don't both have to go in. Do you want me to go?'

'You're being very nice today,' says Dinah, suspiciously.

'Am I?'

'Feeling a bit guilty about Smith?'

She raises her eyebrows.

'Stop it.'

The museum looks like someone's house, which it is. Amassed by Vina and her husband Charles over forty years, the largest collection of dolls in Britain is housed in the museum. Vina shows me around, pointing out a copy of the Cliff Richard doll she made and presented to the singer in 1959. It was shortly afterwards that Cliff himself began collecting dolls and not long after this he recorded 'Living Doll'. Coincidence or not? Vina lets me decide.

There are pictures of bygone celebrities on the walls including those of several, like Reginald Bosanquet, who died just as Vina, not at all menacingly, was preparing to make dolls of them. Vina learned to make dolls out of socks and her husband used to construct them out of porcelain. Now a major player in the doll world, she tells me she only makes them by appointment for large fees 'that I will not disclose'.

In one room upstairs, hundreds of dolls are all turned eerily to face me as I enter the door. More scary is the workroom downstairs, where, laid out face down on a lace draped dining table, there is a plastic doll, its detached arms and an ominous pair of sharp scissors lying close by.

It's the 'operating table' of what Vina calls the 'the doll hospital'. They mend dolls, new and old. They remake eyes, reattach limbs. It's in this room I realise I'm being referred to, when Vina and her husband Charles think I'm out of earshot, as 'the man'. As in, 'The man wants to know about the Shirley Temple letters.' And, 'The man is asking about The Beatles dolls.'

Back in the car, Dinah and I decide a doll museum curator would be a great new Royston Vasey character in *The League of Gentlemen*. We pad the character out as we drive back.

'Silence, dollies. We agreed that would never happen again.'

'I am sorry you have upset the dollies. NOW YOU WILL HAVE TO GO.'

Returning to Center Parcs, it takes me a while to realise the road signs have all moved. It's like World War Two when the Germans needed to be confused in case of invasion. Entry signs are now exit signs and vice versa. Where we turn right for Red Maple, there's now a No Entry sign. Whatever we do, whichever way we turn, we cannot return to the villa. Defeated, we're forced to abandon the car in the main entrance car park.

We spend the rest of the afternoon riding around on bikes with tag-alongs. The kids love it. It's 26 degrees. I'm so hot I tie my jumper round my waist. Dinah does the same.

'This is nice,' Dinah admits, cycling beside me.

'I know, we should have done this earlier.'

Later I see a VW Passat creeping around the village square. I dismount my bike way before I have to and stare after the driver in a hyperbolic display of anger and protection. He shrugs and gesticulates. And I have to stop myself saying to Dinah, 'God, that's selfish.'

That night, sat outside, it's comforting watching other parents performing the rituals we've just completed – feeding their children, putting them to bed. The smell of barbecued meat wafts through the trees, there's a cackle of moorhen, distant threads of laughter. We're wrapped in blankets drinking wine, and I'm editing the day's photos when Dinah says, 'What you told me last night.' She gives me an arch look. 'It does make me wonder what else you haven't told me.'

I tap my nose.

'There's a fifteen-year rule,' I say. 'It's like government papers. That's how long until they're released. I'm doing all sorts right now you won't know about for years.'

She flicks the end of her blanket at me.

'You wouldn't dare.'

'I know.'

'Seriously, though?'

'Dinah!'

I fetch some crisps and two locally brewed ales. I sit back down. Dinah leans forward, wrapping herself more tightly in the blanket.

'Come on, what stopped you? Being serious now. I don't mind. It was years ago.'

'You.'

She nods. 'Good answer.'

I remove the cap on her beer and pass it to her. She looks away, biting her lip.

'God, I was a bitch. Your family really hated me, didn't they?'

'My dad didn't.'

'Pen and Buster?'

'Yeah, they did.'

She laughs.

'Thanks for softening that for me.'

'That's all right.'

She holds my hand across the table. She twiddles my wedding ring.

'Although, you were horrible to me.'

'You wanted to settle down. I didn't and I didn't take you seriously. My mum was ill. I took my eye off the ball. And we were very young and… why are you looking at me like that?'

'I'm not,' she says. But she carries on with the same piercing look.

'Dinah, I'd hardly tell you about something that almost happened that you had no idea about if something really had happened, would I?'

She picks up a crisp.

'That's true.'

She pops it in her mouth.

'So your dad supported me, did he?'

'Of course.'

'He saw how much you loved me?'

'Plus he was always going to take the opposite side to me in any dispute.'

Dinah laughs.

'Your family are so funny about you.'

'I'm the baddie, it's my role.'

CHAPTER 11

When I was a teenager and my dad took us on family walks he'd sniff the air or suddenly stand stock-still and pull me back by my elbow and say, 'Listen!' And when I said, 'What? I can't hear anything,' he'd walk on, saying, 'Exactly – wonderful isn't it?' and it just irritated me, making me wish I was back at home zapping Starship Battlecruisers on my Atari. When he read me poetry I felt embarrassed because he was becoming so ecstatic about the unusual placement of the word *bough* in a sentence, and his preference for black and white war films, usually featuring a submarine, where there could be up to five minutes of total silence only punctuated by a sonar bleep, alienated me. When he reverently stroked the label on a bottle of wine and said, 'Life's too short for bad wine', or sucked a piece of tender meat in a rich sauce and said, 'This is the life', I thought, 'No, it's not, it's rubbish – I want Coke and crinkle chips.' He gave me old classics to read, their pages crisp as toast, and he tried to teach me geography and enthuse me about space. 'So the light you're seeing now has come from the past, don't you find that amazing, my son, *my son?*' he'd have to say, as my eyes would have wandered enviously from the dining room this took place in to Buster outside playing keepy-uppy. And it's painful now to remember his sunken head in the driver's seat of the camper van as Mum would eject Beethoven's Fifth from the cassette desk and I'd pipe up from the back, 'Can we have Bananarama now?'

That said, adolescent rebellion then meant to me stealing a hot hatch, drugs, anti-social behaviour, maybe some under-age sex. All I had to do for my dad to think I was The Wild One when I was sixteen was to leave, despite being told not to, used tea mugs in my bedroom, then deny they were there when challenged about this. He'd go to bed convinced I was on the fast track to a young offenders' institution because I wore trainers *most of the time*, didn't enjoy *Circus Act of the Year* on TV 'quite as much as I used to', and spiked my hair with Country Born gel rather than paste it to my head in the Lego-style side parting he'd insisted on for the last eight years because it was like his and could be done at Roy's in Chesham for £2.50. I wound my dad up so much somehow just being a teenager under the same roof as him, the night he dropped me at college he wrote a only half jokey letter stating, 'I am now opening a bottle of champagne. I shall drink it very slowly, with a very large smile on my face. I am by turns proud and appalled by you, my son. I reckon based on your sister's experiences you might well visit home three times this term, where I would have felt inclined to give you on each occasion £50. In the bottom of your bag I hope you found a cheque, for £150. Please, let's not see you until Christmas. I don't think my heart could take it. Love you to death, you utter menace, Dad.'

Staring closely at the swollen red behind of a Barbary macaque monkey in the Trentham Monkey Forest, Phoebe tells me: 'Daddy, they've not got our bums, have they? They have their own bums.' They have indeed got their own bums. And also one of Charlie's Roary the Racing Car socks. We're in Staffordshire at a 60-acre reserve of 140 free-ranging monkeys not exactly sure why we've come – but that isn't unusual. Our itinerary was compiled weeks ago, and with no spare time to adjust it, or even to read it until the day we're supposed to do it, we quite often turn up at places blind with only two or three written words to go on. In this case it just says beside the address and phone number in the blue file: 'Monkey Forest, the Trentham Estate, Southern Entrance, Stone Road. Pick up passes from Monkey Forest ticket office. They're not in cages.'

We've been away six weeks now, have driven 2,000 miles and eaten out so often Phoebe's come to believe everything laminated is a children's menu. In PC World buying a replacement Bébétel lead the other day she attempted to order spaghetti from a flyer for the Samsung M1640 laser printer. And we've stayed so briefly in that many cities and large towns – Hereford, Worcester, Gloucester, Northampton, Warwick, Cardiff, Swansea, Newport, Coventry, Birmingham, Leicester, Nottingham – we're starting to feel like a touring rock band minus the fans, the glamour, the adrenalin rush of performing, and with Organix Goodies Organic Alphabet Biscuits instead of hard drugs.

Veterans of the road, we drive in the mornings after check-out when the kids are fresh, and late afternoon when Charlie and Phoebe are liable to sleep. To cheapen and quicken lunchtimes we steal rolls from hotel breakfast buffets. We did this secretly to start with, slipping them into the buggy basket when waitresses were out of the room refilling butter dishes or fetching coffee. Semi-feral now, we snaffle large portions of the buffet – not just bread but cheese, yoghurts, cake, fruit. Sometimes we even ask for napkins to wrap it all up in. The censorious stares we've learnt to almost welcome. ('Nosey bat at five o'clock, seen me swipe the camembert triangles, give her a big smile on the way out.') We rejoice in living off the land; pride ourselves on this. We steal every branded pen left in hotel rooms to make notes with. We swipe hot chocolate sachets from refreshment baskets for the days we're in serviced apartments; soaps, toothpaste, bubble bath and hand lotions for the same reason.

If we're all in one room, we've discovered if we screen off Charlie so he can't see any of us, he, and therefore we too, will sleep better. It's the first thing we do now – rearrange our hotel room. We'll move beds, bookcases, wardrobes if we have to. We've learnt never to be without treats. To be without sweets in a car with two under-fours is the imprudent equivalent of walking through a vampire-infested graveyard without a silver cross. OK, you might get away with it – but why the hell risk it?

A routine's finally emerged. While Dinah dresses the kids in the morning I call my dad. He tells me what he's eaten for breakfast, how he slept. I tell him where we are. I clean Charlie's Avent bottles from the day before in the bathroom sink using free shampoo sachets in place of washing-up liquid. I fill up two water bottles, pack a day bag of their favourite toys. After breakfast I load the car up while Dinah orders hot milk for Charlie and another load to decant into the flask to keep warm for his lunchtime feed. We're on the road by 9.30 a.m. and, after celebrating the bill, ('Absolutely nothing. Hooray!' High five) we'll hit our first attraction by 10 a.m.

In fact, we've begun to enjoy ourselves. Why not? Each day is different. We're seeing new things. It's become an adventure. We've no household jobs, very little responsibility. All we need do is check out baby-changing facilities at aquaria, Munch Bunch lunch boxes at small breed farms. We give restaurants one to three stars based on their child friendliness, their propensity to supply dinosaur-shaped chicken nuggets and hand out colouring-in sheets. We devise 'Did You Know?' box copy, Frommer's insider tips. I take pictures of the kids looking cute in front of landmarks and furry animals. That's it, that's our whole life.

As the baby monkey chews Charlie's sock, a yellow-shirted guide wanders over. She explains baby monkeys are exceptionally curious about everything (including toddler footwear) and that it's important from now on to keep our children close lest they're kidnapped by these monkeys, assumed into their monkey troupe and taught, who knows, to come running for melon rind at fifteen minutes past every hour.

Phoebe's still looking for closure on the monkey bums issue at the Banana Cafe at the end.

'We have people's bums. And monkeys have monkeys' bums. We don't want a monkey's bum, do we? That's their bums.'

'That's right. We have our own bums, Phoebe.'

'And other animals have their bums as well.'

'They do.'

We eat our stolen buffet cheese inside our stolen buffet rolls. The kids watch a nature film in a hut next door, where the ranger finds us and returns Charlie's chewed sock, and this is the hardest part of the day – when Phoebe's happily debating monkey bums, when Charlie's charging around, and we must bully them on to the next attraction. Charlie squeals like a pig bound for the slaughter house as I strap him into the buggy. In the car seat Dinah must virtually karate chop him in the middle to bend him into it. And the only way to get Phoebe back into the Astra nowadays is to make a mini assault course of the experience. Already allowed to enter via any door and given three minutes to clamber about muddying everything her feet touch before she settles into her seat, today she wants to climb in through the hatchback boot.

'What do you think?'

Dinah shrugs.

'Go on then, pops. But this is a special treat, OK? This isn't happening every day.'

It's at times like this, waiting impatiently as Phoebe scrambles over bags, squashing food in the cool box – becoming more and more like an actual monkey – that I wonder how our world will look further down the line, with so much ground already conceded. Will Charlie, by the time we reach Cornwall, be sitting unbelted on my lap in the driver's seat scoffing through a family-sized bag of Mini Cheddars? Will Phoebe be curled up in the roof box playing Cooking Mama on a Nintendo DS, banging down on the roof every time she fancies a Magnum Feast? It's hard to know what to do about discipline. Half the time we think Phoebe needs reining in; the rest of the time, feeling guilty we've dragged her on such an arduous trip, we give her more leeway. In Brighton a solitary chocolate button was a treat. Now Phoebe has a chocolate croissant for breakfast, sometimes Coco Pops as well, normally a buffet-swiped blueberry muffin when we set off, and every afternoon she expects a Cornetto or a vanilla ice cream with a flake. At dinner if chocolate ice cream isn't a dessert option, there's more trouble. Before this trip she watched ten minutes of *In the Night Garden* before bed. Now it's CBeebies every morning as we pack, an afternoon film in the car, more CBeebies when we get in, and last night she wouldn't go to bed until she'd watched *Gok's Fashion Fix*.

In the Wedgwood Visitor Centre in Barlaston, just outside Stoke-on-Trent, we're in the Ivy House cafe eating a complimentary buffet lunch waiting for our factory tour to begin when Phoebe insists on a high chair for her cardigan.

I look at Dinah. She sighs. I fetch the high chair. Anything to avoid a scene. In the absence of the toys we had no room for in the car, Phoebe's been making do. That's another thing worrying us.

She plays with attraction leaflets, pay and display tickets, gravel, wild flowers she collects in a pink beach bucket. She plays with sugar sachets and mini milk cartons that she takes from hotel rooms and calls 'my treasure'. It shows a degree of creativity, I've argued up until now, to make a game out of tea and coffee-making facilities, but maybe, I think today, watching Phoebe strap her cardy into the high chair, it's gone too far.

Trying to get into the game, I ask Phoebe, 'Does cardigan want dinner?'

Phoebe spasms with anger. 'No, Daddy – she's not called cardigan. Her name's Ella. And she's my baby and I'm her mummy and she's three.'

I ask if *Ella* wants dinner and Phoebe shouts. 'No, she's had dinner you silly billy and now Ella's tired and you're waking her up. You're very naughty, Daddy, and there will be no mint Cornetto for you ever, *ever* again.'

'Is she doing me, or you?' I ask Dinah.

'I don't know. Phoebe!' says Dinah, 'Please don't talk to Daddy like that.'

Phoebe folds her arms in the learned pose of the huff.

After dinner, Phoebe and Charlie are gifted sessions in the demonstration area, making pots. While Dinah supervises this I complete the factory tour. I'm led through a series of open-plan booths, where I learn about the fettling process, jigger heads and the 1764 fluting lathe designed by Josiah Wedgwood that's still used today as no computer works as accurately. I'm told Paul McCartney's a fan of the Asprey Collection and that Josiah Wedgwood had a leg amputated after a childhood infection and was the grandson of Charles Darwin. The factory floor's split into small work stations. Craftsmen listen to headphones as they work, the atmosphere reminiscent of college art classes.

Returning to the demonstration area, I find things aren't going well. Ella's now ruling the family with an iron fist. As Phoebe paints a ceramic plate, Charlie attempts to sweep £5,000 Asprey Collection teapots off the shelves while munching through an assortment of modelling substances like he's at an all-you-can-eat clay buffet.

'Charlie, take that out of your mouth. I'll put you in the buggy.'

'No good!' says Dinah.

He's already been turfed out of the buggy, she explains, because 'Ella needs more sleep'.

Not only this, Ella is also demanding she be allowed to press a rabbit in clay for £5. It's one thing to be bossed about by a three-year-old, quite another to be bossed about by a three-year-old's cardigan.

'OK, Phoebe that's enough.'

'NO!'

'Phoebe, if you want ice cream for dinner.'

'NO!'

'Right. We're going.'

'NO!'

As I carry her rigid body through the remote-controlled double doors under my arm like a surfboard, Dinah laden with gifts – key rings, Peter Rabbit toys, gift-wrapped Portland thimbles – the head of publicity's shoulders visibly un-tense. If we'd threatened to stay to watch the life of Josiah Wedgwood film in the Experience Centre, she'd probably have given us a £5,000 Asprey Collection teapot as well to get rid of us.

We take the A53 north through Leek. The Old Hall Hotel in the spa town of Buxton is a large, square, brown-stone ivy-clad building beside the beautiful Victorian opera house. The hotel has creaky, sloping floors and boasts it's the oldest hotel in the world, the claim dubiously resting on the fact Mary Queen of Scots stayed here under house arrest, the equivalent of calling Wormwood Scrubs the largest hotel in London.

After checking in, we ascend to our room on the top floor in a wooden lift so jerky we arrive feeling like we've been physically thrown upstairs. Dinah flops on the bed, exhausted. We have two beds, separated by a curtain. There's a round window overlooking the opera house. I throw the bags down and before I even unpack I march Phoebe back to the lift. Out of the hotel we turn left past St Ann's Well. We cross Terrace Road and I march her down pedestrianised Spring Gardens, where I buy her, from various charity shops, a dolly, four teddies, a *Princess Diaries* jigsaw and a bucket of Lego bricks.

In the oriental-themed Pavilion Gardens, opposite the hotel and next to the opera house, Phoebe plays with these new toys. The River Wye meanders through the park and I can see Solomon's Temple on top of Grinlow Hill across the main road. A brass band is trumping out Beatles tunes from a bandstand and there are several strange red-faced turkey-like birds looking at me as I talk to my dad. There's good and bad news. The bad news is Dad's stent definitely needs refitting. There's something wrong with the plug. The fluid's not draining properly. But on the upside he's been told there's a small hope that if his liver functioning improves he'll be able to have some targeted chemo.

'I'm not hopeful, my son, but we clutch at this and if this falls through our fingers we clutch at something else.'

'That's great news,' I say focusing on the positive.

'And where are you now, my son?'

'Buxton.'

'Ah, the lovely opera house.'

'I'm looking at it right now. As well as some very strange ducks.'

'Muscovy ducks,' says Dad.

'Dad, I was wondering if you played here.'

After Cambridge my dad was going to be a history master, but during his teacher training at Wroxham College, he auditioned for the Cambridge Footlights. In 1963 he was part of its revue show, *A Clump of Plinths*, which, renamed the *Cambridge Circus*, transferred from the Edinburgh Festival to the West End before Dad ended up performing off Broadway. The show was made into the radio series *I'm Sorry, I'll Read That Again* and from this platform most of Dad's contemporaries went on to become household names in comedy: John Cleese, Graham Chapman, Graeme Garden, Bill Oddie and Tim Brooke-Taylor. My dad moved to the other side of the mike and became a light entertainment producer at the BBC. 'I played the straight men, my son. That was my role. The army majors, the policemen, the headmasters. The authority figures. I knew where talent was and it wasn't with yer old man. I was a good producer, though,' that's what he used to say.

'You're thinking of the Georgian Theatre Royal in Yorkshire,' says Dad, coughing before he's finished the sentence. 'Are you going there?'

'I'm not sure.' We're not but for some reason I don't want to disappoint Dad.

'And where's next, my wandering boy?'

'Chester via Knutsford tomorrow.'

'Ahhh, Knutsford!'

'I've never been back, have you?'

'Not for thirty years,' says Dad. 'Happy times there, my son. Like yours now with your wonderful family.'

Every hour Dad's bag fills up and needs emptying. The egg timer goes off now.

'I'm being summoned,' he says.

We say goodbye and, walking back though the gardens, I notice I'm doing Dad's walk again.

At dinner in the George Potter Bar Dinah tells me she's noticed something.

'What's that?'

'You are getting more like your dad.'

'His walk?'

'No. But I have seen you copying it.'

'It's comforting. I don't know why. Why is that?'

'I copy the facial expressions of people I like sometimes. What I was going to say is you make the best of everything,' she says.

It's what my mum used to say about my dad and it makes me feel so ridiculously proud for a second I struggle to blink back a tear.

'I mean, obviously you're a terrible bully as well...'

CHAPTER 12

Draft Copy for Guidebook:
The good people of Chester have three main hobbies: shopping at Browns of Chester for scatter cushions, dressing up like Romans and murdering the Welsh. Chester folk have been murdering the Welsh for centuries and are so keen on it they have ensured, despite many significant advances in human rights, that it's still perfectly legal to slaughter Welshmen with a crossbow within the city walls provided it's after 9 p.m. Chester has other impressive claims to fame. It has the best preserved Roman city walls in Britain and is also where the teen Channel 4 soap Hollyoaks is based. Besides (if you are my wife) looking out for actor Jeronimo Best (the annoying Spanish dance teacher Fernando) from the top deck of a City Sightseeing bus, families can boat along the River Dee or have their picture taken with one of the many costumed Roman centurions sweating like greasy pasties near the Eastgate Clock. Within striking distance are the aquarium in Ellesmere Port and Chester Zoo, where our daughter's highlight was watching a schoolgirl from Rainhill getting wedged in the Marmot Mania tunnel because of her overlarge sandwich bag, prompting mournful shouts from the darkness to her concerned/highly amused friends,

'Get Mrs Harris – I'm stook.' My own top moment, however, was overhearing a man with a heavy German accent at an ice cream stand near the elephants asking for 'Von Nobbily-Bobbily', a phrase that has become a family joke as in: How many Nobbily-Bobbilies do you want? 'Von Nobbily-Bobbily.'

We drive round two sides of Knutsford common and make a right onto Northwich Road and then another right up Ladies Mile. And there it is. The house we moved to when I was eight is squat, red brick and set back from the road with a strip of common land between it and the front garden that Buster and I used to play headers and volleys on.

'What are we doing?' says Phoebe.

'We're looking at the house Daddy used to live in.'

'When I was a little boy, Phoebe.'

She grins.

'Hard to believe, isn't it?'

'You lived here when you were a little boy?'

'When I was a little boy.'

'What were you like when you were a little boy, Daddy?'

'I was like Charlie. I liked football, cars and trains. I had ginger hair over my ears and lots of freckles.'

And as I say this a memory returns. I'm sitting in a white T-shirt with a picture of a tiger on the front on the living room floor with Buster swishing cars across the parquet floor. The Living Room Grand Prix, the Dining Room Grand Prix, and Our Bedroom Grand Prix. 'Well,' I'd say into my mike fist. 'Would you believe it? Lorry, under the telly yesterday, written off with no chance, *takes* the Dining Room Grand Prix!' Buster tried harder for cars he preferred. He'd put more into their swish, make sure they went straighter. When his favourites lost, he'd be supportive. 'Scooby van, did well, didn't he?' And if I felt there was a story I'd back him up. 'Scooby, on his first Bedroom Grand Prix wins *third place*, but that long ginger hair of Mum's wrapped round the wheel axle that his team can't get rid of, might cost him dear in the living room.'

'What else did you do when you were a little boy?' asks Phoebe.

'We always played Monopoly on Sunday afternoons after my mum's roast beef. Monopoly's a board game like Tummy Ache, Phoebe. My dad made the loser do a forfeit.'

'What's a forfeit?'

'If we lost all our money in the game, my daddy made us do something silly. Something to make everyone else laugh.'

One forfeit I remember was standing in the middle of the road about where we're parked now in my pyjamas and having to sing 'Baa, Baa, Black Sheep' at the top of my voice while the family watched from the doorstep, Dad laughing and shouting, 'Louder, we can't hear you. How many bags full?'

'Maybe we should play Family Monopoly,' I say.

'And do forfeits?' says Phoebe.

'Yeah.'

'Although maybe not ones in the road,' says Dinah.

Our first attraction of the day is the Chester City Sightseeing bus. We love City Sightseeing buses for two reasons, a) because they give a great overview of a city, allowing you to work out where everything is in relation to everything else, and b) because the kids are always gifted a packet of Haribo sweets when they board and we get to sit down for five minutes while they eat them.

On the bus the commentator mixes historical context with tittle-tattle about, for example, the planned House of Fraser that will increase the city's retail pull. He tells us about the Airbus A380 super jumbo that flies low over the city and that it was while visiting a cottage called Nowhere near City Road, where

The Beatles played at the Royalty Theatre in 1963, that John Lennon was inspired to write 'Nowhere Man'. We exit the bus outside St John the Baptist church. The Norman church, which used to be the city's cathedral, is where Dinah and I tied the knot on 8 December 2001, the rationale being it was the nearest nice place to her hometown of Widnes.

'Fancy a peep?' says Dinah.

'We can't really not.'

Inside Charlie shrugs off his Ben 10 rucksack, pours out its contents and begins constructing a circular rail track. Every time we stop now, even for just a couple of minutes, off comes his rucksack and Charlie lays rails.

'Bless him!' says Dinah.

'Any chance he gets.'

The church is empty and, walking down the nave, I can vividly remember the moment I saw Dinah at the back of the church on her dad's arm, her white dress merging with the sunlight. There hadn't been as much traffic on the Runcorn Bridge as her mum suspected and for the first time in her life Dinah had been early, catching the organist out. Phoebe lies down on the stone floor and starts colouring beneath the altar and I can remember walking from the vestry after signing the register trying not to stand on Dinah's train, the confetti being thrown as we'd stepped into the Roller, and the conversation we had after we pulled away.

'It was shit. I wish I 'adn't gone through with it,' she'd told me.

'It was a sham,' I said.

'We don't love each other.'

'We'll get divorced now.'

'What do you think of my dress?'

'I prefer you in pyjamas.'

'And the terrible thing is you mean that.'

Driving home the next morning, I'd kept wanting to hold her hand across the front seat of the car as we discussed whose was the best speech, who was best dressed. That afternoon before setting off for Heathrow we'd unwrapped the presents and rifled through our cards hoping for vouchers.

'Anything?'

'Nothing. "To Dinah and Ben, wishing all the happiness in the world, hope you have a wonderful day," etc. Sue and Pete. What's in there?'

'The same. "Always knew it would work out. Have a wonderful life together now and for always," blah blah, no vouchers.'

Dinah had blagged two weeks in Mauritius in exchange for an article she was writing for *Business Traveller* magazine and at the BA check-in desk her travel connection got us upgraded.

'I don't have to tell you how clever you are, do I?' I'd said, as we sat down.

'No, but do it anyway.'

'You're so clever. I'm so excited.'

'What about?'

'Everything.'

'The flight?' she asked.

'No, everything. Being married, the honeymoon, the flight.'

'We'll have a glass of champagne before take-off.'

'Great idea.'

In that business cabin we fiddled with everything.

'Look how far back the seats go.'

'Have you seen the lumbar position?'

'Look, I've put my socks on already!'

'Let's see the film choices.'

'Could the cabin crew take their stations for take-off.'

'Oh Dinah, I'm not ready for take-off. There's too much to sort out.'

'We don't want to take off,' said Dinah.

'I really am so happy to be married.'

And Dinah had kissed me, then leant forward and kissed me again before making notes about the Butler's Secret cheese on the menu for her article. And waking up from a micro snooze a short while later my wedding ring had knocked against the meal tray, instantly reminding me what had happened, that I was married to Dinah now, and I don't think I've ever felt so happy in my life.

We pass under the city's famous Eastgate Clock on our way to the Dewa Roman Experience on Bridge Street, where, according to the blue file, kids can fire Roman catapults, build hypocausts and sit in a recreated Roman galley. But there's a problem. The Northwest Regional Development Agency hasn't cleared our visit and now the museum's too full of school parties. Dinah's response to conflict is to out-polite people. This passive-aggressive stance unfortunately rarely succeeds because nobody apart from me (and often not even me) can detect her voice rising half an octave, the only aggressive bit of her passive-heavy passive-aggressiveness.

'That's fine,' she informs the ticket booth man. 'We'll come back later. Come on, kids.'

'I can't guarantee it'll be any better later,' he says. 'You're not on the list.'

I try to explain we should be on the list and, when this fails, I ask if he perhaps could ring the Northwest Regional Development Agency. Or let me ring them and pass the phone to him.

'Or maybe you could speak to your manager,' I say. 'And check with him.'

Dinah holds my arm.

'Ben!' Dinah says. 'I'm sorry,' she says again to the man. 'Come on, kids,' and her voice now raising a tiny fraction, 'Let's go to the park where we'll try to find something to write about.'

Walking to Grosvenor Park I try to explain to Dinah, who's now angry with me, that I have different responses to conflict.

'I tried politeness, this failed so I changed strategy and employed curtness. We'd probably have got in if you'd backed me up...'

'Asking the name of his boss. You sounded like an arsehole, Ben.'

'I asked if he could *call* his boss. And at least I didn't thank him to death.'

'You threatened him, that was *your* tone.'

'I was goading him into being helpful. My strategy matched the situation.'

'And asking if he was Welsh and then firing an imaginary arrow at him.'

'He didn't see that. I did that round the corner. You have to stand up for yourself once in a while.'

We've been told there's a miniature railway in Grosvenor Park and when we can't find it, I ask a litter picker by the fountain where it is. He shrugs and picks up a Calypso wrapper, and Dinah says 'Good strategy, Ben' like I've rubbed him up the wrong way as well. On our picnic I'm accused of being 'on edge' because I feel uncomfortable around the crazed squirrels here that approach us fearlessly on their hind legs looking to swipe the kids' Hula Hoops.

'They might have rabies, love.'

'They're squirrels, darling. Calm down.'

Part of our City Sightseeing pass includes a thirty-minute pootle along the River Dee on the Mississippi-style paddle steamer, the *Mark Twain*, that starts near the suspension bridge close to the park, and cruises up to the Earl's Eye along the Meadows. There's on-board commentary and it's quite relaxing until we reach the spot where witches were rolled in barrels into the water to see if they floated. Here Phoebe announces she wants back one of her rabbit pictures she completed in St John the Baptist church and had asked me to look after. My pockets are permanently filled with dirty feathers, flower petals, leaves and stones that Phoebe likes the look of, and also her rabbit pictures. At any one time I've dozens on me. From time to time, at great personal risk, I initiate a cull.

'Daddy, can I see my rabbit picture?'

I rootle through my pockets, find a rabbit picture and hand it over.

'Not that one, Daddy, the one with the ears.'

I stand up, check my pockets and find another.

'That's not a rabbit. That's a puppy, Daddy.'

'Really?'

'Of course, rabbits don't have long tails, Daddy.'

'You're right. Sorry.'

I pull out another.

Phoebe shakes her head.

I try to interest her in Carlton Villa, a house the boat is passing that the commentator's talking about, but she's too canny for that.

'Daddy, I want my rabbit picture.'

'I know, I know, and I will find it.'

She starts going through my pockets herself, reaching down into my jeans and yanking out her hand, scattering feathers, flowers, ticket stubs and coins on the deck. She spins me round to reach the other pocket. 'Oh, you've lost it,' she keeps repeating, as more detritus lands on the deck. 'My favourite picture in the whole world.'

'What's that, Phoebe?'

She stares where I'm pointing.

'It's a cormorant. Did you see that? It was a cormorant.' And, when that doesn't interest her, I pretend I've seen a Nemo fish, 'Look, floating by – a Nemo fish.'

'Let me see your shirt pocket, Daddy.'

'I'm serious, look! A Nemo fish. Did you see it? There!'

Phoebe stares over the railing as an orange crisp packet washes past.

'Oh, yeah! I seen it!' she shouts. 'I seen it! Charlie, I seen a Nemo fish.'

'You see?' I tell Dinah, as the kids point and shout at the crisp packet. 'What you do is apply the right strategy for the right situation.'

After the boat trip I insist we return to the Dewa.

'You'll make another scene.'

'I didn't make a scene last time, love.'

'No, if we're going, I'll do it,' she says.

'You'll be passive-aggressive and he won't even know you're angry.'

'You had your go, Ben. It's my turn.'

I'm taking photos of the eighteenth-century gilt-faced Eastgate Clock, according to our Northwest Regional Development Agency pack the second most photographed clock in Britain, when Dinah returns. Despite her triumphant face, I know straightaway it's actually bad news. For me, anyway. And I'm right. There was a different man on the till, she explains. The manager this time.

'Well?'

'We're barred, my love.'

'What?'

'After what you said. So much for there not being a scene. Maybe you'll listen to me next time.'

'I don't believe it.'

'They won't tolerate verbal abuse. We're barred.'

Except, as I point out to Dinah, I didn't swear at Dewa man.

I cursed around the corner from Dewa man, not *at* Dewa man. And I cursed the unfortunate *situation*. Not Dewa man himself. But Dinah's made up her mind. I was jumpy and cross. I've been jumpy and cross all day, and somehow I transferred this jumpy crossness to the ticket man and made him jumpy and cross as well. I probably made Phoebe jumpy and cross on the boat about her rabbit picture. Maybe the squirrels, too.

'That's outrageous. I need to talk to him.'

'You're not going to talk to him.'

'I didn't swear at him.'

'You'll make it worse.'

'You saw. I didn't swear at him, did I?'

'Can we leave it?'

'No.'

'Ben, from how angry he was I wouldn't be surprised if the Northwest Regional Development Agency's been informed.'

'Ooh, the Northwest Regional Development Agency's after me, is it? I'm really bricking it now. What are they going to do? Rescind our family pass to the Ellesmere Port aquarium? Recall the brochure they sent us on the Manchester Ship Canal?'

'Believe it or not I stuck up for you.'

'I doubt that very much.'

'I did, actually. And have you thought what you're going to do if this gets back to Frommer's?'

'That little shit. He probably panicked because he hadn't let us in and we're journalists, so to cover his arse he made out I swore at him.'

The NCP car park costs a whopping £9 for the few hours we've been here, which I pay very unjumpily and very uncrossly and it's actually Dinah, in Tesco, who decides we need a magnum of Pinot this evening.

Working our way through it with nibbles at our cottage in Helsby later, Dinah tells me her theory about my jumpiness: 'Today reminded you of your wedding day nerves, Ben. You were nervous because you weren't sure about marrying me because I wanted children. After what happened after your mum died. Now you realise if I'd listened to you we wouldn't have Charlie and Phoebe and that would devastate you. You were a huge idiot – you still are in many ways – but I forgive you. Now pass me the Frazzles you curt little shit.'

I pass her the Frazzles.

CHAPTER 13

*D*raft *Copy for Guidebook:*
    A big push by Visit Wales to attract tourists to the 'land of song' recently saw a series of ads featuring the fictitious Drake family engaging in wholesome family activities such as horse riding in the Brecon Beacons and camping in Snowdonia, all set against the backdrop of Sweet Baboo, a Welsh artist, singing 'How I'd Like to Live My Life'. Gravel-voiced TV comedian Rhod Gilbert starred in it, too, highlighting little-known facts about the country of his birth ('Who knew there was wine made in Wales?'). We must confess that prior to this research we had little experience of Wales. The first time my wife came, she and her brother and sister all contracted impetigo from filthy bed linen in the caravan they rented in Rhyl (Who knew there was impetigo in Wales?). Her second time, in Prestatyn, aged sixteen, she was clouted round her (thankfully tightly permed) head with a 1,000-megawatt torch by her dad after she returned to their static caravan post-midnight smelling of Lambert & Butler cigarettes with 'borstal boy Lee'. My own Welsh memories hinge on a week camping in the Brecon Beacons aged eight, where I was forced to amuse myself in an empty field with just a peacock

feather and the prospect of my dad's proffered 25p reward for finding a four-leaf clover (a plant I now realise doesn't exist). We now know, of course, that Wales has much more to offer than non-existent plants from the leguminous pea family and highly contagious bacterial skin infections. You can, for instance, descend 140 feet into a coal mine in Torfaen, hear a male voice choir in St David's, and see paintings at Cyfarthfa Castle Museum & Art Gallery in Merthyr Tydfil that are by a small, curly black-haired man prone to playing the wobble board and singing about being one of two little boys who had two little toys (have you guessed who it is yet?). Yes, of course, we're talking about Rolf Harris, whose grandfather (doesn't it all make sense now you picture him?) was Welsh. Elsewhere you can visit the town with the longest name in the world, **Llanfairpwllgwyngyllgogerychwyrndrobwllllantysiliogogogoch,** *visit a Baked Bean Museum of Excellence and have fun channelling T. E. Lawrence at Merthyr Mawr sand dunes where the famous David Lean biopic was made: So long as the toddlers fight toddler against toddler, so long will they be a little people, a silly people – greedy, barbarous and cruel.*

Crossing into North Wales all we've learnt to regard as the truth about our surroundings is surrendered within less than a mile of leaving Chester. Just as the radio reception scrambles into the Welsh voice of a man from the Friendly Garden Association talking excitably about a UFO spotted over Newport, we're bombarded with confusingly insistent signs in ever larger white bold writing on the road saying something like 'Cadwch Eich Peleter!'

'What the hell's *cadwch*?'

'I don't know. What's *Peleter*?' asks Dinah.

'Can you see any signs in English?'

'No. I'm looking.'

'It's the *eich* that worries me. We're going to have to *eich* something soon. Jesus! Look at that one!'

The signs cross the entire road now, each letter 10 foot wide. It's sort of like how you shout increasingly loud instructions in English to a foreigner hoping he'll understand, only it's being done with white paint on a B-road.

'Pull over,' says Dinah.

'Maybe *cadwch eich peleter* means *don't* pull over.'

But then as quickly as they materialised they disappear. More strange now is that in the space of a few seconds we've gone from day to night. Moments before, it was morning in Chester. Now it's dark, already evening in Wales.

'Are we in Wales?' says Phoebe.

'We think so.'

'Why is Wales so dark, Daddy?'

'We don't really know, Phoebe.'

'Whales?' says Charlie, making a swimming motion with his hand.

'Not *whales*,' says Phoebe. '*Wales*, Charlie. There's Wales the country and whales in the sea. We're in Wales, the country.'

'Dinah?'

The rain pounds down from the enormous black cloud overhead.

She turns the map 90 degrees.

'It says straight on but the sign says left.'

'I need to know where to turn, love. I'm at a junction.'

'I don't know where to turn, my love.'

Charlie makes the swimming motion again.

'Charlieeee, Wales is a country. Like England,' says Phoebe. 'Not whales in the sea.'

'Just carry on. Hang on, no,' says Dinah. 'That's not right. Turn around.'

'Charlieeeee! Daddy, Charlie's not listenin' to me. Charliee, listen to me. That's very rude, isn't it Dad?'

'What?'

'Turn around at the next roundabout.'

'Charlieeeeeee!'

'What, love?'

'GUYS! I can't hear Daddy. Will you be quiet? Go back on yourself. Turn around. I want to see what the sign said on the other side of the road. Oh hang on, no, A425. Ahhhhh, this map is so shit!'

'Daddy,' says Charlie, in a sing-song voice. 'Phoebe's lookin' out my window. STOP LOOKIN' OUT MY WINDOW!' shouts Charlie.

'Charlie, everyone can look out of everyone's window, OK? You don't own the windows. Kids! Please! Daddy and Mummy are lost, it's all gone weirdly dark and we need a bit of quiet.'

We drive up through Flintshire on the scenic A548 coastal road and spend the day at the beautiful seaside town of Llandudno, a sort of Welsh Eastbourne. We visit the famous Punch and Judy show on North Parade run by generations of the Codman family since the time of Queen Victoria, and after this, the Victorian tramway to the 679-metre-high summit of the Great Orme. We wander round the visitor centre, with its sweeping views across the Irish Sea, learning about limestone pavements, cashmere goats and the rare silver-studded blue butterfly that only exists here and in a handful of other places in the world, while the kids, surrounded by history, beauty and rare wildlife are interested solely in riding the 30p Mr Blobby Seesaw in the Summit Complex arcade.

In the days that follow, driving through the slate hills of the Snowdonia National Park, it feels like we're finally travelling properly now, away from big cities and out in the countryside.

We visit the National Slate Museum in Llanberis, and watch a traditional craftsman using a hammer and chisel to splice Welsh slate into slices so thin you could roll them up like ham. We walk round Portmeirion, a ridiculous, saccharine, over-the-top Italianate village created on the estuary outside Porthmadog that's full of garishly bright three-quarter-sized villas and churches painted so like the brightly coloured homes on Balamory Phoebe asks, 'Where's Archie's house, Dad?' We buy buckets, spades and a crabbing net in Porthmadog and on Black Rock Sands beach Phoebe orders me about the rock pools. 'Don't stand on the seaweed, Dad. Dad you're standing on the seaweed. Stand on the sand, Dad – like this.' Meanwhile, Charlie runs about poking everything with his spade and I net a tiny fish half the size of a finger joint. 'You got one Dad, well done. Let me see. Now put it in the bucket, Dad. You're standing on the seaweed again, Dad.'

We round the Llŷn Peninsula. No mountains or fir trees now, just rolling green countryside, isolated farmhouses and fields of aimless looking sheep in the area where in the 1970s and 1990s Welsh nationalist group Meibion Glyndŵr set fire to English holiday homes. We take a boat to Bardsey Island to see the seals, we swim at Aberdaron. It's the night after we walk across the Whistling Sands at Porthor beach that I start to panic. The panic comes from a feeling of immense pleasure I'd had at dinner that night. Sat opposite Dinah and me, Phoebe had been speaking, her eyes widening with interest, about the plot of a *Scooby-Doo* episode involving some stolen puppies. Charlie was every now and again trying to interject with his own less detailed knowledge about what he'd seen; 'In their basket', for example, or, 'He had a tail.' I'd finished my steak, was sipping a glass of wine and I'd felt such a piercing love for my family and the particular time we were at in our lives, it felt entirely fitting that just a few hours later Charlie should become quickly so very badly ill.

We're at a B & B in Rhayader, undressing Charlie for his bath, when we notice how hot he is. Then in the water he shivers.

'He's ill.'

'Definitely,' says Dinah.

Half an hour later Charlie's violently sick. I drive to the local Spar for paediatric Nurofen. They have none but let me use their phone to call the Spar in the next town. When I get back, Charlie points at his mouth.

'Yes, you were sick.'

And his tummy.

'Your tummy hurt. But you're better now, aren't you?'

Nod.

But he's not. That night he deteriorates. Sleeping between Dinah and me, he begs for water and brings it back up almost immediately as we try to hoick him out of the bed to be sick in the bin, on a towel or, if we have time, the sink.

The next morning Charlie listlessly shakes his head at spoonfuls of Coco Pops. It's Saturday morning. No GPs are around. The nearest out-of-hours service is in Carmarthen, the West Wales General Hospital, and we're on the way there when it happens. We're listening to Beatrix Potter, are up to the Jeremy Fisher story, and about to drop our bags at the cottage we're staying at next that's en route to the hospital, when I miss the turning. It's a country road – no pavements, windy, undulating. There's a small turning left up ahead and an even smaller turning opportunity opposite on the right. I slow down, indicate and start to make the right turn and just have time to say, 'Shit!' before it hits us. The sound is like a bomb going off. My head smacks the trim of the driver's door. I come around a second later. In my driver's side window there's now a man's face. He's in a black car that's filling up with smoke. I swing my head round to check on Dinah and the kids. I shout, 'Is everyone all right? Is everyone all right?' At the same time I'm aware Dinah's shouting, 'Get out of the car. Get out of the car.'

I open my door. The lady driver's out of her seat. I shout, 'Is everyone all right?' at their car. The lady looks into the back of our Astra, sees Charlie and Phoebe and starts to say, 'I'm so sorry. I'm so sorry.'

The man, whose face was next to mine, gets out. Their daughter climbs out with a red long-haired dog. She sits at the roadside stroking the dog, rubbing her neck. Our front wheel on the driver's side is at right angles to where it should be. The front of our car has caved in a metre. There's plastic trim over the road. The other car's windscreen and side windows are shattered. Their airbags have inflated. I pull Phoebe out. Dinah does the same to Charlie. We check them over for cuts and bruises. The man tells me his partner saw us indicate right too late. They thought we were going left, tried to overtake. But there wasn't enough room. She steered for the wall but the gap wasn't big enough. They bounced off the wall and hit us broadside. He calls the police. Sat on the bank by the road, Phoebe strokes Dinah's arm. Dinah's crying. In my arms Charlie's still not made a noise.

I feel woozy. I can't think straight. There are things we should do – insurance companies, getting details, but it seems insurmountable to imagine something as small as where a pen might be.

When the second police car arrives they park at either end of the two wrecks. They put a sign up to slow down the traffic and I'm led to the driver's seat of the police Range Rover. As I'm giving my account of the accident an air ambulance settles in the field next to us and the fire brigade arrives. The woman driver, composed before, is now in tears. I climb out of the police car and Phoebe's excited now, 'Daddy, I want to sit in the police car with you… Daddy, I want to go in the helicopter… Daddy,' whispering now, 'Tell the policeman I can wink. Daddy, Daddy, Daddy…' And as

I lower my ear to her mouth, 'And that I can hop. Daddy, Daddy, Daddy. On both,' holding up two fingers, 'legs.'

Firemen open the buckled bonnet using a crow bar to check there's no fire. They clear an oil patch. Villagers slow down as they drive past to ask, through their windows, if everyone's all right. One lady stops, offers to take Dinah and the kids to the cottage while the WPC, who's been dealing with the other family, agrees to take me and all our things. But it takes a while to make this decision. It's like a puzzle, a puzzle moments after waking when you're groggy. I have to wade through the treacle of my mind. There are countless options – which is best? There's the air ambulance, police cars, recovery vehicles arriving, Charlie who needs hospital, and we need our valuables from the car.

It feels a huge achievement to be at our cottage. It's not ready yet so we drop the valuables with the owner, the policewoman returns for the kids' car seats and I ring the insurance company. The woman's abrupt.

'Have you any speeding tickets you've not told us about in the last three years?'

'Yes.'

I change my mind. No, the ticket I'm thinking of hasn't gone through yet. They haven't deducted the points.

'Is the car insured for business use?'

'I can't remember.'

Were we on business writing the book? I stall. She keeps asking the question.

'Do you use your car for business, Mr Hatch?'

'I don't know, I don't know.'

'Mr Hatch, do you use your car on business?'

'I don't know, I don't know – we're on holiday.'

The policewoman, back with our car seats, takes the phone from me. She gives the insurance company the name of the recovery agent and hangs up for me.

I keep having to think about everything I say and do. It's like when the policewoman says I need to hand my documents in at Hove police station within seven days, including my driver's licence. I explain I can't do that – because it's already at Swansea about to be endorsed with points – and she just keeps saying, 'You have seven days,' and I can't get the problem across.

'So that's seven days, Mr Hatch.'

We look a strange sight in the Green Suite at West Wales General Hospital lugging our car seats around. We're transferred to the Cilgerran Ward, where we commandeer a consulting room. There are bricks for Phoebe ('Dad, there are BRICKS!') and books ('and look I've seen a Thomas book Charlie might like'). The doctor says Charlie needs an X-ray. He's pale, slightly yellow. When I hand him the Thomas book his eyes widen slightly but he doesn't open the book – he just holds it. Meanwhile, Phoebe's reaction is to go hyper. 'DAD, DAD, there's two Mickey Mouses on the walls. LOOK!' But if she bangs her leg or if we're slow giving her the sip of water she's asked for, she bursts into hysterical tears.

They want to keep Charlie in overnight on a drip to put some sugars back into his body. In the meantime they take blood tests and do their X-ray.

'It sounds like a virus but he is very lethargic and that's a worry to us.'

It's around this point they discover we've just been in a car accident, have come directly from it. A nurse advises I have the bump on my head looked at. In fact, we should all go down to A & E, she says. Charlie's wheeled away in the buggy for more tests, seemingly oblivious to our going. The wait at A & E is three hours and it's here I think of something. The day before arriving in Rhayader I'd pointed out to Dinah the comically bad way a woman on the wrong side of the road was trying to make a right turn. Simultaneously a lorry on the mini roundabout got stuck unable to make a tight right turn himself. I'd had my own trouble driving into the B & B making a right turn. The whole thing had been like a Mr Men book about bad driving.

In A & E the doctor feels every one of our vertebrae. Phoebe, still skittish, says her back hurts. We're strict when the doctor leaves to arrange further X-rays on her.

'Does it really hurt? Was it a joke, tell us? You mustn't fib to doctors. Was it a joke?'

Nod.

'Was it really?'

Nod.

'We don't mind.'

Big smile.

'Was it a joke?'

Nod, another big smile.

'OK, never mind. Come here for a cuddle.'

Charlie is wheeled back with a cannula fitted for his drip. He's given a metal-sided cot and put on a ward with two young chemo patients and at 10 p.m. Phoebe and I are given a room off the ward with two single beds. Dinah has a fold-out camp bed next to Charlie's cot. Phoebe can't sleep. She comes in with me and eventually drops off, her head on my chest, the first time she's slept like this since the day she was born, the day we brought her back from the Royal Sussex County Hospital. In her sleep Phoebe scratches her eczema. I find the duty sister but she won't give me hydrocortisone.

'I have to cover myself. You can go to casualty if you want.'

'It's three in the morning. I can't leave her alone. She's three. She might wake up and panic if I'm not there.'

'Politics, I know,' she says, in a vague attempt at empathy.

Back in bed, listening to Phoebe scratch, I go through the accident again and again. I keep making the right turn. I keep trying to picture the seconds before the impact.

In the morning Charlie's sitting up in the raised cot with a jumper on but only over one arm. The other arm is covered by a bandaged splint protecting the cannula. He's eating tiny squares of toast.

'I was just wondering where you were,' says Dinah. 'He has more colour, don't you think? He hasn't been sick. How did you sleep?'

I show her my flea bites. Dinah has five of her own. It must have been what Phoebe was scratching.

Phoebe plays in the pre-school area. They have a lava lamp. 'LOOK, DAD! It's pink and it goes purple. LOOK! SEE! Purple. NOW IT'S TURNING BLUE.' Charlie plays with his Thomas train. He says his first words other than 'Mummy' and 'no' for almost a day and has already adapted to using one arm, the other having just a finger and thumb protruding through the bandages protecting the cannula in his wrist. When his X-ray results come back we're led into the side room. The nurse stares at a computer screen. I see a white patch on his lung. 'Don't worry,' she says. 'It's just a chest infection.' Shortly after this Charlie comes off his drip. He plays with Phoebe in the pre-school room until the pharmacy opens for his antibiotics. It's lovely seeing them together. It makes me tearful. Dinah too.

We've been looking forward to this cottage in the Brecon Beacons all week. It sounded so idyllic. Throughout difficult nights in one-room-only Travelodges and Best Westerns we've tried to imagine its dry stone walls, the log fire and the beamed ceilings. The cottage, however, turns out to be a bungalow. It has sliding OAP style doors. There's no washing machine, dishwasher or toaster.

The floors are lino, even in the living room. The double doors into the bungalow have that cross-hatched wire between the double glazing you get in institutional buildings. The bathroom has an orthopaedic handrail and there are wardrobes in the kids' rooms so tall and thin and topple-risky we lay them flat on their sides like patients in the recovery position.

On the dining table there's the producer form the WPC forgot to give me yesterday, along with a note ('Hope everyone's well'). It tips Dinah over the edge.

'It's the kindnesses,' she says, in my arms. It's the woman who gave us a lift, the people who stopped to ask if we were all right. The lady at the hospital who called the taxi for us earlier on. ('If you know the way, fine,' she told the driver. 'If you don't I'll call another company. This family has been through enough.') And the disabled couple in the next door bungalow who offered to buy us food at the supermarket and gave us their Sunday papers, which we read after lunch while the kids watch CBeebies and are kissed by us every few seconds.

That night I try to explain to Dinah about the fabric of events leading up to the accident, how there seemed a pattern we should've been able to read – the inability of everyone the day before to make a right turn, the obsession with the cottage we'd never get to. The military jet we'd been buzzed by a few days before in the Dyfi Valley – the bang we'd heard when it passed overhead.

'All of it was there – the sounds, the facts. We just didn't read them. And that pause before I turned right. If I hadn't have paused.'

'Don't say it.'

'I don't know why I paused. One more second and...'

'Ben, I don't want to talk about it.'

The next morning our insurance company says our car will be towed to a Brighton garage where an assessor will judge whether it's worth repairing. If it's not – and of course it won't be – they'll provide a comparable hire car until we're made an offer. The hire car place is in Carmarthen. We take a taxi. 'Blue car,' Charlie immediately nicknames the Vauxhall Astra we choose. It's the same as ours apart from the colour and one other crucial aspect: the smell. It has no smell. We drive it to the breaker's yard. There are thirty wrecks in five rows of six, all with dents, smashed windscreens, crushed bonnets and missing wheels. The Astra is three quarters its normal size. Every window is smashed. One of its doors now hangs off. I take off the roof box and reattach it to the hire car and salvage Phoebe's ZhuZhu Pet from the glass strewn floor, and a couple of DVDs from the glove box.

'So what we doing, then?'

'Now or later?'

'Both,' says Dinah.

That night, the kids in bed, we're trying to work it out. The holiday letting agency has explained there's a penalty fee of £200 for each cancelled booking. But Dinah, I suspect, still wants to abandon the trip.

'Now, we've got no choice. We've nowhere to stay, love. We have to carry on.'

'Drive all the way to Liverpool tomorrow?'

'What else can we do?'

'And later?' she asks. 'We can't drive around in a hire car for the next three months. What are we going to do afterwards?'

'I know you want to abandon it.'

'I haven't said that.'

'But it's what you think, isn't it?'

'I just can't see how we can carry on without a car, my love. It might cost us more to abandon it.'

'How?' she asks.

'Not writing the guidebook, not renting the house. Hiring the car might be the cheaper option. We just need to think about it.'

'Let's sleep on it.'

'OK.'

She kisses me.

'What's that for?'

'Yesterday. I was hopeless. I was all over the place. You were really calm. Thank you.'

'I had no idea what I was doing. I was a bit concussed.'

She strokes the bump on my head.

'You looked after us.'

I imagine what it would be like arriving back home in a few days, abandoning the guidebook, unpacking the house, explaining to the kids the holiday's over.

'Maybe we can get a deal on the hire car. Frommer's might help out. The insurance could come through really quickly. Things might happen.'

'I don't think it's fair on the kids.'

My phone rings. It's my dad. I walk into the bedroom to answer it. He wants to know about the accident. He's heard about it from Pen, who I called in the hospital. I explain what happened and the dilemma. Dad's adamant.

'Oh, you must carry on,' he says.

'It's tricky.'

'What's tricky?' he says. 'You've been commissioned to write a guidebook and that's what you must do. You have a contract. Honour that contract.'

'Dinah's a bit spooked.'

'Of course she is. But she must understand that this is your job now.'

'I know but...'

'The family were pleased when you got this assignment, my son.'

'The family?'

'My son, when did you last finish a book?'

'A few years ago.'

'How many years ago?'

'Four.'

'Four,' says Dad, leaving the word hanging.

'It's a difficult story and I've been looking after the kids and...'

'Don't waste opportunities. Life is about taking them.'

'I know but...'

'Anyway, I'm very glad you're all right.'

'And how are you?'

'I'm fine. Carry on with the trip, my son. Goodnight.'

CHAPTER 14

On the banks of the River Mersey, amidst a landscape of rusting cranes, East Float Quay in Birkenhead was the departure point for migrants on ships bound for Australia. It's also where in 1879 the world's first submarine, the *Resurgam II*, was launched. Our two-bed apartment is in a rundown area of Birkenhead on the second floor of a converted mill. The streets are deserted. There are rows of red-brick terraced houses boarded up and the only shops open besides the Tesco Metro are Happy Shopper newsagents and tanning studios selling diet pills. Already I've counted seven kids in number eight Steven Gerrard Liverpool football shirts.

We drop the bags off and head for the Seacombe ferry terminal. Ferries operate as commuter shuttles in the morning and early evening, but between these times become river explorer cruises with tourist commentary. The *Royal Iris* stops at Woodside and Birkenhead before Pier Head on the Liverpool side of the Mersey. A ferry across the Mersey conjures up images from 1970s sitcoms. I'm expecting squawking seagulls, tooting ferries and women in electric blue miniskirts and mop-topped men eating chips from the *Liverpool Echo*. But it's raining so hard we can hardly see the Royal Liver Building through the haze and instead of cool 1960s people in polo necks and beehive hairdos there are tourists in pacamacs and bobble hats reading guidebook entries about the World Museum. The commentary isn't particularly inspirational either ('The vessel is 42.7 metres long with a gross tonnage of 747 tons... A ventilation shaft was opened here in 1934 by King George V...') and it's all slightly disappointing.

It's a short walk from the Pier Head to Albert Dock, where our first attraction is, The Beatles Story. It's a modern museum with a disability lift that takes so long descending the five steps it'd be quicker to break both our own legs, reset them, wait for the bones to knit and then walk down the steps unassisted several months later. Inside, the museum's rammed with school kids looking bored while their spellbound teachers hungrily consume every word on the information boards. I have an audio guide which Charlie delights in pinging away from my ears while Phoebe spills her Ribena in shock when 'Twist and Shout' comes on in the mocked-up Cavern room. The tour, conducted partly through the voices of John Lennon, Paul McCartney and Brian Epstein, is made up of recreated scenes, models and mementos from the era while the final room is all white. The piano is white, the floor's white, the walls are white, the ceiling's white. Everything is white except for Lennon's round glasses on the piano that has a small sign on top of it – 'This is not here' – that we read as the lyrics to 'Imagine' are piped into the room. It gives us something to debate in the Starbucks we come out into – was the display not there as it was all in our imagination? Or was John Lennon not there as he'd been shot dead? Or was it something far deeper and impossible to decipher when you're spooning HiPP Organic Spaghetti Carbonara into the reluctant mouth of an under-three while his sister's running around shouting, 'Daddy, I want that biscuit what I saw with chocolate on it and icing on it.'

After a picnic on the cobblestones outside the Tate Gallery, overlooking the stretch of water Fred Talbot famously fell into leaping across a floating map of Great Britain and Ireland to give the weather forecast on *This Morning*, we try what proves to be a highly embarrassing tour with the Yellow Duckmarine. The Yellow Duckmarine is an amphibious 1960s landing craft that was used in Vietnam to put marines ashore. Refashioned, it now doubles as both a city sightseeing bus and, for the second half of the ride, a boat that cruises around Salthouse Dock. What it isn't, is the submarine Dinah, for some reason, assumes it to be. Having misunderstood its purpose she's understandably unhappy, when we board, with the Velcro straps holding shut the plastic windows, whose strength she guesses is about to be severely tested with a few thousand pounds per square inch of water pressure when we dive.

Dinah sometimes gets 'urges'. These urges are irrational premonitions of doom that necessitate often quite mundane acts to prevent them. 'Look at me,' she will say out of the blue, very seriously. 'It's an urge,' and at this point I'll have to drop whatever it is I'm doing to stare at her for a few moments while she nods, say, or drums her fingers on a table. In the old days I used to ask what these urges were about. What terrible accident would befall me or her or someone we loved if I did not touch the side of my nose six times and pass her a saucepan from the cupboard handle first? Nowadays I just go along with them. 'Touch your head. Quickly, it's an urge.'... 'Look round that bend and open your eyes really wide.'... 'Hold up a pen. Now stick it behind your ear and clap.' I'm assuming it's one of these urges that makes her insist we put on the life jackets. I don't question why we must do it, even though the first twenty minutes of the tour is on dry land, and thus still have no idea she thinks we're on a submarine. It's quite a humiliating hour in truth. In our bulky orange float suits we're pointed and laughed at a) by passers-by at traffic lights outside the World Museum and

b) by the tour guide himself. 'Someone's got a lot of faith in us,' he says, walking past us to set up his mike. Later, as we splash down in Salthouse Dock and float, rather than submerge the 20,000 leagues Dinah was expecting, he says, 'And finally ladies and gentlemen before I leave you, a big hand please for the Safe Family,' and then when everyone's looking round at us, 'Yes, ladies and gentlemen. They've been wearing them since Gower Street.'

Caught in a rain shower we miss the last tourist ferry back to the Seacombe terminal and expect to pay a supplement on the next one because our Livesmart card is no longer valid but instead we're waved through by the steward. Unbeknown to us the return ferry stops at places in a different order and, as a result, in classic sitcom style, thinking we have longer to wait than we do, we miss our stop. It turns out to be a blessing in disguise. Going round again, this time there are genuine Scousers reading the *Liverpool Echo* in boiler suits, seagulls follow us and the Royal Liver Building looks magnificent in the oily black sky. In the main saloon, Phoebe and Charlie are in the middle of a game of 'weddings' (hugging until they both topple over), when a woman, seeing Charlie has no socks on (his were drenched in a puddle), walks over and hands Dinah a pair. They're brand new and the gesture is so transparently good-natured and unadulterated, it's one of those moments that simply bowl you over.

We're still marvelling at this when two middle-aged women start taking photos of Phoebe and Charlie. They ask if we mind, we don't and they take our address to email them on to us. A few minutes afterwards Charlie wanders over with a microphone toy.

'Charlie, where did you get that?'

He points at another woman. She shouts over that her son already has one.

'He can have it. It's not'n'.'

At Birkenhead we again don't have a ticket but the collector waves us through, and even gives us two helium balloons left over from some corporate gig in the terminal.

'It's unbelievable,' says Dinah.

'Imagine that happening anywhere else.'

'It wouldn't.'

'In Brighton.'

'No way.'

'Everyone's so nice. I feel humbled.'

'Me too.'

Our final attraction is a tour of Anfield, the home stadium of Liverpool Football club. It's an atmospheric ground that rises above the roofs of the terraced houses of its supporters in a neglected area of the city close to Stanley Park. It's nearly teatime and Dinah's not keen. But Liverpool is the team I've supported since Knutsford infants. Petty rules again don't apply because although the 5 p.m. tour is full and has left, we're squeezed on anyway. We catch up with it in the home team changing room. Dads with their football-mad sons cluster around the pegs from which Jamie Carragher's number two shirt and the number eight of Steven Gerrard are draped. Although I notice there's not much action around Sotirios Kyrgiakos's number sixteen. The guide makes jokes. The floor is made of a special rubber to prevent players sliding around on their studs, he says. It's different in the away changing room. There it's quite slippy. 'Yet Ronaldo never fell over in thuz,' says the guide. 'Evun whun we painted a punalty spot.'

I translate these jokes for Dinah: 'Ronaldo used to play for Man United, and was well known for feigning injury, particularly in the penalty area.'

Before we walk through the players' tunnel a tape is played. It's a recorded crowd roar from the Liverpool heyday in the 1970s when the team was winning European Cups. It's what opposing teams were subjected to before running out onto the pitch. Often, says the guide, opposition players were kept here for ten minutes listening to that. The noise, even diluted through time and the speakers, is like the cacophonous roar of an army. We pass underneath the famous 'This Is Anfield' sign that players touch for luck. 'Although Michael Owun wuz ter short ter do dat,' jokes the guide.

'Michael Owen used to play for Liverpool and is very short,' I tell Dinah.

I hold Charlie up to touch it. As we're sitting in the dugout Liverpool legend Sammy Lee (He's fat, he's round, he bounces along the ground, Sammy Lee, Sammy Lee) walks past. Now a coach, he's with a much a taller groundsman. 'Me dad,' jokes Sammy Lee.

'Sammy Lee is another short Liverpool player. The other man is much taller so he's making out...'

'I get it,' says Dinah. 'I'm not an idiot.'

After a walk round the Kop, the tour ends in the museum. Trophies are displayed, old players' signed shirts are framed on the walls and there's a video of Liverpool's 1977 European Cup Final triumph against Borussia Mönchengladbach. In the film the grass looks impossibly green and long. The players are in tight shorts with bouffant hair. And I can remember staying up and watching this match with Dad as a special treat in Knutsford. We nip into a chippie down a side street. The windows steam up from the piping hot chips. I finish mine and, waiting for the kids to do the same, to save time later, I edit the photos on my camera in preparation for downloading them onto the laptop. Flicking backwards through the internal memory over the last few weeks, deleting rubbish pictures, cropping others, seeing the kids in different settings, doing so many different things, I feel nostalgic for what we've done and sad for what we won't now be doing.

In the distance, below us that night as we lie in bed, we hear boats on the quay chugging along, the grinding noise of a swinging crane.

'That was a really good day.'

'It was lovely,' says Dinah.

'It seems a shame. Just as we got into the swing of it.'

'We can't hire a car for two months, love. We can't afford it. I do know what you mean, though. I was just thinking today how lucky we are to be doing this.'

'It is incredible. Despite everything.'

'It is,' she agrees.

'We might feel failures giving up, slinking back home. Imagine unpacking the house.'

'I'm not looking forward to that.'

'And there *are* some nice places coming up.'

'The Lake District,' she says.

'I know, and Kielder Forest.'

'We promised Phoebe Legoland.'

'And what about Scotland? We don't have to make a decision now, do we?' I ask.

'But shall we?'

'What do you mean?'

She looks at me.

'Fuck it,' she says.

'Really?'

'Yeah, let's go for it.'

'You sure?'

'We'll manage somehow,' she says. 'It might bankrupt us but I'm enjoying myself too much. What do you think?'

'Definitely.'

She kisses me.

'What swung it?' I ask afterwards. 'The free socks?'

'I think it was.'

She laughs.

'It was nothin', love,' I say.

'It's not'n.' Dinah spells it out. 'N-O-T-apostrophe-N.'

'Dinah, it was not'n.'

'I feel better now,' she says.

'Me too. Hey, we're back in business.'

She smiles.

'It was nottin.'

'NOT'N! Apostrophe N,' she says.

'Now tell me,' I ask, leaning up on one elbow and looking down at her. 'Because I'd really like to know – why did you think the Yellow Duckmarine was a submarine?'

'Well, it was yellow.'

'And…?'

'We'd been in The Beatles museum.'

'OK.'

'Where we heard the record "We All Live In A Yellow Submarine".'

'Ahhh, I see. You put the two together.'

She laughs. 'Plus I don't think I really understood the word amphibious in that context. I thought it was a war word.'

'And the first submarine in the world *was* launched at Birkenhead quay. The *Resurgam* thing. So you had submarines on your mind.'

'Yes.'

She laughs.

'There's still one thing, though.'

'What?' She looks up, sensing a trap.

'You thought it was a submarine?'

'Yes.'

'And because of this you were worried about the Velcro straps holding those plastic windows shut?'

'I knew if it went underwater they wouldn't be strong enough. I'm not daft.'

'But you still got on.'

She laughs and shoves me across the bed.

'I was looking out for us.'

'Knowing we would all die if it went underwater you still got on. That's like knowing the plane you're getting on is certain to smash into the Alps and instead of changing your travel plans merely packing an extra cardy.'

'I didn't know for sure it was a submarine.'

'So why didn't you ask?'

'I was embarrassed. Leave me alone.'

CHAPTER 15

I was seventeen years old when my dad tried something else with me. He was the controller of Radio 4 and very much a management suit by the 1980s, but he still liked to keep in touch with his comedy roots. He put it to me that Mum could do with a break from 'clearing up after you'. That's how he sold me on the week in Blackpool. He was scouting out a couple of up-and-coming acts appearing at the city's Grand Theatre for the BBC and we had to meet with the Grumbleweeds, a comedy troupe he was thinking about bringing back to Radio 4. Although I only grudgingly accepted his offer, I remember my slight disappointment when it emerged that it wasn't to be just Dad and I, but that we'd be joined by his two greatest friends – John Ithell and Duncan Thomas – from his BBC Radio Manchester days. Duncan was a very precise engineer, and John was a gentle, very tall, softly spoken Man City supporter from human resources. I worried a little that they'd spend their time discussing the beeb. Instead they spent the week taking the piss out of each other. They'd take it in turns to gang up on one of their group until this person reached breaking point and was about to lose their temper and then they'd switch sides and it became someone else's turn to take the flak. When it was my dad's turn he was mocked for his control freakery, and his sense of self-importance. Given a free pass because of my age, I wasn't targeted at all and was allowed carte blanche, for the first time in my life, to join in and make fun of my dad. I loved it. And so, to my surprise, did my dad. I was only forced onto the back foot once during a mock serious debate about handkerchiefs. They each carried one up their sleeves and couldn't understand why I didn't. What would I do if I needed to blow my nose, cut my finger, or a woman needed grit removing from her eye? 'Benj, how will you help her? With toilet paper? I think you need to listen to your father.'

I struggled to match their drinking, the enormous Chinese meals they consumed as well as the hectic show schedule Dad had lined up. 'He hasn't got us down for the matinee as well, Dunc?'

'He bloody well has, John.'

'He's like a machine your father, Benj.'

Dad and I shared a room in the Blackpool Hilton and amongst other acts we saw that week were Ben Elton, Lenny Bruce and Jasper Carrott. I'd never seen live comedy before or my dad laugh so hard. After we returned from Blackpool he showed me some of the old sketches he'd written during his own comedy days. There was one about a sheepdog partial to a nice bit of lamb and mint sauce that made me laugh out loud. After this I began to watch TV sitcoms and listen to radio comedies with Dad like they were the Picture Box documentaries in school. *Not The Nine O'clock News*, *Blackadder*, *Butterflies*, *Yes Minister*, *The Hitchhiker's Guide to the Galaxy*, *The Good Life*, *Dad's Army*, Monty Python, Pete and Dud. It's still vivid the day we watched *The Young Ones*, the one programme I tried to turn him on to, but which left him cold. 'Vulgar – why did they have to do that with the bogies?' When my dad talked about comedians he always referred to them like friends because many of them had been or still were. Kenneth Williams: 'Oh Ken – a genius.' David Jason. 'David is the best comic actor... in... the country.' Aged seventeen the praise I most valued was, 'Great line!' His greatest show of love became a belly laugh. Soon I was writing my own hopelessly derivative sketches and Dad would give me advice. 'It's boom, boom, joke. Not boom, joke, boom, joke. There's a rhythm to it, my son. Like great art, it's about light and shade. I hope you'll be a funny boy.' It's what I wanted from then on – to make Dad laugh. To hear him roar like he had in Blackpool.

We arrive in Blackpool with our hire car and most of its occupants caked in sick thanks to Phoebe being violently ill on the Preston New Road after eating a whole punnet of strawberries. Normally you'd worry about checking into a hotel with your clothes covered in spew, but thankfully there's nowhere in the country that at midday you can be seen swabbing vomit off your shirt and feel more at home than Blackpool. Instead of repugnant stares from passers-by we're actually proffered knowing smiles as if to say, 'That could so easily have been me in Yates's yesterday.'

Staying at the Big Blue, we're in our room that overlooks a rollercoaster ride at the Pleasure Beach, changing and preparing to go out when Buster calls.

'Have you heard?'

'What?'

'Dad's been back in hospital.'

There was some problem with the bag, a build-up of fluid on his stomach so he went in to have it drained, but when they sewed Dad back up the wound leaked, soaking his bed. The catheter then hadn't worked properly either. Dad had been through three nightgowns and spent most of the night soaked in his own body fluids and was now exhausted. He was home but the wound was still seeping. Steve, Mary's brother-in-law, a surgeon, had been to the house. He'd tried clotting the opening without success.

'Just thought I'd let you know.'

'Jesus!'

'I know.'

'How is he?'

'He's talking about the pilot light going out. He sounds very tired.'

'When are you back in Cyprus?'

'Depends on this.'

'Do you want me to come back?'

'No point until we know the score.'

'How's Mary?'

'Worried.'

'What's going to happen now?'

'He's going back in later.'

'The one morning I don't phone.'

'I know. Oh,' says Buster. 'I know what I meant to say. The other day I was with Dad when Aunty Edna called. He pulled a face. He's been getting lots of calls. He's really, really tired. It's why he doesn't say much. I was just wondering…'

'I know what you're going to say. I ring twice a day Buster, but we don't speak for long.'

'I know you don't. I know. He's so fucking tired, though. It's why he's watching telly the whole time. It takes less out of him.'

'No way, I'm carrying on ringing morning and evening. It's all the contact I get.'

'OK, OK. I just wanted to say that.'

'He doesn't pull a face when I call, does he?'

'No. Of course not.'

'Has he said anything?'

'I promise he hasn't said anything.'

'I'm not there like you and Pen.'

'I know.'

'It's like yesterday. I should have known about the leak.'

'You're right. You're right.'

There's a pause.

'You OK?' he asks.

'I'm fine.'

'I heard about Wales.'

I go through what happened.

'Where are you now?'

'Blackpool, cleaning up sick.'

'Livin' the dream. I'd better go. I said I'd call Mary.'

'Yeah, and keep me in the loop from now on, OK?'

'I will.'

'You little shit, trying to freeze me out.'

'He's my dad. Not yours. He loves me more.'

'He hates you.'

'Fuck you.'

'And fuck you too.'

'Love ya.'

'Love ya too.'

He hangs up.

Blackpool's new concrete flood defences block out the sea views, and, as we rattle into the centre of town on the tram, Dinah points out interesting *Coronation Street* snippets ('This is where Alan tried to push Rita under a tram'), as we also compete to find the tackiest advert on the seafront – 'Slots of Fun'… 'Time Out Striptease'. There's even an invitation to take part in/watch/ sponsor an organised Pot Noodle food fight. Meanwhile, Charlie and Phoebe enjoy the colourful processions of people walking up and down the promenade.

'Look at that one, Dad!'

Men are dressed as women, women are dressed as cowboys. There are groups of men all in the same coloured T-shirts, their nicknames printed on their backs, almost always, it seems, including at least one 'mad dog'. Hens in wedding veils and L-plates struggle to light cigarettes as the wind rips off the sea and, for some reason, there are lots of people carrying 5-foot-long cuddly sharks under their arms.

'Another shark, Dad! Look!'

Horse and carts clip along beside us, and as we get off the tram, we see the beach donkeys for the first time, walking from pier to pier in their pink coats, almost as brashly dressed as the hens and stags. The garish lights hanging above the street transfix Phoebe as we cross the road to the Blackpool Tower.

'Look, I can see a pig. Look, Daddy, a cow!'

She wants to go on everything, even things that aren't things to go on.

'Phoebe, that's an iron railing. Calm down. Circus first. On the way back we'll go on the rides.'

At the top of the 318-foot-high Blackpool Tower there's the Walk of Faith, a glass floor through which there are views clear to street level that only our children and a group of stags from Huddersfield seem keen to demonstrate their immortality by traversing. Downstairs, after this, we have seats in the west stalls for Mooky and Mr Boo's International Circus Carnival. Upstairs in the tower it was tacky. The carpets were dirty, the air was filled with the plink and beep of arcade games. Nestling between the four ornate iron feet of the tower, however, the circus has a huge big top and a sawdust-filled circular ring. We watch a woman spinning inside a metal cube, the Vavilov tumbling troupe. Mooky the clown appears with Mr Boo. The kids shout their heads off ('Behind you, Mooky!'). A sparkly outfitted Miss Elizabeth dangles 40 feet on a silken rope. Charlie claps. Phoebe's spellbound. But our favourite moment comes towards the end when we attempt to feed Charlie in situ because neither of us wants to leave the circus and miss anything. Phoebe's on my lap. Charlie's on Dinah's.

'Are you sure we can do this?'

'Pass me the thermos,' says Dinah.

'OK.'

I reach into the day bag and take out Charlie's baby bottle and the thermos. I pass the thermos to Dinah and remove the baby bottle lid. Dinah unscrews the thermos cap and I hold the baby bottle away from me, as Dinah decants hot milk into it and pauses whenever Charlie or Phoebe shifts position. When this is done, I retrieve the bottle lid from my chin where I've stored it, screw it on one-handed, then pass the bottle back to Dinah, who tilts Charlie into the feeding position just as the final tumbling act in the ring reaches a crescendo and one of the troupe jumps onto the head of another with a great bouncy fanfare of music from the show band.

The audience clap and wave their light sabres.

'Thank you very much,' says Dinah, dipping her head.

'Thank you, thank you,' I say, waving one arm to the crowd.

'And for our next act...' says Dinah, laughing.

'We will extract a miniature PACKET OF RAISINS.'

'From the INSIDE pouch of the DAY BAG,' I say.

'Are they real pirates, Daddy?' asks Charlie, warily.

'No, Charlie, they're dressed up,' says Phoebe. 'If they were real pirates they'd be killing people, wouldn't they Dad?'

'Yes, and they're not, are they? They're just taking people's coats and showing customers where to sit. Guys, you see that?'

In the middle of the room there's a massive treasure chest full of sweets.

'Come on, Charlie. Charlie, there are sweets in there. SWEETS!'

Tonight we're at a pirate-themed restaurant back out near the

M55. It's based at a Premier Inn on the Whitehills Business Park. Unprepossessing on the outside, inside it's like something out of Vegas. At the cost of £3 million, the interior has been transformed into a huge medieval town complete with Tudor houses, a ruined castle, a running waterfall and life-sized fibre glass trees underneath a starry night sky. The staff are dressed as buccaneers.

As the kids run to and from the Ben Gunn soft play area, Dinah talks about the day. She speculates on the sheer amount of guys we've seen with significant bits of their ears missing. Were they bitten or torn off in fights? But I can't concentrate. I keep thinking about Dad. Near Keswick in a couple of days' time we're staying at Armathwaite Hall. We're there two nights. It's the first time we'll have spent longer than one night anywhere. And there's a reasonably fast connection from Keswick to London.

Mary answers when I call. Dad's asleep. I tell her my plan to surprise Dad.

'But he will sleep a lot of the time, my darling.'

'I know, but I'm also coming for you, Mary.'

'I know my darling.'

Mary seems at times to be together and others not to be coping at all. Towards the end her voice falters. 'He tells me these things,' she says. 'He's losing his eyesight,' she whispers and starts to cry. 'I tell you, the last two days...' She breathes heavily, carries on. 'And you know what a fastidious man you father is. The bag filling up. He was on his hands and knees, so brave...'

When Mary breaks down the temptation is to try to comfort her, but it happens so often in the end I just stare at the dummy pirate hanging in a gibbet above our table and wait for her to recover.

'I don't ask questions any more,' Mary says. 'Nor does your father. I don't want to know anything else. It will happen, let it happen. Some people use activity to keep the devil away. Your sister and her meals. Buster and his DIY.'

'Me and this trip.'

'You, my darling, and your trip. We do what we have to do. He understands that. But I don't want to know any more. But I do know your father didn't deserve this.'

'He didn't.'

'He did not deserve this. A few weeks ago...'

'I know, Mary. I know.'

CHAPTER 16

*D**raft Copy for Guidebook:***
The Lake District, England's largest national park, is widely considered the most romantic spot in England. Containing the country's highest summit, Scafell Pike, and its deepest lake, Wastwater, the area's rugged beauty and crystal clear lakes have made it the most common English location for couples to pop the question. Bill Clinton proposed here to Hilary in 1973, as did Sir Paul McCartney to Heather Mills in 2001. Your children will, of course, know it better as the setting for John Cunliffe's classic, if extremely dull, children's series, Postman *'My black and white cat is more interesting than me'* Pat. *The main family attractions are a zoo, an aquarium and Keswick's Cars of the Stars, highlights of which include Del Boy's three-wheeler from* Only Fools and Horses, *Mr Bean's pea-green mini and Michael Keaton's Batmobile that our son ducked under a security rope to touch, prompting a harsh Dalek-like voice to bark out over the tannoy, 'Stay away from the cars.' In the gift shop you can buy an autograph of Mr T from* The A-Team *and be told by the curator that the tannoy announcement 'was for his own safety', as if the Batmobile's front-mounted machine guns were maybe actually loaded and*

capable of being triggered by a chocolatey hand. There are also two former homes of poet William Wordsworth. Dove Cottage is where he spent his time of 'plain living and high thinking'. He returned here after long lakeside walks to write some of his best-known works including his famous 'I wandered lonely as a cloud' line. There's an education room where, during school holidays between 9.30 a.m. and 5.30 p.m., kids' activities include making up poems using fridge magnets. There was also a poet in residence, Adam O' Riordan, when we visited, who does readings at 2.30 p.m. on Wednesdays, and can be talked about by your smitten wife at 8 a.m. the next morning and also again at 9 a.m. and 10 a.m. and then half-hourly following lunch after she has googled him and discovered, according to reviews, that he 'engages the reader with meandering narratives which zoom in from cosmos to coffee cup whilst still having the subtle facility to turn his attention to woozy landscapes that capture the broken dreams of cities and love affairs'. The other Wordsworth property, Rydal Mount, has rooms full of period furniture including a cutlass chair (designed so you could take the weight off your feet without removing your sword) that we suggest you sit on to finally have your say about Adam O'Riordan. 'He's a loose-buttoned fop and, no, we will not be visiting the Ledbury Poetry Festival as part of this book's research so you can steal up to him and ask for his autograph and show him your own work about that cornfield we saw in Worcester, where you rhymed evanescent fields of barley with Salvador Dalí.'

'It's all about pensioners,' Dinah's saying.

'I know, I'm sick of it.'

'Leaning on their bloody anti-shock trekking poles staring at Helvellyn, communing with nature.'

'I'm starting to hate them.'

'Buying those stupid pieces of slate with their house name on it. The Brambles, Honeysuckle Smug Cottage.'

'And all the horrible upper-middle-class families.'

Dinah shakes her head contemptuously. 'Oh, I've got a Toyota Prius. Haven't you?'

'We bought it for the all-round visibility, darling,' I chip in, 'On the way to the farmers' market we can see literally four cars ahead of us. And we do so like looking down on people. It's what we do all the time. Fancy a wedge of salted Swedish liquorice?'

'It's so, so yummy.'

'Wankers!'

Bowness, on the banks of Lake Windermere, seemed, at first, a welcome relief after the litter-strewn streets of Blackpool, although its own streets were slightly too narrow and clogged up with well-heeled pensioners scoffing Coniston Fudge to push our huge Maclaren double buggy comfortably along.

But we should have realised we weren't going to be welcome in the Lake District when the swans on the banks of Lake Windermere, probably raised on focaccia or Roquefort and almond sourdough, turned their snooty beaks up at our Kingsmill bread.

'Daddy, why aren't they eating it?'

'Because they're very, very spoilt, sweetheart and it's not wholegrain.'

'They're probably gluten intolerant,' says Dinah.

On our first day we were tutted at in the Beatrix Potter exhibition after the kids shouted excitedly at a model of Miss Tiggywinkle. On the second day you'd have thought we'd detonated a cluster bomb on an orphanage, the way we were stared at when Phoebe opened a packet of Walkers cheese and onion near the Ruskin Museum. ERGHHHH! NORMAL CRISPS!!… CRISPS WITHOUT SEA

SALT AND CHIVES, IN A PACKET THAT HASN'T BEEN MADE TO LOOK LIKE IT'S MADE OF ACTUAL WOOD! STAND BACK EVERYONE. IT'S THAT FAMILY WITH THE KINGSMILL AGAIN.

We're at the grey stone village of Grasmere ranting as we struggle to find somewhere that'll heat up Charlie's baby food. Today it's been more of the same and we're reaching breaking point after being shunned aboard the steam yacht *Gondola* on Coniston Water, where I spent forty-five minutes holding on to the back of Charlie's shirt so he didn't topple over the edge into the water after Donald Campbell, who died attempting to break the water speed record here. And while it was fun at the Laurel and Hardy Museum's small cinema in Ulverston witnessing the kids laughing at the bowler-hatted slapstick ('Daddy, he just bit that man's tie'), it ended in tears when Charlie accidentally broke the head off an Ollie statue and we were asked to leave. To cap it all off, in the last half hour we've tried to sit down in three restaurants for lunch but each time have been told, despite the empty seats, none of which were marked reserved, that, 'Sorry, we're fully booked.' Meaning, 'Get out scumbags, we don't want your noisy kids in here taking up space, chucking homemade cheese and ham galettes around when there are stacks of minted grey heads prepared to pay £15.75 for a chicory salad.' And now we're struggling to even get Charlie's baby food heated up because nobody will admit to having a microwave. ('I'm sorry, we don't believe in bombarding our organic apple confit with non-ionising radiation. The Lake District is a national park, you know.')

In the end Dinah leaves me with the kids on Grasmere green and moves round College Street to try a few more places. She returns fifteen minutes later looking upset.

'Nope,' she says, punching the baby food jar into my hand.

'Really?'

She shakes her head.

'Someone must have one.'

'They did, love. But they thought I was a pikey.'

'What do you mean?'

'They wouldn't let me use it.'

'Are you all right?'

Nottingham's aberration aside, it's a lunchtime courtesy we've become accustomed to. People, generally, don't mind heating up baby food. It's been the case throughout Wales, the Midlands and the whole of the North-west. Cafes, restaurants, pubs; they don't mind if you're eating with them or not, they'll help out. It's something to do with it being baby food – the universal regard for the welfare of a child – because I doubt it would be the same if it was, say, a Barbecue Beef Pot Noodle.

Dinah sinks to the grass and twists her head away from me. I crouch down.

'You're really upset.'

'Why is Mummy crying?' asks Phoebe.

Phoebe comes and sits in her lap. Charlie does the same.

'Poor Mummy,' they say.

Dinah laughs and hugs them towards her.

'Is it because you banged your toe?' asks Phoebe.

Dinah laughs. 'Yes, I banged my toe.'

She kisses Phoebe's head and laughs.

'*I* cry when I bang *my* toe,' says Charlie.

'I know, sweetheart.'

In the end I give Charlie some yoghurt instead of milk. And Dinah tells me about what happened. She saw the microwave in the kitchen on the way into the cafe and so went up to the man behind the counter and asked if he'd mind heating up the food.

'But he just said no.'

'Just like that?'

'He was horrible. I practically begged him, Ben. I was so polite too. You should have seen me. I actually grovelled. I was so humiliated. "It will just take twenty seconds." "Sorry, we're busy," he said.'

'He knew it was for a child?'

'I told him. They weren't even busy. I felt this big.' She holds up her thumb and forefinger. 'He was leaning on the counter chatting to his chi-chi looking wife. They're probably laughing at me right now. I really, really hate this place.'

Pretending I'm going to the dustbin on the other side of the green with some rubbish I peel off and go to find the cafe. It's a trendy-looking wooden-floored place with shiny metal tables inside and out. I see the microwave and the man at the till Dinah described. A handful of people are drinking tea, one or two are eating. I walk up to counter. The man serving is about fifty, with a checked tea towel draped over his shoulder. He's standing next to a woman with a flower in her hair, the chi-chi wife I'm guessing. I take out my Frommer's card, introduce myself and go into my spiel. I'm writing a guidebook, *Frommer's: Britain With Your Family*, I am compiling the 'North-west and Around' chapter and looking to include ten family-friendly places to stay, eat and visit. Their cafe has been recommended to us by a number of people.

'Do you know Frommer's at all? We're the American equivalent of TimeOut. Frommer's has one of the biggest travel websites in the world.'

The lady steps forward.

'I know Frommer's,' she says.

'So do you mind if I ask you a few questions? I see you've got high chairs.' I indicate a stack by the till.

'And colouring-in books and pens,' the woman froths. 'We also have a children's menu.'

Tea towel man hands me one.

'Thank you.'

I glance at it and make some notes, nodding as though impressed.

'And we also do half portions of adult meals for half price.'

I make a note of this.

'And how about staff attitude?' I ask.

'Sorry?'

'You know, some places they claim they're child friendly but deep down...'

'Oh, I see. No, we're definitely child friendly.'

She looks at tea towel man, who nods.

And that's when I do it. I know it's unprofessional. That it's vindictive and petty. But I do it anyway.

'Well, that's funny,' I say, looking puzzled, 'because my wife was in here five minutes ago and you wouldn't heat up some baby food.'

There's a momentary silence before the woman backs away from the till like I've punched her in the face. I close my notebook. She starts babbling about ten orders they had at the time. I pat the top of the counter with my pad as she changes tack and tells me she can't be held responsible for heating the food up of anyone who happens to walk past.

'Of course not and it wasn't a test,' I say, 'sending my wife in like that,' although I realise I'm making it sound exactly like one.

'I will not to be held hostage to that incident,' she says, her voice quavering, and I slide the menu back towards tea towel man.

'Of course not. It's a pity, though. You were highly recommended. Highly recommended,' and I walk out, feeling like a gunslinger spinning revolvers back into his holsters.

'I am a boy with a pet dog, who changes into a cartoon character whose first name begins with T?'

'Tommy Zoom.'

'That's right, Tommy Zoom, Phoebe.'

'Give me another one.'

'OK, I am a pretty woman with seven small friends whose first name is what falls from the sky when it's cold and isn't rain?'

'Snow White.'

'That's right, Phoebe.'

'Let me do one for Charlie, Daddy,' says Phoebe. 'I have a trunk, what am I?'

'Efant.'

'Well done, Charlie,' she says.

'Let me do another one. Charlie, I have stripes what am I?'

'Tiger.'

'Well done, Charlie.'

'Charlie, I am yellow with a long neck?'

'Orange, Phoebe.'

'I know, I know, Charlie, I am orange with a long neck, what am I?

'Efant.'

'No, Charlie.'

'I am orange. Elephants aren't orange.'

'Tiger.'

'No, Charlie,' says Phoebe, and whispering now, 'Giraffe, Charlie.'

'Rarf.'

'That's right, Charlie.'

'Phoebe, don't whisper it to him.'

'I didn't.'

'You did. We heard you.'

'It was too hard.'

'Well, you set it.'

Phoebe laughs. 'OK, OK, I've got another one...'

After my small victory it's a heart-lifting drive to Keswick. We cross Dunmail Raise, the scene of the defeat of the last king of Cumbria by King Malcolm of Scotland. The sun's out, the trees have a startling cartoon greenness that pings out while the hills shooting past us are perfect brown ovals. In between playing guessing games with the kids and staring at the scenery we relive the confrontation.

'And they'd actually heard of Frommer's?'

'That's what made it so perfect. You should have seen her face, Dinah.'

'I wish I'd been there.' She giggles. 'The little shits.'

She slaps me five, gets out her Frommer's business card.

'Frommer's,' she says, holding it up like a cop. 'A Wiley imprint. Sir, I am writing you down for no stars. You will have no smiley-faced emoticon next to your kids' menu. You will not make a hundred and fifty words in the "North-west and Around" chapter.'

'Charlie, I am a C,' says Phoebe from the back seat, 'and I have hump. What am I?'

'Efant?'

'No, Charlie.'

'Tiger?'

'Charlie, not every answer is elephant or tiger.'

'Legend has it that in the early 1500s, a violent storm in the Borrowdale area of Cumberland led to trees being uprooted and the discovery of a strange black material underneath. This material turned out to be graphite, which shepherds began using to mark their sheep.'

The Cumberland Pencil Museum is based at the Southey Works on a bend in the River Keswick, north of the town's high street. The kids are asleep and we're parked outside and Dinah's reading from the blue file.

'A cottage industry of pencil-making soon developed, culminating in the formation of the UK's first pencil factory in 1832. That factory is now the Cumberland Pencil Museum.'

'I think you have to admire that.'

'What?' says Dinah.

'The sheer audaciousness of it.'

'What do you mean?'

'It's not even a museum about stationery, or a museum about pencils and pens. It's not even a museum about pencils per se. It's a museum about pencils FROM CUMBERLAND!'

'But, have you seen the sign?' Dinah points to the large red and black lettering down the side of the building that reads in capitals: SEE THE WORLD'S LARGEST PENCIL!

I smile and close my eyes with pleasure.

'I thought you'd like that,' she says, and reads on. 'The factory has had various owners in its 175-year history, but became the Cumberland Pencil Company in 1916. The Lakeland children's range was launched in 1930, followed by the Derwent brand of fine art pencils in 1938.'

'So do you think that's a big deal in the world of pencils, then?'

'What?'

'Having the world's largest pencil? It's probably like skyscrapers. Rival pencil manufacturers all around the world are probably shaking their heads with wonderment right now at the incredible news. They've just broken the record in Keswick!'

Dinah puts on a German accent. 'Add ten feet of graphite, Hans, we're taking zis 2B up to sixty-five feet.'

Not only does the museum contain the world's largest pencil, another sign claims it also has: A SECRET WARTIME PENCIL.

'A secret wartime pencil!'

However many times we say it we just can't envisage a secret wartime pencil.

'It sounds like a children's story. *James and the Giant Peach. Tommy and His Secret Wartime Pencil.* But what can be secret about a pencil?'

'I don't know,' says Dinah, who has her eyes closed now.

'What's secret in wartime?'

'Weapons,' says Dinah, yawning.

'So it's a weapon.'

'Not an ordinary weapon,' she says still with her eyes closed.

'Or else it wouldn't be secret,' I say.

'A *secret* terror weapon.'

'Dinah, do you think Churchill planned to fire giant HB pencils at key German cities in the dying days of World War Two?'

'I do.'

'Are you going to sleep?'

'Trying to.'

'Huge very sharp pencils raining down on German cities, fired from secret stationery silos. Our response to the V2 rocket. Dinah, are you imagining plucky, cockney British munitions workers turning huge pencil sharpeners in factories in the East End to create these ultimate terror weapons? Dinah?'

'I am.'

'Are you picturing Churchill on military rallies inspecting these giant pencils, testing their sharpness with the tip of his gloved index finger? And, of course, they had one other great advantage, pencils over traditional military hardware, didn't they, Dinah? Dinah?'

'I'm listening.'

'They could scribble on buildings on their downward trajectory. Doodles on the Brandenburg Gate sapping Jerry morale. Scribble on the Reichstag. Air raid wardens with giant mobile rubbers racing around to get rid of the daubings. But then it would escalate. It always does. A new arms race for the next terror weapon. Who gets it first? Us or Hitler... The BIRO. Dinah?'

'I am awake. I'm just resting my eyes.'

'Are you bored of this?'

'A bit.'

'Do you want me to shut up now?'

'I am a bit tired, love.'

Entering the Cumberland Pencil Museum via a mocked-up mine we learn about Borrowdale graphite, the drawing material of choice of Michelangelo, 450 years ago. I take pictures of Phoebe and Charlie standing beside the world's largest pencil (26 feet long) while the secret wartime pencil turns out to be a pencil manufactured with a disguised compass and map inside to help downed allied pilots during World War Two find their way home.

At the end of the museum there's a small theatre. The big screen plays an extract from Raymond Briggs's animated cartoon, *The Snowman*, which was drawn using Cumberland pencil products. I bought *The Snowman* DVD for Phoebe last Christmas. We've watched it so many times she still recognises the Howard Blake score, 'Walking in the Air', when it comes on the radio. Or as Phoebe always corrects me, 'Not walking in the air, Dad. Flying in the air. You can't *walk* in the air, Daddy.' Phoebe climbs on my lap and puts her thumb in. Although we've seen it dozens of times somehow I've never noticed the frame before showing Brighton Pier. It's unmistakably the Palace Pier lit up at night. The snowman and the boy fly high above it holding hands on their way to Lapland. It's such an unexpected reminder of home, it makes me shout across to Dinah, 'Look!'

We all stare at it.

'That's where we live,' I say to the kids. 'That's home. Do you recognise it? The pier.'

'Where they have rides?'

'Where they have the rides, that's right, Phoebe.'

The film ends, we leave the museum and on the way to the Castlerigg Stone Circle, a few miles off Penrith Road, Phoebe says, 'Daddy, when are we going home?'

It's the first time Phoebe's asked this. In a way it's a question I've been dreading.

'Not for a while yet, pops.'

'I thought we were going home soon.'

'Well, we were going to go home, Phoebe.'

'When we had the accident?'

'When we had the accident, yes. But then...'

'We got blue car.'

'Yes, we got blue car and we thought we were having such a good time we'd carry on.'

'And Daddy,' says Charlie, seriously. 'Blue car doesn't smell, does he?'

I smile at Dinah. 'No, he doesn't smell Charlie.'

'Although it will start to,' says Dinah. 'If we carry on dropping our sandwiches on the floor, guys, and if Daddy doesn't give me his apple cores and stuffs them in the driver's side door.'

'Because red car,' says Charlie, 'smelled yucky. Didn't he?'

'He did.'

'So we got a new one.'

'Well, it didn't happen exactly like that, Charlie.'

A few minutes later I park in a lay-by on Castle Lane. We cross the road and walk up to the Neolithic stone circle. At 3,000 years old, it's one of the oldest in the country. There are thirty-eight stones arranged around a 30-metre diameter with ten standing stones inside this forming a rectangle. On a low flat hill there are views to Skiddaw, Blencathra and Lonscale Fell. We play hide and seek for a while and grandmother's footsteps, the kids have running races and afterwards I'm lying prostrate on a stone bathing my face in the sunshine when Phoebe jumps on my stomach. I ask her what Mr Nobody thinks of the holiday, if he's enjoying himself.

'He likes doing some things,' she says.

'But not everything?'

'He doesn't like everything.'

'What doesn't he like?'

She sighs. 'He doesn't like it when his sandwiches are cut into little squares. He wants big long sandwiches.'

'I can understand that.'

'Daddy,' says Phoebe, 'When we go home and I start school I'll be a big girl, won't I?'

I look at her white, finely boned, bird-like face and feel a tremendous pang.

'You will, sweetheart.'

And from feeling homesick earlier, I now want to stay away longer. In fact, I don't ever want to return. I want us to live on the road forever. Phoebe won't need to start school then; Charlie won't have to go to nursery. We'll simply freeze the way we are right now, stay the same, and just carry on driving around the country – the four us – staying in different hotels, reviewing family-friendly attractions for the rest of our lives.

Armathwaite Hall Hotel opposite Bassenthwaite Lake is a former sixteenth-century country house. The hotel has mounted tiger heads on the wood-panelled walls and the press pack mentions a kids' weekend programme, so posh it includes cooking with chocolate, falconry and young etiquette sessions organised by Walpole, the butler, where kids are shown which knife and fork to use for certain courses, how not to shovel peas, 'And probably what the correct glass is for a highball,' jokes Dinah.

On the lawned grounds the kids play their first ever game of croquet (they pull up the hoops and throw them in the car park) while, in the chandeliered dining room, Charlie turns me into a slip-catcher during his main course, forcing me to constantly dive from my chair to catch the tiny morsels of food he flings to the carpet. Phoebe, meanwhile, midway through her bangers and mash turns to two ladies behind us to ask, 'So where are you from, then?' Startled by her precocious urbanity they're about to reply when she maddeningly ruins it by discarding her teaspoon then beginning to eat her mashed potato using her hand like a bear paw.

We're back in the bedroom after a glass of wine on the terrace downstairs and getting ready for bed when Dinah shows me her phone. 'I almost forgot. I found this earlier.'

She calls up a web page entitled 'world's tallest pencil'. It's a story about a 76-foot pencil that was built in 2007 in Queens, New York. The pencil commemorates the life and work of artist Sri Chinmoy.

'So it wasn't the biggest pencil in the world.'

'It's not even the previous record holder. That was a 65-foot Faber-Castell in Kuala Lumpur.'

I hand the phone back to her.

'Good research.'

'I thought you'd laugh more.'

'Sorry.'

'Thinking about tomorrow?'

I nod.

She looks at me, guesses talking about my dad will stop me sleeping, and leaves the room.

'Just make sure you keep tabs on the Wadcrags,' I call out after her.

Earlier, when we couldn't find Armathwaite Hall and rang the hotel for directions, the receptionist had for some reason gone on and on about the village of Wadcrag.

'Have you been through Wadcrag yet?' she'd asked.

The road didn't go through Wadcrag, I'd said.

'If you've been through Wadcrag you must be close,' she'd said. 'Have you seen the sign?'

I'd said again we were on a different road and hadn't been through Wadcrag. She'd asked which road we were on and, after we told her, 'How far away from Wadcrag are you?' she'd said.

We didn't know, we were a bit lost.

'When you see the sign for Wadcrag, you'll be close,' she said.

I said again the road we were on didn't go through Wadcrag.

'Just go to Wadcrag and ring again,' she'd said.

'She's fucking mad on Wadcrag, that woman,' I'd said to Dinah. And we'd decided over dinner it would be Dinah's mission tomorrow when I was with Dad to see how many more times she could get her to say Wadcrag.

CHAPTER 17

Dad's wearing a checked jacket. The checks are lime green, pink and blue. The yellowness of Dad's eyes is the colour of an unhealed bruise and his breathing has a background sound to it. It's like the hum of a fridge at night. We're in the living room, Dad has two friends over and Mary's face is fidgety like a sparrow's head. It moves in and out, back and forwards, catapulting out the bullets of fear she confides as the day wears on. 'Is he looking worse to you?'… 'Do you think he's fading?'… 'The blockage has made him so tired.' Dad's friends are telling stories and Dad's head moves slowly towards their conversation. He sits stiffly in a simulacrum of relaxation – an arm over the back of the sofa, legs apart slightly. When he smiles it's slightly too late. His teeth seem larger as well, too heavy for his jaw. He gulps before he says anything and I feel his loneliness from across the room and I want to get up, go over and touch him.

After they've gone, Dad plays the piano. 'The Lord's Prayer'. I stand in the doorway of the barn conversion where he can't see me. It's too much. The tears twist up and I blub in the bathroom. I dry my eyes, wait until they're less red, and come out. I move behind Dad and hold his shoulders. I feel the notes resonate through his flesh. Dad's quiet on the way to the hospital. Mary and I hoist him out of the passenger seat. Leant against the car door he pants and winces. His belly hurts. I ask if he wants a painkiller. He shakes his head without looking at me and widens his eyes. We stay this way for a few moments. Then he nods. 'Clear the path.'

I swing open the main hospital doors. I come back.

'Ready?'

'Not yet.'

I wait until he puts his hand out. I hold it and we steer him. Dad proceeds in the scared, stop-start way you move across a ship's deck in a storm. He falls into a seat at reception, exhausted, bent forward slightly, his cold clammy hands on his knees. We pat his still heavy shoulders, stroke his damp head and tell him how brave he is, how much we love him, and he occasionally looks up and blows us a kiss between pants.

In his room on the ward I stand outside the bathroom like a guard while Dad changes into his hospital gown. Five minutes later when he hasn't emerged I shout, 'All right, Dad?' I walk in. Dad's standing up, his boxers round his ankles. He can't reach down to take them off. They're caught under his feet. I pull them off for him. I slip his gown on, do it up at the back as he leans on the washbasin.

'Now put some toothpaste on a brush,' he tells me.

'You want to do your teeth?'

He nods. 'Not too much and wet it.'

I do what he says. He brushes his teeth. Again his eyes are wide with pain.

'My dressing gown,' he says, turning round.

I find it in his bag.

'You've got paste round your mouth, shall I wipe it?'

'Yes.'

I wipe his bottom lip. Dad winces.

'Not so hard. My lips are sore.'

I do it again lightly.

'Thank you,' says Dad.

The procedure to relieve the swelling and do something – nobody's really sure what – to the stent near Dad's bile duct will last twenty minutes and Dad's first on Gorhard's afternoon list so Mary and I go for a cuppa in the hospital canteen to wait. Sitting at a Formica table sipping tea, Mary hands me a sheaf of letters addressed to Dad from her handbag. There's one from Nora, a friend of Mary's. How could someone so ebullient and full of life have been laid so low? There's a letter from the author P. D. James. There are letters from cabinet ministers, high court judges, former archbishops, TV stars, writers and entertainers. But it's during the letter from Kieran, Mary's nephew, that I start to feel lost. The letter is impossibly grown up for a twenty-year-old. It expresses Kieran's upset and regret that Dad's been so unlucky, especially as they formed, what he felt, was a special rapport in South Africa. I picture Dad on the balcony at his and Mary's second home in Cape Town establishing this relationship with Mary's nephew. At the end of each letter I say 'What a lovely letter' or 'That's so kind', or something like 'I didn't know Dad knew Cardinal Hume', and I hand it back to Mary as she passes me another.

My dad's a great letter writer. Come rain or shine the first thing he did when he got into work at the BBC at 6.30 a.m. was dash off six letters. He did this for thirty years. When he ran short of colleagues to praise or offer encouragement to, he wrote to public figures in the news he felt were unfairly under fire in the newspapers. Now all these people are writing back to my dad. The letters are kind, thoughtful, respectful, heartfelt and they worry me about the last letter I sent to Dad. Dad was a great building, large on my horizon, impossible to replace, that had been detonated and was about to be received spectacularly into the earth. That was what I wrote. It seemed a clever analogy at the time but now it seems heartless, negative, the opposite in tone from all these other much more upbeat letters.

At 4.10 p.m. Dad's back in his room. We sit about the bed on low chairs. Buster and Pen have arrived by now. Buster holds Dad's arm on one side. Pen wells up on the other. At one point I try to hold Dad's hand myself when he lets go of Buster's to undo a plaster over his wedding ring but Dad shakes his hand free of mine. He's just looking for Buster. Buster's not long back from Cyprus. Of course he's looking for Buster.

'Was it good for you, doctor?' Dad asks Gorhard, when he does his round.

'Yes it was.'

'And can I go out for dinner on Friday, doctor?'

'Yes.'

Pen laughs. Everyone laughs.

'Can I go for dinner on Friday!' says Pen, shaking her head with wonder.

'Yes,' says Dad. 'He said I could.'

'What's he like?' says Mary.

He'll be kept in overnight and can expect an improvement in the next couple of days. The oncologist will visit in the morning. Back at Mary's everyone's ecstatic.

'Dad was bouncing around the room,' Mary says.

Pen thinks he already looks less yellow.

We drink wine and look for the positives. 'It's not Alzheimer's.'

'It's not a stroke and life like Uncle Dick's.'

I hear myself saying, 'He's a great man and he's led a great life,' and on the word life my voice cracks in half and everyone holds their faces up for a second and after this silence we leave. We each hug Mary. She says she will go on loving us. We say we will go on loving her. I'm in Buster's hire car. We follow Pen in hers up Nightingales Lane. I've changed my plan. I was going to stay the night at Pen's with Buster. We were going to stay up late and chat. I'd been looking forward to it. I'd take the train back in the morning – but now in the car I change my mind. Buster tries to dissuade me, but eventually signals to Pen. In the car park outside Dr Challoner's Grammar School, Buster pulls off the road. Pen follows. She draws alongside us and lowers her window. Buster does the same with his.

'I'm going back tonight,' I shout across him.

'OK, hon,' she says.

'I'll be so tired getting up early for the train tomorrow otherwise.'

'Do what you think is best, hon.'

She blows a kiss. I blow one back.

'Tough night,' I shout and I feel a crack in my voice. Tough night, it's a Dad phrase.

'Tough night, hon,' Pen shouts across the car park and Buster drives me to Little Chalfont station.

The journey back takes six hours. I sleep, read, but most of the time I just look out of the blackened window. Dinah's waiting up for me when I get in. She puts her book down when I come through the door. We hug and she hands me the glass of wine she's saved in the bottle. I down it in two gulps, undress and put my pyjamas on.

'That feel better?'

'A bit.'

We sit on the edge of the bed and I tell her how I felt in the hospital – excluded. I tell her why I hadn't gone back to Pen's like I'd phoned her to say I was doing. I felt I deserved to be excluded.

'Why my love?'

'Because I've not been around.'

'I'm sure your dad doesn't think that.'

I tell her about the letter to Dad I'd written, not to comfort him, the purpose of every other letter he'd received, but merely to impress him. Even on his deathbed I was selfishly scampering about hoping for a pat on the head for an elegant turn of phrase, thinking of myself.

'You're tired. Let's go to bed.'

'Tell me something nice.'

Dinah says that on the Ullswater Steamer earlier that day they passed the hotel where Paul McCartney proposed to Heather Mills.

'And I got the kids to boo. Everyone on the boat laughed.'

'Tell me another nice thing.'

She talks about Trotters World of Animals park.

'You'd have been ashamed of me.'

'What did you do?'

She laughs.

'We missed the otter feeding encounter because I wouldn't pass an enclosure of pancake tortoises. And I had to force the manager of the birds of prey section to radio a woman called Esther who was about to give a reptile talk to make sure she wasn't going to be handling a tortoise after the monitor lizard.' Dinah puts an imaginary walkie-talkie to her mouth. 'Andy to Esther – are you using a tortoise this morning?'

She nods at the kids' room.

'Go and have a look at them. But be quiet, they've both been a bit shouty.'

I stand in their doorway. Charlie and Phoebe are sleeping in pretty much the same positions they were when I left them that morning, although it now seems weeks ago.

'Something else to cheer you up.'

'What?'

'We're up to twenty-one Wadcrags. A massive volley when I asked her the way to Hexham tomorrow.'

And in bed I think of my dad. My fear is vulnerability. With Dad in the world I can cope with any disaster – financial, emotional, physical. I know how to react through Dad's reaction. I'll behave the way he behaves. Without Dad I'll be naked, newborn, helpless – a house without a roof. It takes my breath away, the fear of there being nobody above to look out for me.

CHAPTER 18

*D*raft Copy for Guidebook:
Northumberland was once a popular mediaeval dragon-slaying destination, but is now such a sleepy backwater they recently reintroduced the barn owl just for something to talk about. Home to about ten people mainly called Gawain, the county is basically a giant national park run by a few eider ducks and a couple of part-time otters. We are, of course, joking. Northumberland is an extremely vibrant county, with the most diverse wildlife in Britain, and one bursting with varied attractions to walk around, that are fun and would also be illuminating if you could understand a single word your Geordie tour guide was saying. Interesting places to visit include Berwick-upon-Tweed, which until 1966 (because of a treaty signing oversight), was still officially at war with Russia, the Kielder Forest, recently voted the most tranquil place in England, and Alnwick Castle, seat of the ancient Percy family, where during the state room tour in the library, we were informed by a visitor/nutter/local witch/ possibly even a member of the Percy family themselves that it was perfectly legal to urinate on the kerbside wheel of your own motor car. We are still, to this day, wondering at how strangely we must have been standing to have been told this. Lindisfarne

Priory across the causeway, meanwhile, was founded by Irish monk Aidan in 635, making it one of the earliest cradles of Anglo-Saxon Christianity. To keep the kids amused here there are jigsaws of the Lindisfarne Gospels and although climbing the priory ruins isn't strictly allowed, Bob in the kiosk turns a kindly blind eye to toddlers running about the lower walls with packets of chocolate gems shouting, 'This is so boring, I don't believe it.'

We're heading north on the A686 into Northumberland's Cheviot Hills. It's a beautiful, gently climbing road lined with drystone walls, flanked with green valleys, sudden vistas opening up all the way to the Solway Firth and Phoebe and Charlie are not only ignoring me when I indicate pretty sights they're actually telling me, 'Daddy, please be quiet. You told us that already 'bout a hundred times. And it's not beautiful. It's boring. It's *trees*.'

Kielder Leaplish Waterside Park is set against the tree-lined banks of the Kielder Water reservoir, which, at 28 miles long and 3 miles wide, holds 4,000 million gallons of water; enough, according to our Hoseasons stay-pack, for every person in the world to flush the toilet at once.

On the banks of the reservoir, down a windy shingle road, we find the park's reception. I go in alone to collect our lodge keys and a site map. A Geordie man behind the desk recommends I buy a bottle of Avon Skin So Soft, a hand and face cream used by the British Army, which trains here. It's to protect against the midges and is apparently better than any insect repellent.

'The army use Avon Skin So Soft!'

'Aye, tha one wi'ya green bottle. Not tha pink one, mind. That'll make yer skin soft alreet, boot they'll bite yer al tha same. Ya knaa, that's the good thing aboot tha bats,' he says.

'What is?'

'They eat tha midgies. Now, yer knaa where ya gannin – turn reet, past this building…'

'You actually have bats?'

'Aye, an' buzzards. Tawny ools, barn ools, grey ools, otters, goldin eagles, puff adders, rinbow trowt.'

'Puff adders! What, in the forest?' I ask.

'No, al'orver. They bask in tha road sometimes. Ah found one doon by tha lodges las' week. Aye, but divvent worry pet, they wern't harm yee if yee divvent harm them.'

'What could they do?' I ask.

'Bite.'

'And what would happen then?'

'Yer OK unless yee hev a weak hort or,' and he looks past my head towards the kids in the car, 'well, it's not for young bairns, mind. Were yee not warned afore yee came?'

Dinah and I have an argument on the way to our lodge about whether or not we were warned afore we came. I included Kielder on our route but Dinah found the accommodation through a Hoseasons contact.

Was she warned afore we came?

'No. He sent me an information brochure about the lodge and the reservoir. It didn't mention puff adders, Ben. We're not going to see one anyway. He was probably winding you up. What's this?'

She holds up the Avon Skin So Soft.

'It keeps the midges away. The army use it, apparently.'

'What do they use for camouflage – Smokey Brown Eyeshadow? I think he was pulling your leg. What did he actually say about the adders?'

'He said he'd seen one down by the lodges last week.'

'He definitely said that?'

'Why would I panic you? You panic all the time. What's in it for me? It's what he said.'

It's already been a difficult day. Our first attraction had been Eden Ostrich World at Langwathby Farm just outside Penrith, although calling it Ostrich World is a bit like calling our car Banana Skin World. After all, in it we have, amongst many other items, two banana skins. Eden Ostrich World was home to a pair of ostriches in a back field, but there were more emus than ostriches, more goats and more sheep and more chipmunks and more rabbits than ostriches, so why wasn't it called Goat World or even Guinea Pig World? It was annoying for other reasons. There were insidious signs everywhere as well warning that pregnant women shouldn't touch sheep and lambs, that the emus, rheas and goats might peck. We were warned we couldn't eat our own food when the cafe was open and, several times, that we must 'supervise children at all times'. As Dinah said when we left: 'Nanny World, more like.'

Crossing the Pennines, the scenery was staggering – great sweeping views, drystone walls going on forever – but I couldn't get out of the car to take photos because Phoebe was so bored she started doing the toddler equivalent of self-harming with razors. She shouted every five seconds she wanted a cuddle, clung to me when I tried to return to the driver's seat and then started scrawling over her face and arms with a black felt-tip pen. On top of this we missed the fort at Housesteads in Northumberland set against Hadrian's Wall as well as the nearby Roman Army Museum because we were under time pressure after stopping in Alston to buy Charlie his third new pair of shoes of the trip. He likes to hook them under the buggy footrest when we're not looking, prise them off his feet and hope we don't discover there's one missing until we're 50 miles away and it's too late to go back for them, at which point he shouts, 'Daddy!' his eyes lightening with delight as he highlights his shoeless socks. 'Look!'

The temperature rocketed as well. Phoebe was roasting but I couldn't work the air-con in the hire car. It was slightly different from the one in our old Astra. Opening the windows to cool down, Phoebe lost the balloon she was given for being 'patient' at Shoezone in Alston. She went mad even before her long fringe started whipping her face. Craziness reigned.

'I can't scratch my leg. I need to take my tights off.'

'I want my colouring book.'

'Charlie has taken my teddy bear.'

'It's taking a long time.'

'I want another biscuit.'

'I want my box of felt tips NOW.'

'I want to get out.'

'My hair is HURTING MY FACE. SHUT THE WINDOW!'

They did it in shifts for 100 meandering miles, taking it in turns to cry out for something, anything – a banana, Weetabix, toys, sweets, cuddles, treats. Phoebe was so fed up when we reached Chollerford she was pressing the ignition button over and over again on a toddler driving game of Charlie's with the deadened eyes of a shark. The only respite came from topping her up with half-melted chocolate Aero Bubbles from the driver's side pocket. When she finally fell asleep, Charlie woke refreshed and took over the baton, angry he was still in his bucket seat and we weren't there yet. We teetered on the edge of madness down the tiny unmarked roads on the way to Kielder, the lowest moment coming when I took Phoebe for a wee in a field of potentially live ordnance in Otterburn, a few feet from a friendly roadside sign warning: 'Do not touch any military debris. It might explode and kill you.'

And what do we find now we're here? The place is overrun with puff adders.

Dinah, after being sanguine before, in a panicky volte-face now insists she and the kids wait in the lodge while I unload the car alone.

'I see, it's OK if Daddy gets bitten, is it?'

'Do you want me to do it too and the kids run out?'

'No, I'll do it.'

'Why are we waiting here, Mummy?'

'Never mind, Phoebe.'

'But why?'

'Phoebe, just do as you're told.'

'But why, Mummy?'

'Because of the puff adders, OK.'

'Puff adders?'

'Snakes, Phoebe.'

'Dinah, is that wise?' I shout from behind the boot.

'In real life, Mummy?' Phoebe asks in a quieter voice.

And Dinah, too tired and beleaguered to filter stuff now, replies, 'Yes, in real life.'

'Love, can I have a word?'

'If there are the snakes you say there are, Ben, I think the children ought to know.'

'OK, OK. You know best.'

'Charlie, there are snakes here,' says Phoebe. 'Loads of snakes.'

'Not really!' says Charlie, fear crossing his face.

'In real life,' says Phoebe, nodding. 'There are snakes, aren't there, Mummy?'

'Yes.'

Charlie thrusts his arms in the air, demanding a cuddle. It sets Phoebe off, who demands the same.

'Mummy! Mummy!' Phoebe shouts, jigging up and down on the spot with terror.

'Cuddle, cuddle,' shouts Charlie.

The situation's just calming down when something else happens. I'm in the middle of feeding Charlie when I hear a buzzing noise coming from what I think is the failing battery in a pendulum clock on the wooden wall of the living room. But how silly of me to assume it could be something as innocent as an AAA battery? It's a bat, of course. A live bat trapped in our lodge. It's officially the lowest point of the day, maybe the entire trip, as the bat I've disturbed begins to whip around the living room at great erratic speed. It doesn't bump into anything because, of course, it has echo location, but that doesn't stop the children crying and besides it's a rather hard concept to explain, echo location.

'Phoebe, stop crying! It's OK. They won't fly into you because bats send out sonar bleeps through their larynx that bounce off objects, sending differing rebound signal frequencies back to the bat's ears giving them a clear picture of what's in front of them.' It also doesn't help that I'm involuntarily ducking every few seconds myself as I'm saying this.

Some days it really doesn't pay to be the man. I'd suggest fleeing from the lodge but outside there are not only midges but puff adders.

'Ben, do something. Get it out.'

'What?'

'I don't know. God, this is so rubbish,' says Dinah. 'We should have gone home when we had the chance. I don't know, wave something at it.'

Fat tears spring from Charlie's eyes. His wailing is muffled by Dinah's shoulder. Meanwhile, Phoebe's in my arms, hiding her face in my chest.

'I don't like it, Daddy. I don't like it,' she says. 'Get it out. Get it out.'

'Sweetheart, it'll be fine. Please, no one cry. We've been here five minutes!' I shout. 'Five minutes! And we're already at crisis point. This is ridiculous. *Ridiculous!* Just open the door, Dinah. It will probably just fly out.'

'You open it.'

'You're nearest. I'm holding Phoebe.'

'Well, I've got Charlie.'

'Phoebe...'

'Don't ask her!'

'I wasn't going to. I was going to say, go to Mummy, actually.'

Phoebe runs to Dinah, where she begins to whimper.

'Ben, for God's sake!'

Dinah's dad, Bert, is six foot five, a former club rugby player and electrical engineer who, over the course of his thirty years keeping a roof over his family's heads, received several near fatal high voltage shocks from generators and faulty wiring. He once threw a boyfriend of Dinah's sister over a 3-foot hedge. This is who I'm being judged against.

'OK, OK.'

And it comes back to me. The reason I really, really hate bats. Growing up in a windmill, bats used to fly around the sails at night. Once, aged eleven, in the middle of the night, I'd sat on the toilet and heard a high-pitched squeaking noise. Unable to work out its source, I'd eventually stood up and peered down the bowl. A few inches from where my bum had just been, from where my face was now, there was the most disgusting thing I've ever seen – a bat covered in my shit flailing about in the toilet water. It must have flown in through the open window.

'AHHHHHHH!' I shout now, making a dash for the door. The bat arcs towards me but at the last moment banks away. It now hangs from the curtain before beginning another looping trajectory. I duck, slide open the door and dart back behind the sofa. Now the bat drops to the ground and crawls across the floor. Its wings resemble a crumpled parachute. It's a hideous sight, but I find the strength to run at it shouting again, flapping my arms. 'Ahhhhhh!'

The kids hide their faces.

'Daddy!' calls Phoebe, dramatically, an arm outstretched as if I'm sacrificing my life.

The bat takes off, swirls round the room once more and flies through the open door. I slam it shut and turn to face my family expecting – I'm not sure what: cheers? Congratulations? Indebtedness? I've saved us and slain personal demons in the process. I've done what a man must do.

Dinah, rising and shepherding the kids toward the bathroom, just says, 'God, you're a coward.'

'They're my tortoises,' I shout after her. 'I got rid of it, didn't I?'

She looks round and raises her eyebrows as Phoebe whimpers, 'But what if it comes back to get us, Daddy?'

'It won't come back. And it won't get us. Bats don't get people, Phoebe.'

'But what if this one does?'

'I promise you it won't.'

In the bath Charlie pretends his sponge is a bat and waves it in my face, laughing. Phoebe does the same with her flannel. It's all family folklore now. Except it's not. At bedtime Phoebe has to sleep with the light on, while Charlie refuses to go to bed until we put on his Spiderman slippers.

'Charlie, there's nothing in your bed!' I pull the covers back. 'See! Nothing. You can't wear slippers in bed. Nobody wears slippers in bed.'

He falls to the floor, writhes about on his stomach like he's having an imaginary judo bout with Brian Jacks.

''Lippers. I wan' 'lippers,' he shouts.

'Is it the bat, Charlie?'

''LIPPERS. I wan' 'lippers.'

'Charlie, you can't wear slippers in bed because if you wear them tonight you'll want them tomorrow night and the next night and the night after that and sooner or later we'll lose them like we have lost every pair of your shoes and then you'll go crazy like you're doing right now.'

'I won't. I won't.'

'The bats won't get you.'

''Lippers, 'lippers.'

'He's two, Ben. There's no point reasoning with him. I can't bear this,' says Dinah.

She leaves the room.

''Lippers,' shouts Charlie. 'I wan' 'lipperrrrs.'

'Charlie, is it the midges? They're outside, they've gone to sleep. Midges go to sleep *before* children. Didn't you know that?'

''Lippers,' he sobs. 'Lipperrrrrs.'

'Is it the puff adders, Charlie? Look at me. Stop shouting and look at me.'

I hold his head at both sides. I fix his brown eyes in mine.

'Is it the puff adders?'

He nods slowly and heartbreakingly.

'Is it the puff adders, Charlie? Is that what you're scared of?'

He nods again and leans forward to wipe his tears on my shirt.

'It's the puff adders,' I shout to Dinah. 'Come here, you little fool.'

I pull Charlie into my arms.

'You won't get puff adders in your bed,' I tell him. 'They're outside. And anyway they're more scared of you. Did you know that? Puff adders are scared of little boys.'

'I wan' 'lippers,' he says, softly.

'What shall I do?' I shout to Dinah. 'Help me here, love.'

'It will become routine,' she shouts back. 'Then we'll lose them.'

Phoebe pops her head down from her top bunk. 'You could let him wear them this night,' she shrugs.

'It's not as simple as that, Phoebe.'

'Then he can go back to bare feet the nextest night when there are no puff adders around,' she says.

'Thank you, Phoebe. Dinah?' I shout.

But all I can hear in the kitchen is the sound of wine glugging out of a bottle.

'OK, you can wear your slippers for one night. Just one, OK?'

He nods.

'But tomorrow it's bare feet. Do you understand?'

He nods.

'And if they fall off in the night, I'm not coming in here to put them back on.'

I read him a Thomas the Tank Engine story. I kiss him good night. I re-check the bedroom window is shut at Phoebe's insistence and in the kitchen I pour myself a large glass of wine and flop down on the sofa beside Dinah.

'To be fair on him it was quite a scary half hour,' I say. 'If I was his age, I think I'd want 'lippers on.'

'How did you get out in the end?'

'I let him wear them.'

Dinah closes her eyes.

'I had to make a decision.'

'Fine,' she says.

'He looked me in the eye. He understood the deal. It's tonight only.'

'Well, it's you who's getting up when they fall off in the night,' she says.

'They're quite tight. They won't fall off. And if they do, I've told him no calling out. Trust me. I've dealt with it.'

I get up three times. The first two times to replace a slipper. The third time it's 2 a.m. I don't know where I am. I stumble about banging into things. Eventually I'm standing over his bunk. I've scraped my shin on the ladder. I'm exhausted, furious.

'Charlie, we had an agreement. I am very cross with you. Very cross. This is the last time. The LAST TIME.'

I lift his covers to check which slipper needs replacing. Both are still on his feet.

'Charlie, they're on your feet, man! Jesus! You just woke me up for nothing. It's the middle of the night. I'm sooo tired.'

A tiny hand sneaks from underneath the covers and points. I follow his hand.

'Other 'lippers,' he says, indicating Phoebe's slippers by the door.

'What! You got me up not to put a slipper *on*. But to *change* your slippers!'

''Lippers,' he shouts.

'NO WAY, matey! You've lost me. That's it. No more slippers. Slippers ARE GONE. I'm not coming in again. And if you call me in again I will take *off* a slipper.'

''LIPPERS!'

'Have a tantrum, I don't care. You can do what you want. I am very, very cross with you. GOODNIGHT,' and I slam the door.

I stand the other side of it, leaving him crying for three minutes before I go back in.

'Fworry, Daddy,' he says.

He holds his arms out. I hug him.

'That's all right.'

I pull his covers up.

'Now, I meant what I said. That's it. No more slipper nonsense, OK?'

He nods, turns over.

I return to bed and although it's dark and there's no movement from her side of the bed I'm pretty sure I detect the ghost of a smile on Dinah's sleeping face.

The accident happens the following afternoon. We'd planned to take the Osprey ferry to the visitor centre at Tower Knowe that morning, but it was cancelled because it was too windy so instead we'd driven to Housesteads Roman Fort, which we'd missed the day before. The fort, manned by Tungrian conscripts and abandoned in AD 400, was on a windy ridge near Hexham off the B6318. On a tour with an English Heritage guide that started in the small museum, we'd visited the former barracks, the commandant's house as well as the Roman latrines. But the kids, still jumpy from yesterday, kept mistaking falling leaves for bats and were scared of the free-roaming sheep and it was so freezing on the exposed ridge we left early.

We're back at the park when this nervousness causes the accident. The kids are looking at the owls in the Birds of Prey Centre, when, returning from fetching the tickets for the now operating ferry to Tower Knowe, I hear Phoebe's wail. I rush there and discover her whole face washed in blood. Dinah's looking concerned pressing a tissue to her chin.

'She fell over,' she says. 'Get more wipes from the car, will you? Quickly. It's a nasty one.'

The bird-keeper says: 'Sheh bit hor lip reet through.'

I race back to the car.

'Let me see, popsy,' I say, when I'm back.

Dinah wipes Phoebe's face while I tilt her head and roll back her bottom lip. 'I'm just going to…'

And the bird-keeper's right – there's a tooth mark that goes in one side of Phoebe's lip and right out the other.

At reception, the first-aider gives Phoebe a lolly while Dinah goes through what happened. A five-year-old, southern white-faced owl called Willow on the gloved hand of the bird-keeper had made a tiny movement towards Phoebe, who'd leapt out of the way, slipped forwards and gone down chin first on the loose gravel path. Phoebe has the placidity of a beautiful doll as various interested hands tilt her head back to see her bottom lip, all agreeing on two things. Firstly: 'She's bit har lip reet through.' And secondly, 'She's being reet brave, mind.'

Phoebe's given three further lollies, a plastic key ring and is patted so kindly by up to half a dozen Geordies from all corners of the park, all cooing 'Dint worry pet – such a brave bairn' with such genuine affection, Dinah eventually bursts into tears and has to be told 'Dint worry pet' herself.

We're advised to take Phoebe to Hexham General for stitches. Phoebe's white with shock on the drive. Given treats to perk her up, she can't shake her natural suspicion at the fact that she's getting a choccy Aero Bubble for free, without having to, say, eat a Marmite sandwich, first.

'But I don't want a sandwich, Daddy.'

'You don't have to have one, sweetheart.'

'But I do want a choccy.'

'You can have a choccy.'

'But this is my third one.'

'I know.'

'But no sandwich?'

'No sandwich.'

It's an hour back the way we came this morning. The same road we drove yesterday. At Hexham General we're seen by the A & E duty nurse, who says the wound will probably heal well but wants us to see a doctor. Waiting in the kids' playroom, the Wimbledon ladies singles final between the Williams sisters is on the telly. At one set up to Serena the doctor takes us into the consulting room. The cut has crossed the vermilion of Phoebe's bottom lip so there'll be a small scar when she smiles. He asks if we want to see a plastic surgeon.

'What would they do?'

'Knit the lip back,' he says, although they might not think it worthwhile. We return to the playroom and agree it's a no if Phoebe requires a general anaesthetic. We watch the next set go to Venus. The duty nurse returns and ushers us back into the consulting room. Charlie hoofs around trying to snatch needles and a roll of bandages from an equipment tray. The consultant tells us we can see a plastic surgeon at Newcastle General tomorrow but we might wait around all day and they'll probably stitch the day after this. Plus it will be a general anaesthetic because they don't suture under-fives with a local. She might as well add 'and they'll waterboard her'.

We tell her our decision. She agrees it's the right thing to do, and ushers us into the corridor, where we half wonder about slipping back into the playroom to see the last few games of the final set before we drive back to the park.

'Sheh bit har lip reet through!'

'No, it's sheh bit hor lip reet through!'

We're copying the beautiful way the sentence sounds in Geordie leaving the park the next morning when I see the belt in the road. Whenever I see clothing in the road – a kid's glove, a sock, an old trainer – because of our chaotic lives, I always naturally assume it must have come from one of our cases. I'm slowing down for a closer look when it straightens out. The belt coils and moves in a looping S shape off the dirt road, disappearing into the long grass at the verge.

I look at Dinah.

'Was that what I think it was?' she says.

I nod, putting my finger to my lips.

'Why are you laughing?' says Phoebe.

'We're laughing at you guys,' I say. 'You're such lovely nutters.'

Dinah wipes her brow.

'What's a nutter?' says Phoebe.

'Someone slightly crazy but in a nice way.'

'So am I a nutter, Mummy?'

'Yes.'

'And is Charlie?'

And, before I answer, as if to confirm this, Charlie shouts at the top of his voice, 'NUTTTTTTTTTTTERRRRRR.'

CHAPTER 19

Dad hated losing and hated even more losing to Buster or me. He never gave us a quarter, always put 100 per cent into every cricket ball delivery, every swing of his racquet, and every penalty kick he punted our way. It made beating him far more real and enjoyable, although for many years an awful lot less likely. It must have been the mid 1980s because Buster and I were spending most of our time perfecting our impressions of Percy and Baldrick from *Blackadder* and my sister wasn't with us. Dad had decided, clearly forgetting he wasn't very outdoorsy, that we'd spend a week in Scotland. He'd hired a log cabin in a wood near the small town of Lochgilphead in Argyll that might have been idyllic if it wasn't for the rain and the mosquitoes.

I remember we tried walking the first day, got soaked trudging to the town's war memorial and spent the next six days engrossed in a marathon Family Olympics. My dad could turn something as simple as buttering toast into a competition. It was his answer to any lull – Family Olympics. Events in these particular games included trivial pursuit, card games and various activities available at the Mid Argyll Sports Centre, such as badminton, table tennis, tennis and squash, where Dad, overweight, unfit and well into his forties, came so close to killing himself playing Buster, Mum had to bang on the glass: 'Badge [short for 'Badger', her nickname for him because he worked like one], you'll have a heart attack. For goodness' sake – it's just a game.' I can picture it now – Buster shrugging apologetically at Mum, Dad red-faced, eyes ablaze, returning to his court position, crouching down ('Eleven–seven. Your serve.').

The final event was a round at the nine-hole municipal golf course. Dad had never played golf before, but with his natural aptitude for ball games unrealistically assumed he'd pick it up straightaway. He didn't. We were on the eighth hole of what had been a miserable hour and a half and it had just started to rain again. The hole before, Buster had become the first of us to lift the ball more than a couple of inches off the ground. We'd humiliatingly daisy-cut our way round the entire course; nevertheless, the spirit of competition was alive and well, and we were still carefully keeping track of each other's scorecards. ('Dad, I think that was actually eleven on the last hole. Remember, you hit that tree.') We'd each taken our fair share of air shots so it wasn't that unusual when Dad missed the ball entirely trying to run it down a hill on to the green on his seventh shot. The second and third times he played and missed, Buster and I had to stop looking at each other. The fourth and fifth times this happened it became excruciating. On the failed sixth attempt, an enraged Dad, in slip-on shoes, the ground sleek with the fresh rain, fell over. He picked himself up very quickly, too quickly, and before setting his feet right took another, even mightier swipe. The force of his swing was such that he fell over again. Buster and I were openly pleading now, 'Dad, come on. You'll never hit it like that.' As was Mum from the bushes, where she was still looking for his last lost ball. 'Badge! Stop it. Badge! For goodness' sake.' For his final swing Dad resembled a polo player as he ran at the ball, windmilling his club. Eventually he kicked the ball down the slope in disgust, called it 'a fucking stupid game' and refused to play the final hole.

It wasn't until later that night we dared bring it up and not until a day after this I reminded him, technically speaking, I'd won the Family Olympics and was entitled to my £5 reward. The episode entered family folklore as a synonym for sulking: 'He's Lochgilpheading.'

We're in Edinburgh, staying at the five-star Balmoral Hotel in room 522, where J. K. Rowling finished *Harry Potter and the Deathly Hallows*. This morning we've been spying on tourists buying tartan tea towels on the esplanade from the 150-year-old Camera Obscura periscope on Castlehill, and now we're at Arthur's Seat having a picnic, perched high above the city, when Pen calls.

'Have you spoken to Dad?' she asks.

'No.'

'Give him a ring.'

'What's up?'

'Give him a ring.'

'You sound pleased.'

She giggles. 'Give him a ring.'

I call Dad.

'Daddy-boy. What's the news?'

'Well, my son, I saw the oncologist this morning and now it's probably the steroids so we're not getting too carried away just yet, but – and I use the word but – my liver tests seem to have improved again.'

'That's excellent.'

'By fifty per cent.'

'That's brilliant, Dad.'

I hear panting. 'Dad, where are you?'

'Walking round the garden, my son.'

'That's amazing!'

'Fifth lap.'

'Dad, I'm so pleased. How are you sleeping?'

'OK.'

'And the bag?'

'Sore, but OK.'

'What's Gorhard said?'

'He's... surprised.'

I laugh.

'And what's he said about chemo?'

'Still a way to go.'

'But still.'

'I know,' he says.

'From what it was before, Dad.'

'I'm doing all right. And when am I seeing you next, my lovely boy?'

'When we get to Lincolnshire in a couple of weeks. I'll get the train down again.'

'I shall look forward to it. Kisses to everyone please.'

'And to Mary from me.'

And when I hang up and look down from the summit past the new Scottish Parliament building 250 feet below and the Palace of Holyroodhouse at the bottom of the Royal Mile, it seems impossible it could have gone any other way now. Nobody gets the better of my dad. He'll wear down anyone and anything, even cancer. It's also perfectly in sync with our charmed existence in Scotland. Our good luck had started the day we crossed the border and received our offer from the insurance assessor: £2,000. Exactly what I'd paid for the Astra three years earlier. We'd been expecting half this and to celebrate we immediately treated ourselves to a TomTom satnav that quickly cut mine and

Dinah's arguments down by half. From then on, whenever we were lost, instead of turning on each other, we united against Jane, the woman with the newsreader-like voice giving our directions. 'Jane, you told Ben to cross the roundabout and take the second turning on the left. That's an access road, you silly cow!'

We spent our first few days in the Borders mainly visiting ruined abbeys. Phoebe and Charlie aren't that interested in lower niche corbels or lierne vaulting and Dinah and I couldn't care less about delicate foliate tracery, yet all it took was one mildly interesting historical fact about an abbey (in the case of Melrose Abbey, that the embalmed heart of Robert the Bruce is buried there) and off we'd go, forgetting the abbey would be just the same as the last one. I'd take a few photos of the kids running through the cloisters, we'd hear its copycat history (burned down, rebuilt, burned down, rebuilt, burned down, dissolved) and back in the car we'd renew our vow.

'No more abbeys!'

But a few miles on there'd be a sign for another one.

'Dinah, we're not going to Jedburgh Abbey.'

'I know. I know. Although it does say here...'

'Please, don't tell me what it says there... OK, tell me what it says there.'

'It's where Alexander III married Yolande de Dreux in 1285.'

'Dinah, you fool. You should never have told me that.'

We headed north, bypassing Glasgow and Edinburgh, and explored the Trossachs. I don't think I've ever been anywhere more beautiful than the central Highlands on a sunny day. For days all we passed on either side of the road were breathtaking tree-topped mountain slopes perfectly reflected in crystal clear lochs. The weather, normally changeable in Scotland, was always warm and never wet. Or at least it always was whenever we stepped outside. If it was raining when we set off, by the time we arrived at an attraction and stepped from the car it was magically dry. It happened so often we started taking it for granted. 'OK,' we'd shout to the clouds. 'We'll be inside for a bit now so fire away, guys.' And often within minutes they would, right up until we stepped outside again. 'It's no fluke we didn't bring coats,' we began telling each other. 'We don't *need* coats.' It was the same with traffic. The odds were we'd run into the odd jam. It didn't happen. Not even entering major cities. Like the weather, bottlenecks magically disappeared when we came through and tightened up when we left.

We cruised lochs, scaled Munros. We climbed the Wallace Monument and at Doune Castle, the setting for the film *Monty Python and the Holy Grail*, we shouted from the ramparts in our best John Cleese voices, 'I fart in your general direction,' and that your mother was a hamster and your father stank of elderberries. We rolled into Perthshire and then up through the Highlands, where we clocked up our 5,000th mile of the trip, and along the Glen Coe pass, scene of the infamous MacDonald clan massacre, which we brought to life by listening to the gasp of pipe bands on the local Gaelic BBC radio station, the road sign warnings that thieves operated in the area, as we wound through this steep, desolately bleak road, conjuring up images of wild Scotsmen in kilts brandishing broadswords emerging from the heather on horseback.

In Fort William, at the end of the West Highland Way, we rode the Jacobite steam train to the fishing town of Mallaig, from where Bonnie Prince Charles fled to France dressed as a woman. Later we walked the Culloden battlefield. We dolphin-spotted in the Moray Firth at Chanonry Point. We rambled through forests, we windsurfed and fished. We ate Forfar bridies, tried haggis and Ecclefechan cake. And just outside Inverness, overlooking Loch Ness, we stood in the Grant Tower of Urquhart Castle looking for a break in the waters, irritating professional Nessie hunters who were nattering about plesiosaurs, Operation Deepscan and the Dinsdale film by loudly telling the kids, 'Don't be silly – they proved it was a giant sturgeon years ago.'

We returned to England via the north-eastern coast, where we toured the oil town of Aberdeen and the jam, jute and journalism city of Dundee. We played on the Old Course in St Andrews, saw the Burrell Collection and fell in love with Charles Rennie Mackintosh in Glasgow. And now here we are, on our last night in Scotland, at Edinburgh's Balmoral Hotel.

We eat downstairs at Hadrian's Brasserie, the Balmoral Hotel's super-swanky Michelin-starred restaurant. It's Phoebe's favourite place we've stayed in and Dinah and I have already agreed when that conversation comes up about who'd look after your children if you both died in an accident, our answer has changed from my sister or brother, who'd accept Phoebe and Charlie as their own, to the Balmoral for their junior accessories. Waiting for us on check-in was a bag of toys, a bottle warmer, steriliser, a changing mat and a stack of different sized nappies that we felt like lying on the bed and flinging in the air like stolen money. For Phoebe there was a gift (*The Gruffalo* book) and, in the bathroom, a Balmoral plastic duck, children's bubble bath, and her own fluffy white dressing gown with slippers. After dinner each night a bellhop has even been delivering her a complimentary banana split to have in the bath.

At the table three members of the staff management team, recently trained in making kids feel welcome, cluster around the children asking how Phoebe's food is and if there's enough of it, whether they have enough crayons, if the crayons are the right colours, what they've done today, whether they enjoyed what they did today and whether they know what they'll be doing tomorrow, leaving Dinah and I to quietly enjoy super-chef Jeff

Bland's traditional Scottish mixed grill. After dinner we put the kids to bed in their complimentary monogrammed pyjamas after reading them their complimentary reading books and then we come downstairs to the bar to drink the complimentary bottle of Prosecco left in our room.

In my twenties, whenever I met a girl I really liked what I always wanted to do was run off with her in a camper van. It was a recurring fantasy, this romantic image of freedom. Real life – falling in love, settling down, marriage, kids, a career – never seemed enough. I wanted something heightened. Desert island feelings, I used to call them, this urge to escape the real world. I wanted to run off with a girl I was in love with and spend all my time with her in a camper van. In my head we'd drive around playing hippyish music. We'd get into scrapes and fall hopelessly in love against some beautiful backdrop. Chatting over fires in the evening, we'd get to know each other. We'd do crazy things, too, like adopt emblematic pets of whatever country we were driving through – a Dalmatian in Croatia, a whooper swan in Finland. We'd be away for years, grow old together and never be bored.

In reality, the closest I came to recreating this was the weekend in a Premier Inn near the Tebay services I spent with my ex-girlfriend Julie on a 2-for-1 Easter mini-break deal during my second year at university. The element of travel: I drove us there from Sheffield in a hired Mazda 323.

But in a way what we're doing now feels more like this than anything else I've ever done.

'Even with the kids?' asks Dinah.

'Especially with the kids.'

'Sort of an adult version?' asks Dinah.

'It's a hire car not a camper van and we have kids rather than guitars. And we don't listen to Joan Armatrading but Charlie's *Dig Dig Digging* CD. But apart from that...'

'It's exactly the same,' says Dinah.

We drink a toast to my dad. Then to Mary, who's whipped him into shape. But eventually I swallow a yawn.

'Am I boring you, love?'

Dinah yawns too.

'I think we're boring each other.'

'Bed?'

But we don't go straight to sleep upstairs. We find a DVD to watch. *The Bone Collector* is about a paraplegic NYPD forensic scientist. Denzel Washington plays the main character. The top man in his field, he's been paralysed on the job and is worried his next seizure will leave him in a permanent vegetative state. He's already arranged self-termination but agrees to defer it to help the department solve a horrific and baffling serial killer case. It's scary, but also unintentionally funny in places. Dinah's either snuggling up holding her hand over her face, or laughing, like when the killer turns off Denzel's life-support systems towards the end shouting, 'Which vegetable to do you fancy being – a carrot?' He shuts off a monitor. 'You'd like to be a carrot? What about a zucchini?' He presses a button and more lights go off. 'You wanna be a zucchini?'

When Dinah's scared by a film she never acknowledges this is what's frightened her. That just makes it worse. Before she turns over to go to sleep she says without referring to the movie, 'Have you locked the door?' She says it matter-of-factly, pretending it's routine. It's better if I play along with this because if she has to tell me she's scared it makes her even more terrified and she'll want to sleep with the light on. I tell her I've locked the door.

'Better check it,' she says.

I pretend to and come back to bed.

Our bed's huge so we needn't be anywhere near each other.

'I'm going to sleep closer to you tonight,' she says, moving to the middle of the bed. Every now and again her hand comes out to test I'm still within touching distance. The third time she does this, after tapping my knee a couple of times, she says: 'It's an urge. Touch your nose three times?'

'Don't worry, there are no bone collectors in Edinburgh, love.'

'Touch your nose three times,' she says, more insistently.

I touch my nose three times. I don't ask what it is about because I know what it's about: Dinah's worried I'm getting carried away with my dad's good news.

CHAPTER 20

We're in the Gateshead Metrocentre shopping for Phoebe's very specific fourth birthday present wish list which includes:

A Hello Kitty lunch box (not a problem)

A jumbo set of pens (easy)

And:

A medium-sized pink rabbit that can walk and talk and goes chut chut chut when it chews a carrot. Not a small pink rabbit that can walk and talk and goes chut chut chut when it chews a carrot. Not a large pink rabbit that can walk and talk and goes chut chut chut when it chews a carrot. A medium-sized one (more tricky).

This morning we were at the eleventh-century Alnwick Castle, the boyhood home of Harry 'Hotspur' Percy, immortalised by Shakespeare in *Henry IV*, although nowadays more famous as Hogwarts in the Harry Potter films. We went on a magician-themed tour led by a guide with an impenetrable Geordie accent, who spoke in incredibly fast, short sentences like someone recovering from a near drowning who's trying to tell rescue workers whereabouts other endangered swimmers might be. It began at the Lion Arch, where the forbidden forest started in the films, although I only found this out later because all I heard at the time was this: 'Harry Potter ag ig ag aye. Aye cran oer toooer. Follow me to the courtyard now.' There were around thirty Italian schoolchildren on the tour. Their teachers kept hoping in vain to make things clearer but gave up as we did at the inner bailey. 'Quidditch aahe canne ig gannin. CGI special effects hoawn hwhol. Hagrid masks £15.50 in the gift shop.'

We'd crossed town afterwards and popped into Alnwick Gardens for a tour of their famous walled poison garden. 'The purple flower is aconite; the only way to tell a victim had been poisoned with it in the nineteenth century was by tasting the victim's vomit. It had a peculiar tang.'

'Charlie, stay away from the aconite, please.'

We learned angel's trumpet was the favourite poison of assassins ('No spasms. No vomiting. Slip a tiny bit into their food and they just drift off to sleep and don't wake up'), that the laurel plant releases cyanide gas. Henbane, meanwhile, emits so powerful a smell every year three or four kids pass out from it.

'Charlie, put the henbane down, please.'

We learnt rosemary can give pregnant women miscarriages and finally that the leaves of the rhubarb plant, although common in gardens, contain oxalic acid, which is capable of inducing kidney failure, coma and ultimately death, if ingested.

'Charlie, do NOT put that in your mouth. STRAP HIM INTO THE BUGGY, BEN. THIS IS RIDICULOUS!'

'But you said I could have what I wanted because I'm not having a party, Daddy.'

Still looking for Phoebe's present, we're now in the Early Learning Centre and I'm trying to modify her wish list by suggesting an alternative to the medium-sized pink rabbit that can walk and talk and goes chut chut chut when it nibbles a carrot.

'Yes, we did,' says Dinah. 'And we will have a look for your medium-sized pink rabbit, I promise you.'

'But if we can't find one, Phoebe...' I say.

'But you said.'

'We will do our best, sweetheart,' says Dinah.

'But Daddy, you said.'

'We'll look in one more shop, OK?'

But we've done our best. We've been to the Build-A-Bear Workshop (rabbit too big), the Disney Store (rabbit too small), Mothercare (rabbit couldn't talk) and finally the Early Learning Centre (rabbits didn't go chut chut chut).

I draw Dinah to one side in Toys R Us.

'Love, we're not going to find one. This is the largest shopping centre in Europe and if we can't find it here...'

But Dinah isn't prepared to give up.

'We promised her, Ben. Phoebe, come here. Tell me again, where did you see the rabbit?' Dinah asks. 'On the telly? On an advert? Can you help us? Did it have a name?'

'Dinah. We're not going to find one. I've got another...'

Dinah raises her hand like a white-gloved traffic cop.

'Phoebe, what's its name?' she asks.

'Fluffy,' she says. Phoebe's voice goes fey, as it does whenever she discusses teddy bears, mermaids and other mythological creatures. 'She was called Fluffy because she's sooo fluffy.'

'OK, but was Fluffy its real name from the advert or the name you gave it because you thought it looked so fluffy?'

'Dinah, why don't we...'

The hand comes up again.

'I call it Fluffy because it's fluffy,' Phoebe says, dreamily.

'Phoebe, what would happen if we couldn't get Fluffy?' I ask.

She starts to blink, about to make herself cry.

'You see, you could make a bear in the Build-A-Bear Workshop and we could wrap it up for you and you could call it Fluffy because it would be very, very fluffy,' I say.

Phoebe shakes her head.

'Building your own bear? You decide what it looks like! And what colour it is!'

She looks away, thinking.

'Really, you don't want to build a bear?'

'Actually, I do want to build a bear.'

'Are you sure?'

I look at Dinah.

Phoebe nods and we set off back to the Build-A-Bear Workshop until she stops in her tracks.

'But I want Fluffy,' she says, blinking again.

'But we can't find Fluffy, sweetheart,' I say.

I can sense Dinah's about to go insane. Phoebe raises her eyes to think for a second – we wait, holding our breath – before she pronounces: 'Actually, no, build a bear.'

'No more changing your mind. Build a bear?'

'No. Yes. No. Yes, yes.' She smiles, nodding.

'Yes?'

'Yes. Because I can build it. AND I can make it fluffy.'

Behind Phoebe's back I hold out a hand. Reluctantly Dinah slaps me five.

We're staying in a castle owned by the Craster family back up the A1 in the village, famous for herring smokehouses, which bears their name. At the turn of the century Craster was the UK kipper capital, smoking over 25,000 a day. They were gutted by Scottish fishwives, who lived in ramshackle buildings called kip houses, suitable only for sleeping in (hence the saying: having a kip). Today, the herring are still smoked over traditional fires of oak sawdust and heading coast-wards off the main road we can smell the kippers as we enter the village.

The castle, which turns out to be more of a mansion with turrets, is set back from the road down a gravel drive. We're met in the garden by Colonel Craster and his wife, who asks us to call her Fiona and shows us around our penthouse apartment. Craster Tower has been in the colonel's family for more than 900 years. 'Longer than the Percys at Alnwick,' Fiona tells us proudly. The apartment, at the top of the castle with distant sea views, is set over two floors. There are four bedrooms, a kitchen-breakfast room and a playroom.

'Come down and see us when you've settled the children?' says Mrs Craster. 'We'll have some wine. We've got a few questions we'd like to ask you.'

An hour later, we're led into the Crasters' drawing room on the ground floor. Fiona, who looks a little like Christine Hamilton, is sat opposite a burning fire. Colonel Craster fetches crystal glasses and seems unfazed that the wine we've brought down is a Chenin blanc from an Asda promotion. Fiona grills us about the book – what its sales will be, how our review might affect their business, whether we think Wi-Fi would help their occupancy rates – but soon the conversation flows more naturally. Colonel Craster, or Michael as he asks that we call him, is a former grenadier, who served in Eden with the Argyles and is now a military historian. Fiona mentions their daughter. She also has a historical bent and studied the Holocaust at university and this somehow segues into a story about how they all had dinner with the former SS officer Reinhard Spitzy, von Ribbentrop's one-time adjutant, and the last man alive who personally knew Adolf Hitler.

'He's a military historian too,' explains Michael.

'I bet that was interesting,' I say.

'He was a very civilised man,' says Fiona. 'Excellent manners. The Nazis – the high ranking ones – people forget, they came from some of the great German families.'

Michael chips in, as I steal a glance at Dinah, 'But our daughter, she'd studied the Holocaust.' He holds his hands up as if to say, what can you expect from someone who has done this?

'She asked him, sat right next to him, "Why didn't they hang you at Nuremberg, Spitzy?"' says Fiona.

'That's brave.'

'He hid in a monastery and then in Argentina,' says Michael.

'But she wouldn't let him off the hook,' Fiona says. 'She asked him what he thought of Hitler.'

'What did he say?'

'He said he was inspirational. He charmed everyone he met.'

'But that wasn't the worst bit,' says Michael.

I catch Dinah looking at me nervously.

'We were leaving,' says Fiona. 'At the door. Can you imagine? No more questions, he'd already said. But my daughter wanted to ask another. We tried to usher her out. She asked him: "Is Hitler dead?"'

Fiona pauses and, for a moment, I feel we're on the verge of entering a Dan Brown thriller and are about to discover that Adolf Hitler is actually alive and well, maybe living down the road in Craster, smoking herring for a living.

'What did he say?' I almost whisper.

Fiona leans forward. 'He said yes, you can believe it. We went to leave again, but she had one more question. And you can imagine what we were thinking. We were scared now. We wanted to go.'

She closes her eyes.

'But she wasn't scared. "What would you do if he came back now, Spitzy?" she asked. You could see him thinking about it. It was a question he'd obviously never been asked before. He said he'd say, "*Mein führer*, what have you done? There is a chalet in the woods. You will be safe there."'

'To be in the same room,' I say, looking at Dinah, 'with the last man alive who knew the man responsible for the greatest evil ever perpetrated.'

'We drove somewhere quiet afterwards and parked the car and just sat there in silence, decompressing,' says Michael.

It sets the tone for the rest of the night and the spooky conversation drifts somehow onto the ghosts that live in Craster Tower. 'Although none in your rooms, of course,' laughs Michael.

Fiona tells us they often talk to the ghosts.

'You talk to them?' I ask.

'We say hello. Sometimes they make a bit of a racket.'

'They're friendly though,' says Michael, who reminds Fiona of the rule they have: no talking about the ghosts in the house.

'You can talk *to* them but not *about* them?'

'We don't like to talk about them in front of people,' says Michael.

'Some people are funny about ghosts,' says Fiona.

I have to stop myself from looking at Dinah, who is not just scared of tortoises. She's also frightened of, among other things, cats, dogs, spiders, disembodied voices, bees, horror films, woodlice, sudden loud noises, burglars, zombies, plastic ketchup containers with dribbled relish down their sides (pocky, she calls such things). And ghosts. More than anything, ghosts.

'They move furniture around,' says Fiona. 'They get up to all sorts of tricks.'

She tells us how five guys stayed once. The Crasters heard a terrible fight in the penthouse but when they went to investigate no one was there. The next morning they found out the lads had all been at dinner.

'So what was the noise?' I ask.

Fiona shrugs.

'The ghosts?'

She shrugs again.

I ask if they have names.

'There's the one we call the old lady ghost. She likes to settle children,' says Fiona.

'What do you mean, settle them?'

Dinah's now twiddling her hair, staring into the fireplace with her hand on her chin in a stare.

'When children become untucked she wraps them back up. It happened to our nephew once in the strawberry room.'

One of our four bedrooms upstairs has strawberry coloured bedclothes and strawberry themed wallpaper.

A few minutes later we thank the Crasters and leave.

'It's fucking haunted!' says Dinah, the other side of their door. 'Great!'

'Dinah, please!'

'They live here, Ben. They ought to know. Why would they say that otherwise? And it's a nine-hundred-year-old castle. Of course it's bloody haunted.'

'Stop being so dramatic. You'll scare yourself.'

'I'm scared already.'

She grabs my hand, insists on holding it as we walk up the stairs to our apartment.

'Ah, that's so sweet of you, love.'

'Don't laugh at me. I'm not going to sleep a wink now. And you can go and check the kids when we're upstairs. I can't believe there's a settling ghost. Actually, on second thoughts, we'll both go.'

'Worried about the old lady ghost?'

'Shut up.'

Dinah follows me to the kids' room, where they're fast asleep, their covers the way they were when we left. Dinah follows me back to the bedroom. She then tails me to the bathroom where I do my teeth.

'And thanks for asking all those questions. I tiptoe round you when *you* get ridiculous things into your head. You know about me and ghosts.'

'You tiptoe around me, do you? When do you do that?'

'When you get all hypochondriac.'

'You laugh at me for that. That's what I'm doing now. If I took it seriously, imagine how scared you'd get. It would make you worse. I'm more scared about that Nazi.'

Dinah then makes me come with her to unload the washing machine in the downstairs utility room and afterwards even follows me to the toilet.

'Can I have a little privacy? At least stand back from the door a bit. I can hear your panicky little breathing.'

She leans on the door and says: 'No. This is your fault for going on about it. Do you think we should move the kids into our room? Put a mattress on the floor.'

'No, I don't. You're being ridiculous.'

I have to check on the kids again, Dinah again holding my hand on the way there, and finally we get into bed. Only now, the slightest noise – a radiator filling up, a water tank emptying or a seagull on the roof – and Dinah suddenly grips my arm. Twice she hauls me back from the edge of sleep.

'Please, love!'

'I'm scared. I think we should move them in here.'

'I am not waking them up and moving them. None of us will sleep.'

The trouble is it's impossible to be in the same room as someone as jumpy as Dinah without absorbing some of their trepidation and in the end, I start to feel a little anxious myself. To cure myself of this I utilise the same tactic I employ to stop myself worrying about money back at home. What I do when I'm really worried about our financial situation is panic Dinah even more about the problem so that I can then legitimately step back in and be my customary reassuring self. I do the same now about the ghosts.

'Do you remember that film, the Nicole Kidman one, *The Others*?' I ask her.

'Was it a horror film?' says Dinah from the other side of the bed.

'No, it was more of a psychological thriller. They lived in a castle like this one.'

'Ben?' She opens her eyes.

'What?'

'Are you trying to scare me?'

'I'm telling you about the film because the castle reminds me of the one in the film. She lived in a castle, the Nicole Kidman character, with her two kids. The first twist was that her three servants were all ghosts who'd died of TB.'

'Why are you doing this? I'll switch the light on and then we both won't be able to sleep.'

'The Kidman character discovers their graves in the grounds. That's how she knows they're ghosts. Imagine if tomorrow in that little courtyard garden we found two graves inscribed with the names Colonel Michael and Fiona Craster.'

Dinah turns away from me, dragging the covers with her.

'Then we googled the Crasters and found out they committed suicide years ago. In the strawberry room. After their daughter was murdered in the war by Reinhard Spitzy.'

'I can't hear you. I'm chanting something in my head.'

'The second twist was that Kidman and her two kids turned out to be ghosts as well. Do you remember that?'

Dinah puts her fingers in her ears.

I touch her shoulder.

'I have to tell you something,' I say.

'La la la,' she chants.

'I think you've guessed already.'

'La la la!'

'Dinah, the reason we've not talked with friends for such a long time on this trip...'

She whacks me on the arm.

'The reason we alone can talk to the Crasters...'

Dinah puts the pillow over her head.

I yank it off her head and whisper in her ear. I feel real evil in me as I say it. 'Dinah, we died in that car accident in Wales. In the air ambulance we all died on the way to hospital. Don't you remember, Dinah? Dinah, we're ghosts, Dinah.'

She yanks herself away and jumps out of bed. 'You fucking bastard.'

I climb out too. She looks terrified.

'Get away from me. You fucking bastard.'

She belts me over the head with the pillow.

'You're horrible. Get away from me.'

My own black heart is going ten to the dozen now. In frightening her I've frightened myself. And that's when we hear the noise. Dinah wheels round to face the door. 'Whatwasthat?' Her eyes are on stalks.

'Dinah! Calm down. It's nothing.'

But the hairs on the back of my neck have risen too. It's almost like my own fear has conjured up something terrible. Dinah climbs back into bed. I follow her.

'It's OK. It's an old castle. There are bound to be...'

Then we hear it again.

'Footsteps,' whispers Dinah. 'Coming from the...' She gulps, unable to say the words: strawberry room.

We remain stock-still, listening. Heading for the kitchen the footsteps stop. Then they change direction. There's white all the way round Dinah's eyes now. I put my finger to my lips. The knuckles on her hand gripping my forearm are white. Dinah begins to physically cower, slowly raising a hand up to her face, shielding her eyes from who or whatever is about to enter the room. The footsteps move closer and closer until at last a white face appears from the gloom and I hear a little voice.

'I need a wee, Mummy.'

Dinah bangs her head angrily down on the pillow.

'Phoebe! You frightened the life out of me!'

'Why doesn't Mummy want to speak to you, Daddy?' asks Phoebe.

'Mummy and Daddy have fallen out,' I say. 'Like you and Charlie fall out sometimes.'

After we'd said goodbye to the Crasters ('I hope we didn't talk about the ghosts too much?'... 'No. We slept like logs') in the car I'd apologised to Dinah.

'I know you're not going to believe me, but I was scared as well. I was too embarrassed to admit it so I made you more scared.'

'I don't want to talk about it,' she said.

After visiting the cathedral and castle in Durham we'd driven on to Hartlepool. The Tees Valley provided Ridley Scott's inspiration for the apocalyptic backdrop to the sci-fi movie, *Blade Runner*. Coming in from Port Clarence it was all belching cooling towers, flaring oil chimneys and pipe-work. Even the roundabouts weren't decorated with flowers but with metal pipes or steel hoods fashioned into artwork. Lorries carried girders and widgets about and the town smelt so strongly of the fumes from the Lion brewery just walking from the car park to the Hartlepool Maritime Museum made me feel slightly drunk. The museum was on an industrial estate surrounded by barbed wire fences snagged with shopping bags. Shell-suited locals walked about with pit bulls on fist-clenched short macho leads, the atmosphere perfectly reflecting the mood between Dinah and me.

'Why have you fallen out?' asks Phoebe.

We've just walked around HMS *Trincomalee* and now we're in a recreated nineteenth-century harbour-side store, Eustace Pinchbeck's Gunmates, and I'm reading about how the ideal coming-of-age present for a young boy has changed. Nowadays it's a hip flask or maybe the spare keys to your mum's Ford Escort, while in the eighteenth century it would have been a burnished wooden box containing your first pistol and powder horn.

'Because I was naughty last night,' I reply.

I move onto a display about naval slang. 'All my eye and Betty Martin,' is an old phrase meaning nonsense. Another nice one is: 'Whistling psalms to the taffrail'. This one means providing advice that's ignored.

'Why were you naughty?' persists Phoebe.

'I teased Mummy.'

'That's not very nice, Daddy.'

'I know.'

'Say sorry to Mummy.'

'I have done.'

'Say it again, more nicer.'

'You're whistling psalms to the taffrail, Phoebe,' says Dinah. She pulls a flat smile. It's her first move towards reconciliation. I seize it and apologise again.

The sea shanty that's been blaring from a speaker since we arrived seems to grow louder.

Whisky whisky whisky oh
Rise me up from down below

'Mummy, say that's all right.'

I like whisky hot and strong
I'll drink whisky all day long

'Mummy, when someone says sorry, the other person says, that's all right.'

'OK, that's all right,' says Dinah.

'Well, hug then,' says Phoebe.

We hug.

Whisky whisky whisky o
Rise her up from down below

'Let's get out of here, this music's driving me potty,' says Dinah.

Our final stop is the seaside resort of Saltburn-by-the-Sea. Here we ride the nineteenth-century cliff lift, paddle in the freezing North Sea and then wander into the Smugglers Heritage Centre to hear the story of John Andrew, king of the smugglers (or 'hiding people' as Phoebe calls them), who centred his operations 200 years ago on the Ship Inn next door. The tiny museum has wax figures talking unrealistically to each other, often incorporating large chunks of history in their conversation. 'No, I am not feeling very well as the king has introduced new duties on playing cards and dominoes so I might as well smuggle them into the country and make more in a night than I can in a month working the fields. How about you, Seth, and your plans to do the same kind of thing with rum and other products with large import duties designed to raise crown revenue to fight wars that don't concern us?'

That night, in an eighteenth-century former coaching inn off the main A688 road into Bishop Auckland, sitting in the main bar after the kids are in bed with *Channel 4 News* on mute on the wall-mounted TV and an unread newspaper on our table, Dinah admits, after a couple of glasses of wine, that she has the three-month blues.

'I'm sorry I've been ratty today. It's not seeing friends,' she says. 'We've been away ages. We don't get any outside perspective. I need that. We're on top of each other the whole time. And we've still got weeks left, Ben. I just feel a bit glum.'

'One day at a time, remember.'

There's a rule. We're not allowed to read ahead in the blue folder further than a couple of days. It's the only way to handle the enormity of the timescale.

'I know. It's just I keep thinking we've mastered it and then something happens – ghosts, bats – anything can throw us off kilter and straightaway it's back to the chaos.'

'We've been in cities and big towns again. That's what it is.'

'You think?' she says.

The more we talk though, the more we realise we've become unwittingly trapped in a sort of parallel universe. We're in England but it's a different England than the England everyone else is in and reads about in the papers and sees reflected back on their TV. We exist in a bubble because we don't speak to anyone else. Our England is a virtual representation of England made up of no other people we know, no news events, no work-related matters, hardly any telly, and instead just kid-themed attractions, city centre NCP car parks and hotels and child-friendly restaurants. It's like we're abroad but in our own country. In fact, we somehow seem further away here from loved ones and friends than we would do in Egypt even though they're physically only a motorway's length away. It's probably something to do with knowing we won't be seeing anyone for such a long time.

A coach-load of pensioners arrives on a David Urquhart tour bus and, to snap ourselves from the downward spiral, we enter the pub quiz. The landlord has bingo-style showmanship ('Who said let them eat cake during the French revolution? An event some of you may remember.'). Despite being hopeless at quizzes, an hour later the Chaos Monkeys (our team name) triumph. 'The

River Severn', which we were around for several days earlier in the trip, was the answer sealing the free bottle of wine.

We stay up drinking it, and only go to bed after mistakenly watching on a TV over the bar what we think is an old episode of *The Bill*, featuring a long surveillance scene, but which turns out to be grainy black and white CCTV footage of the hotel car park; a fact we only realise when it pans round and we see the roof box on our hire car.

CHAPTER 21

Draft Copy for Guidebook:

Yorkshire, the country's biggest county, is England's Texas only with flat caps instead of Stetsons and Yorkshire puddings and parkin instead of oil and natural gas. Dynamic (well, they set up Asda), brash and hugely sentimental about itself, Yorkshire is also the official nostalgia capital of Sunday night TV, with Heartbeat, All Creatures Great and Small *and* Last of the Summer Wine *all having been filmed here. It's a very friendly place, although be warned: Yorkshiremen, prone to bouts of self-aggrandisement and to starting sentences with the word "Ark", are extremely proud, even if it's only about how it was tougher in their day 'When I had to sleep in't shoebox in't middle of t'road and be beaten t'death by me dad every night.' Often identifying more with their own county anthem 'On Ilkla Moor Baht 'at' (a song about being outside without a hat on) than the country as a whole, the average Yorkshireman will point his pipe in the direction of the historic city of York and remind you George VI famously said 'the history of York is the history of England', although nowadays the history of York is more the history of the elevenses (Terry's, Thorntons and Rowntrees having all been based here). As the county boasts the pretty harbour town of Whitby and the North Yorkshire Moors, why would anyone need t' travel anywhere else, our invented heavily stereotyped Yorkshireman (of whom we're actually rather ashamed now) might ask. For families holidaying here the answer is: they don't.*

There's something slightly decadent but also seedy about celebrating a birthday, even a four-year-old's, in a hotel room: it's half like being a rock star yet also a bit like being Alan Partridge. Thirty miles from Whitby in room 109 of the Gisborough Hall Hotel at 8.30 a.m., Phoebe receives her Winnie the Pooh foldout suitcase of crayons, the Build-A-Bear Fluffy she made and a baby doll, Max, that cries when you press its tummy and makes a sucking sound when you put a bottle of milk to its lips. Max also has a hat that doesn't stay on that will get lost today approximately thirty-five times. Phoebe is also given her Hello Kitty lunch box and Part One of the Ancol rabbit grooming system (a flea comb). Part Two of the Ancol rabbit grooming system (the actual rabbit), we've promised her when we return home. At breakfast two waitresses sing her 'Happy Birthday', their heartiness seemingly undiminished by the fact Phoebe, as they do this, is wiping her chocolate-Coco-Popped hands on their perfect white tablecloth.

'And your birthday treat,' I tell Phoebe, as we set off.

'Don't build it up too much,' says Dinah, under her breath. 'We don't really know what's there.'

'Is that we're going to the place WHERE WALLACE AND GROMIT COME FROM.'

'Where Wallace and Gromit come from?' repeats Charlie, his eyes bulging. 'YAY!'

Dinah stares at me. 'I can't believe you just did that.'

'It'll be fine.'

'What sort of birthday treat is that?' she whispers.

'It will be fun.'

She shakes her head at me.

'Dad, do you mean we're watching a Wallace and Gromit film?' says Phoebe.

'No, Phoebe, we're going to the place where they live.'

'Charlie, we're going to Wallace and Gromit's house.'

'Y-aaaa-ay,' he shouts.

'Where they have those machines,' says Phoebe, 'that make their breakfasts and they slide down into their trousers and have cups of teas?'

Dinah gives me a knowing look.

'Well, it's not strictly their house, guys,' I say.

'It's the Wensleydale Creamery Visitor Centre,' says Dinah. 'Which we were going to anyway,' she says under her breath.

Phoebe looks at me in the rear-view mirror, confused. I explain.

'You know Wallace likes cheese, Phoebe. Well, the cheese he likes best is Wensleydale.'

'Wendysdale!'

'Yes, we're going where they make Wensleydale cheese.'

'Oh,' says Phoebe, then translating for Charlie. 'Wallace likes cheese, Charlie. You know he likes cheese. You remember in the film, Charlie? And the cheese Wallace likes bestest of all is... What is it again, Dad?'

'Wensleydale.'

'Is Wendysdale. So we're going to Wendysdale where we're going to see Wallace and Gromit. The *real* Wallace and Gromit, Charlie.'

'Daddy?' says Dinah.

'Well, guys, we *hope* we'll see them.'

I shrug my shoulders at Dinah. 'It'll be fine.'

It's what I've been saying all week. 'It'll be fine.' It's become my new mantra and on the whole it has been. After the haunted house meltdown things have been better. We've had a little purple patch. The weather's been great, which helps, the kids have slept and we've not been attacked by bats or slept in any haunted castles. This last week we've cut a large scoop out of North and West Yorkshire. In Saltaire we saw the world's largest collection of David Hockney paintings at the 1853 gallery. We descended in a pit cage 140 feet into a former coal mine in Wakefield. We visited the Brontë Parsonage in Haworth and got hopelessly lost in the warehouse room of the National Railway Museum of York amongst the aisles of memorabilia in the company of some strange looking train buffs in brightly coloured pacamacs a little too excitedly handling muffled pop safety valves and signal lever frames. And at the Yorkshire Air Museum in Elvington we had a laugh when Phoebe described a thermonuclear device thirty times more powerful than the one dropped on Hiroshima as 'cute' because it was marginally smaller than the earthquake tallboy bomb stood next to it.

We have two tactics to appease Phoebe on long journeys. The first is adapting well-known children's stories into tales involving Phoebe herself. We do this by replacing the main character's name with hers so it becomes, for instance, 'Phoebe and the Three Bears' ('And then Phoebe tried the medium-sized bowl of porridge…') or 'Hansel and Phoebe' ('And the wicked witch told Phoebe, I will eat your brother, be he fat or thin.'). The thrill of hearing herself thrust into unlikely adventures involving beanstalks, glass slippers and evil witches buys us valuable time. The other game is a variant on I spy except to make the game last longer it becomes: I don't spy, as in 'I don't spy with my little eye something beginning with P', the P capable of being anything in the known universe unobservable from a speeding car, in this case, on the A1.

It's 3 p.m. when we finally arrive; too late to observe the production of the Wensleydale cheese. From the viewing gallery instead we stare into empty, huge, stainless steel tubs, and read information boards detailing the various processes of milling, tipping, blocking, salting, moulding and pressing whilst learning facts the kids aren't really interested in such as this: Wensleydale cheese won the 2002 Nantwich International Cheese Show's supreme champion cheese award. Afterwards there's a film about how cheese-making, brought to England from France in the twelfth century by Franciscan monks, was first threatened by the dissolution of monasteries and then by the Milk Marketing Board in the 1960s until it was saved by a Dalesman with a pipe known as Kit Calvert.

'Daddy, where's Wallace?' asks Phoebe, outside the screening room.

The reason I put the attraction on our itinerary and talked it up was because of the huge picture of Wallace and Gromit on the information leaflet from the Yorkshire Tourist Board.

'We're not sure. He might be out delivering cheese,' I improvise.

'Where's Gromit, then?' asks Phoebe.

'He'll probably have gone with Wallace.'

'When are they back?' she asks.

'We're not sure, pops. But in the meantime why don't we have some of Wallace's favourite cheese in the buttery restaurant? Who's hungry?'

Twenty minutes later Phoebe announces she doesn't like her Wensleydale cheese, cranberry and walnut panini. Charlie's not keen on his either.

'Where's Wallace and Gromit?' she says, for the dozenth time and Dinah looks at me.

'Why am I always right?' she says.

In the hour and a half we've been here the solitary reference to Wallace and Gromit has been a chalk outline of the characters on the specials board.

'Go and play for a minute,' Dinah tells the kids.

They run off and she begins the inquest. 'So, you saw that cartoon image of them both sticking their thumbs up holding some Wensleydale cheese on the information leaflet and, because of this, you *assumed* there'd be life-sized models of the characters wandering about what is actually a working cheese factory.'

'Did your panini taste all right to you? My stomach feels weird.'

'Never mind that. It's an hour and a half back. They're going to go mad. What are we going to do?'

'What about the gift shop?'

'Go and have a look.'

But all I can find that's Wallace and Gromit related in the gift shop are packets of Wensleydale cheese that they don't like. They haven't even got *The Wrong Trousers* DVD.

'Can you believe that? This is where they make the cheese that the global brand that is Wallace and Gromit are *on record* as saying is their favourite, and they don't sell any of the movies. It's like going to Disneyland and not being able to buy a Mickey Mouse toy.'

'Love, just get anything. It doesn't matter if it's Wallace and Gromit themed. You need to get something, though.'

'I know you'll say this is very convenient, but I do feel a bit poorly, love.'

'I know you want me to do this, Ben,' says Dinah. 'But I'm not going to. This is your fault, go and buy them something.'

I return to the gift shop, except not only is there nothing

Wallace and Gromit related, there isn't anything *at all* for kids. It's all aimed at the pensioners getting back on their coaches in the car park: bath salts, expensive cheeses and tins of fudge. The best I can do is a DVD entitled *The Way We Were*. It's about bygone days in the north-east and Yorkshire.

Dinah shakes her head contemptuously. 'How much was it?'

'Twenty quid.'

'You are joking?'

'You said I had to get something.'

'Right, it'll have to do. Round them up.'

'Who's going to break the news?'

'YOU.'

'I feel poorly, love.'

'You're doing it.'

I tell Phoebe and Charlie that Wallace and Gromit's van broke down so we won't be seeing them after all. But there is some good news.

'I've bought you a NEW FILM for the way home.'

The Way We Were is not made by Pixar or Disney. And it rather shows. The film stars old people from Yorkshire reminiscing about some of the north's great industries, including, for several excruciating minutes, the driver of the opencast mining crane nicknamed the 'Big Geordie' talking about the dragline system. Forking south on the A61, Dinah keeps skipping it forward. But every time she presses play it's the same. We're near Ripon, still forty-five minutes away, when we reach the section entitled, 'All in the family. It features fascinating film interviews with descendants of some of our great industrial families including fire hose manufacturers George Angus and Co and chocolate makers Rowntrees of York.'

'The only other option was *Yorkshire Crafts and Traditions*,' I tell Dinah. 'It was about drystone walls. I did my best.'

'What about *Tractor Ted in the Springtime*?' says Dinah. 'I saw that just walking through the shop and I wasn't even looking properly.'

'What, the one with real-life farm footage?'

'It was aimed at kids, Ben – I saw the box.'

'It wasn't aimed at kids. It was aimed at farmers.'

Miraculously the kids hold it together so that a few miles from our serviced apartment in Leeds, I'm able to lean triumphantly across to Dinah: 'Of course, you know what Gromit would have done if Wallace had suggested driving an hour and half to the Wensleydale Creamery Visitor Centre for his daughter's fourth birthday?'

'What?' says Dinah.

I do my impression of Gromit's stern eyebrows.

The next morning I wake at 4 a.m. The pain in my side is so deep I cannot tell where it's coming from. I nudge Dinah. After I've been through my symptoms she says, 'Lie on your back and cycle in the air. It's probably trapped wind.' I cycle in the air but it makes no difference. Dinah tuts as I toss and turn so I climb out of bed. I try to walk it off next door in the kitchen-living room but it gets worse. I feel the need to shed my pyjamas I'm so hot. But straightaway I feel the need to put them back on because I start to shiver. I pace up and down rubbing my stomach, occasionally lying down, sitting up or moving about again. The pain becomes so acute I think I'm going to vomit. I run to the toilet. All I do is gag. I remember Dinah pregnant in the Royal Sussex County Hospital unable to get comfortable. It feels like this. Back in the bedroom Dinah says, with her back to me, her voice muffled by the covers, 'Do some deep breathing? You always think you've got appendicitis. It's wind from that cheese. Or constipation. You said yourself you haven't been for a poo in a couple of days. Please, let me sleep.'

When Dinah was in labour, at her bedside, I offered, albeit useless in the circumstances, energy tablets. I held her hand and said, 'Big deep breaths, love. You can get through this. I love you. It will all be worth it in the end. Nearly there, nearly there.' I wondered if she fancied one of the Marmite rolls I'd prepared, would she like to sit on the birthing ball? On the toilet now, the door closed so she can get back to sleep, I realise what she's thinking. Dinah's convinced I'm a hypochondriac. Despite the fact every time I'm ill there's always something diagnosed as wrong with me, even though sometimes it's not the original thing I thought it was, she's clearly thinking it's all in my head.

I push the toilet door open. 'Before you say anything,' I shout into the room, 'just because we saw the sofa Emily Brontë died on the other day in the Brontë Parsonage, that doesn't mean I think I'm dying of TB.'

I close the door. On the toilet I strain but nothing happens. I try panting to get a rhythm going. Nothing happens. I lie on all fours like a cow giving birth. Nothing. I squeeze my stomach with both hands like I'm a giant tube of toothpaste willing the mass down to my sphincter. Nothing. Off the toilet I grab my phone and google my symptoms: 'An abdominal pain combined with a change of bowel habits can be indicative of colorectal cancer.' So then I google colorectal cancer and out of a checklist of seven symptoms, I have six. Lack of appetite. I didn't have any dinner last night. Dizziness. Check. Fatigue. I am very, very tired. Weight loss. My shorts are practically falling off me. Palpitations – I'm having them now. Pains in abdomen. Check. The only one I haven't got is blood and mucus in my stool. I wake Dinah again. She's level-headed. 'Love, of course you're tired. It's five in the morning. You've lost weight because we've been walking about every day. Trust me, it's constipation. We'll buy some peppermint later. Try to be quiet or you'll wake the...'

Phoebe appears at the toilet door.

'Great!' says Dinah.

'Why are you sweating, Daddy?' she says. 'Have you been for your run?'

'No, go back to bed, sweetheart.'

Charlie puts his head round the door. They both stare at me on the toilet.

'Why is Daddy making that sound, Mummy?'

'He's not feeling well.'

'Are you not feeling well, Daddy?' asks Charlie.

'No.'

'Have you got a tummy ache?'

'Yes. Daddy has a very bad pain in his side that is making him sweat and double up occasionally and he's worried that nobody is taking him seriously and that...'

'Mummy, can we watch CBeebies?'

They climb into the bed. Dinah puts CBeebies on. Another shooting pain courses through me. Desperate now for some relief, I lock the bathroom door and resort to drastic measures. To relieve the constipation, I force a toothbrush up my arse. I picture the poo as a solid mass like a slab of concrete and the toothbrush as a Kango drill smashing it into bits. Except all that happens afterwards is I emit a series of high-pitched clickety farts that sound like a pod of dolphins communicating.

Instead I run a hot bath. Out of the bath the pain returns. I try to be sick again but I can't. I double up on the floor. I straighten out. I breathe deeply. I breathe shallowly. I lean on the kitchen worktop. I picture myself dying while they're watching *Nina and the Neurons*. Ten minutes later it comes upon me suddenly and I have to run for the loo but all that I pass is blood and thick yellow mucus. I open the bedroom door. They're all lined up snugly in the bed.

'Love, you've got to take me to hospital.'

'Really?'

'Yes.'

'But we're watching Ollie the Smell Neuron, Daddy,' says Phoebe. 'I love Ollie the Smell Neuron. He's my favourite neuron.'

'Dinah? We need to go now,' I beckon her towards me and explain what's happened.

'You did what? You just stuck a toothbrush up your bum – your one, I hope – and now you're wondering why you're bleeding. What's the matter with you?'

It takes forever getting ready, preparing milk for Charlie, finding out where the Leeds General Infirmary is from the reception desk. In the car every tiny bump in the road feels like someone punching me in the kidneys. When Dinah takes a wrong turning I find myself shouting directions, 'Red hospital sign straight on, red hospital sign left, red hospital sign straight on', whilst in the back Phoebe complains she hasn't had breakfast.

Finally outside A & E Dinah says, 'Just make sure you tell the doctor about the toothbrush as well. Don't be not telling him now. Ring me when you need picking up.'

I climb from the car but how on earth am I going to explain that one:

'Doctor, I got constipation so I stuck a toothbrush up my bum to loosen it and when I was doing this I felt some resistance and pushed through an obstacle and now there's blood in my stool!'

But the thing is, did the toothbrush cause this or did the toothbrush merely locate a tumour up my bottom that I'd otherwise have been unaware of? Walking to the reception desk I'm having fantasy conversations with friends. I'm telling them, 'Sticking a toothbrush up my arse saved my life.'

At the reception desk another spasm electrifies me. I can't stand up. I have to bend my knees occasionally, and squat down and pop up to finish answering questions.

'Name?'

'Ben Hatch.'

Duck down.

'Address?'

Pop back up. I give our road name.

Down again.

'Where's that?'

Up again: 'Hove, East Sussex.'

In the waiting area the most comfortable position is to squat with one leg half-cocked and the other stretched out behind me on the ground while I rest both my hands on the carpet tiles supporting my forward weight like a 100-metre runner in the blocks. There's one other person here with a Pudsey Bear-style bandage over his eye. As soon as the nurse sees the state I'm in she points into a consulting room.

'In there.'

I'm seen straight away by a young Asian doctor. I sit on a gurney. He tells me the pain sounds colicky, like a kidney stone. But when I tell him about the blood in my stool, he tells me to lie down on the bench and take my trousers and boxers down. I do as he asks. While I'm on my side, my knees bunched into my stomach, he snaps on a rubber glove.

'This isn't going to hurt but you might feel a slightly unnatural sensation,' he says, as he dabs a glob of wax on his index finger and inserts it. It doesn't actually hurt that much, but I wince as if it does, to show that penetration of my arsehole by toothbrushes, or by any other means, is a rare and unpleasant event. Afterwards he asks me a series of questions.

'Work OK?'

'Yes.'

'Married?'

'Yes.'

'That OK?'

'Fine,' I tell him.

'Any kids?'

'Two.'

'They all right?'

'Yep.'

Then the killer question, 'Mum and Dad still alive?'

'OK,' he says after I've told him about Dad. 'I think we have two things here.'

'Two!'

'Firstly, I think you might well have a kidney stone. The blood in your stool, however, I believe is probably stress related. A bit of irritable bowel. But I'd still like it checked out. Have you had a barium enema before?'

He explains what it is, gives me a painkiller and in the Critical Decisions Unit my details are logged again. I'm given a bed and told how to operate the three bed buttons in great detail, like I've been given the keys to a Harrier Jump Jet.

'And the third one marked D is for down. And the one marked U is...'

'Is it for up?'

The nurse shoots me a look. 'Yes,' she says, surprised. 'It is.' She fetches a jug of water. I'm asked to drink it.

'All of it?'

'Yes.'

And I lie there imagining dying of kidney failure or bowel cancer, Dinah being informed in the serviced apartment a few hours later: 'I'm sorry, he was just too far gone when he came in. We did all we could. How he bore that pain...' I imagine her crying, the kids hugging her, Dinah wailing, 'I made him cycle in the air. WE WATCHED NINA AND THE NEURONS. I should have known when he says he's ill he's always diagnosed with something even if it isn't the thing he originally thought it was.'

A large man in an oversized white T-shirt is admitted. He has a shaved head and is linked via a metal chain to two prison warders. Another man is wheeled in, his head fixed rigidly inside what looks like a metal hamster cage. He stares upwards, covered head to toe in bandages.

Half an hour later a West Indian nurse draws the curtains round the bed. She hands me a box of Picolax. I'm to take it after my kidney scan. It will prepare me for the barium enema.

'Dis stuff very powerful,' she says, keeping one hand on the box herself as if I'm not yet ready to be trusted with it.

'Make sure you by de toilet all de day.'

I touch the box. Again she will not release it.

'Don't be leaving da ward. Goin' outside.'

I nod.

Finally she lets go of the box and, opening the bed curtains to leave, she says just loud enough for the woman lying in the bed next to me to hear: 'You're going to be on de toilet all de day.'

I try to call Dinah but her phone is switched off or out of juice and a short while later Buster calls. 'A kidney scan and a whatemma?' he says.

'A barium enema. It's this white radioactive type stuff that shows up on the X-ray and tells you if there's something wrong with your colon. I've had blood in my poo.'

'When you had that constipation, are you sure you weren't straining too hard?'

'It's not piles. I know what they are.'

'OK, but did you put anything up your bum like a toothbrush to loosen the poo?'

Pause.

'Have you been speaking to Dinah?'

Buster laughs.

'I knew it,' he says. 'You've ripped your bum lining, you berk. That's what did it. Now you've got to think up an excuse to tell the doctor.'

'They won't know I stuck anything up my bum, will they?'

'Of course they will. They must get it all the time. Oh doctor, I was in the bathroom and I accidentally slipped over and a toothbrush went up my bum.'

'Are you sure a toothbrush can tear your bum lining?'

'So it *was* a toothbrush?'

Buster laughs.

'Yeah.'

'For God's sake, you can't go sticking things up your bum and expect to get away with it unless you're a qualified poof. Don't tell the doctor, whatever you do.'

'I stuck it up and felt some resistance and just assumed it was the poo blockage so I pressed harder and something seemed to give and although I did go to the toilet I also started bleeding.'

'Of course, that's what it is. I can't believe you stuck a toothbrush up your arse. You really have to think of an excuse if the worst comes to the worst and it's not bowel cancer.'

I laugh.

'Ooh, that's interesting,' he says.

'What is?'

'I just read something. If you don't shit for eight days you die. No! I didn't know that. Have you got your phone with you? Google "Not Shitting plus Dangers" and see what you get.'

'You googled my constipation?'

'I googled your bum.'

'I've got six days to live?'

'Yup. Now go and stick something else up your bum to break it all up. Think of it as gunk wedged in the Hoover nozzle. A coat hanger, a stick. Break it up before you die.'

I laugh again then he says more seriously. 'It is weird how it comes out though. I've been getting a stomach ache the last few days too.'

'I know. I thought I was coping well – being all Dad-like.'

'Then twenty-four hours later you're in A & E with wind...'

'And a kidney stone, Buster.'

'You've got wind, you berk.'

In radiology I'm asked to lie down on a bench with my hands behind my back. A nurse in rubber soles manipulates me into an oblong, coffin-like machine. My legs are bunched up and I'm told to obey the instructions I'll hear on a loudspeaker when she leaves the room. Laser lights illuminate my body around the groin area. The whole thing lasts about ten minutes and afterwards the nurse re-enters the room. She hands me my file and tells me to give it to the ward reception.

Back on the ward the man with the strapped head complains he needs 'ger toilet'. He's told until he's X-rayed he can't move at all. Another nurse draws the curtain round my bed. The doctor pulls it back a fraction, closes it after him and sits at the end of my bed. He tells me I have a 4-milimetre kidney stone. I'll need to be transferred to St James's University Hospital and will have to stay in overnight, perhaps longer if there's damage to my kidney. He leaves and the nurse re-enters to explain things in more detail. The specialist department that will deal with me is called urology. She says the word slowly. She even spells it for me – U-R-O-L-O-G-Y – and then writes it down on a piece of paper.

'UROLOGY. Do you understand?'

I nod.

I call Dinah, half of me feeling triumphant it wasn't wind and half of me worried I've irreparable kidney damage. She arrives at 1.30 p.m. Charlie runs about crawling under beds and Phoebe tells me she can make me better.

'Pretend Fluffy is a stetamope.'

She places the bear on my chest.

'What does the stetamope say?'

'You need medicine. Now pretend this is the medicine.' She passes me an imaginary cup that I drink from. 'So how you do feel? Better?'

'A lot better.'

'See.'

Normally the kids brighten any atmosphere. Their exuberance induces smiles from the hardest of hearts. Here there's none of that. They leave after the nurse, who's been scowling since they arrived, warns Dinah the ward is full of germs and it's not safe for them. Looking at their little round faces staring at me through the glass door as they wave goodbye, I feel like crying.

Two hours later when a bed becomes available, I'm transferred by ambulance to the Lincoln Ward of Jimmy's. In the bed nearest the door is a bald man in his late fifties in so much pain he cannot lean forward to eat his bangers and mash. Opposite him, nearest the window, is Bernard, a Michael Heseltine lookalike, who's in such pain he eats his sausage and mash with his eyes closed tightly. Next to him a man is dying. His mouth is wide open as he sleeps, his lips have vanished and he's curled into a skeletal wiry mass. He's still given his sausage and mash but clearly has no chance of seeing it let alone eating any. To my left are two others I can't see because their curtains are drawn.

I'm clerked, told the doctor won't see me until the morning and told to take my Picolax. I cannot eat because of the barium enema tomorrow and I cannot leave the ward to make a phone call because of the volcanic Picolax. Our ward overlooks the A & E entrance. The game is to spot how many cops it takes to deal with violent thugs being admitted. Everyone cranes over to look whenever a Black Maria pulls up. The record that night: eleven.

At 8 p.m., visiting time arrives but Dinah doesn't. The wife and daughter of the man who's dying show up and in the words of Bernard, 'Woke the old fella up. Gave him a banana. And scarpered after ten minutes, leaving him jabbering. He'll be at it all night now.'

At 11 p.m. the lights are switched off. I put on my overhead light and the bulb goes. At the nurse's station I'm told for health and safety reasons they can't change it. And that neither can I. Will I have to lie in bed all night in the dark? A plucky nurse says she doesn't care about the stupid rule – she'll change my light bulb. I read for a while to justify her bravery then switch it off and try to sleep. An old guy called Christopher shits his bed. The dying man groans until 2.30 a.m. when Bernard's phlegmy snoring takes over. In bed I panic I'm going to die. That I'll hear bad news in the morning – the sort of bad news Dad received. I picture saying goodbye to the kids and Dinah. I imagine my mum's shiny fingers and holding her hand.

The early morning is full of bleeps, of reversing lorries outside, of urine bags that need emptying, of nurse entreaties: 'Just roll on your side, Christopher,' then more bad temperedly, 'Side, Christopher. Side.'

I get talking to the man in the next bed. He came in with a kidney stone too, but it developed into DVT and from there to a massive infection that left him unconscious and on a high dependency unit for a week close to death. After this I'm very careful shaving so that I don't nick myself. To have an open wound here now feels as dangerous as having one in shark-infested waters. I've told the nurses the soap dispenser in the bathroom needs replacing but it's still empty twelve hours later and now the towels used to mop up Christopher's shit last night are here too, lying unwashed in a heap in the corner.

At midday I'm in the radiology department again. I'm told to sit on a chair in the corner because the radiographer wants to explain a few things. I do as I'm told and he leans down, and with a smile that's a mixture of reassurance, *Schadenfreude*, contempt, irony, pity and probably general amusement, he tells me they're going to insert a flexible tube up my back passage and pump barium solution into me. I'll then be given a relaxant to loosen my bowels and air will be puffed into me to open my colon.

'At this point you'll have to do a bit of acrobatics while we take images. Did you take the preparation beforehand?'

I nod.

'How did it do?'

'It did what was expected of it,' I say, and the doctor gives me the same smile.

On the tilting table I lie on my left side and the tube is inserted. The radiographer tells me to take deep breaths while they fill me with the white liquid.

'You'll feel a sensation of being full,' he says.

I'm given the injection, which makes my eyes blur. Air is pumped into me and I'm rotated on the table, feeling now the size of a Space Hopper, so they can take images. On my left side, right side, almost standing up, on my front, and on my back. Every time I move I'm conscious of the tube attaching me to the machinery like an umbilical cord and of the need to grip hold of it with my sphincter muscle in case it comes out and barium starts squirting round the room like it's coming from an out-of-control hosepipe. After twenty minutes I ask the doctor what he's seen. He's vague – he only sees images for a split second.

A second camera is manoeuvred into place to take pictures from another angle. A different radiographer is in charge. This guy makes me feel like a glamour model.

'Over to my side a bit. That's it. Move your bum out. Little more towards me with the bum. Wonderful.' Click, flash goes the X-ray. Then, 'OK towards me, hold that reflecting board up a little more, hips a bit more level. That's lovely, that's better and hold it there.' Click. Flash. 'Oh, could you just hitch up that paper shirt a little more, can we see the tube please? Nice close up of it. Bum out. Further out. Lovely, great.'

When it's over I dress and return to the ward feeling violated.

'The good news is your colon was clear – a little bit of calcification but nothing to worry about.' The registrar is doing his rounds with the consultant. As for my stone, he tells me, in 70 per cent of cases one the size of mine passes naturally. But because there's some kidney dilation they want me in another night. They'll take a further X-ray the following morning to see if it's moved. If it hasn't they'll consider blasting it with a laser. When I explain I'm a journalist writing a book about our trip round England, the consultant says if I were from Leeds he'd advise I stay in at least seventy-two hours for it to pass. But, and he looks at the registrar, if I'm sensible and return to an A & E if I experience pain uncontrollable by normal paracetamol, I can resume the trip. He'll give me my X-ray to show any consultant I subsequently see but if, after two weeks, the stone's not passed, I'll need to return.

Exultant, I call Dinah. 'Where have you been?'

'My phone was out of juice.'

'I'm coming out.'

'Really. What now? I'm in the bath.'

'When they've given me a copy of my X-ray. You don't sound very pleased.'

'I just got in the bath. How was last night?'

'Like something out of *M.A.S.H.*'

CHAPTER 22

It's a week later. We've zigzagged south through the William Wilberforce attractions of Hull. We've seen the John Ruskin paintings in the Sheffield Winter Garden, and crossed the Snake Pass into Manchester, where we spend a day on a City Sightseeing bus, doing a Morrissey tour and visiting the MOSI (Museum of Science and Industry). Now I'm sitting in Gorhard's office on a swivel chair to the right of Dad with Mary opposite, watching Gorhard, his hair combed into a neat side-parting, wringing his hands asking how Dad is. Dad, in a pink shirt and green trousers, is telling Gorhard how well he feels.

'Good,' says Gorhard. 'The bag has stopped leaking. Good. And you're mobile. Now,' and he reaches for a piece of paper with Dad's liver results on them. 'Two hundred and eighty-nine,' says Gorhard. That is good.'

I pat Dad's arm.

'It's halved again,' says Dad.

'Yes,' says Gorhard. He looks at the figures then back at Dad. 'And how do you feel about chemo?'

Mary looks at me, alarmed.

'Is that now an option?' says Dad.

'Yes, I think it is.'

Mary seems tiny in her chair. She looks like a naughty schoolgirl in the head's office. Gorhard looks at her and there's an uncomfortable few minutes where Dad says he's been given a chink of light and should go for it and Mary, against the idea, says things like, 'He's still very weak. A couple of days ago he was as weak as a kitten' or 'It's a quality of life thing. The side effects, you know.'

Gorhard goes through the chemo side effects. Vomiting, but that can be controlled with anti-emetics. Tiredness, although not all patients experience this. He'll need three courses of chemo for Gorhard to tell whether he's amongst the 30 per cent who respond. They'll scan the tumour and after this he'll know if Dad's improving. He'll have his first one in a week or so.

'And I can stop any time?' asks Dad, looking at Mary.

'If it's too much,' Gorhard says, 'of course.'

'And your hair will fall out,' he adds.

'Better to lose my hair,' says Dad, 'than my life. Doctor, what would you do?'

'You may not be responsive but on the other hand if you don't have it you may look back and think "What if?".'

'And if I don't have it, or I do not respond to it,' says Dad. 'How long have I got?'

Gorhard hunches his shoulders. He opens his hands.

'Two, maybe three months.'

'And if it all works well?'

'An extra year,' says Gorhard.

A few weeks before the stent operation Mary wanted for it to be over quickly. I felt the same. I didn't want it drawn out like it had been with Mum. But now, an extra year on the table, I want to shout, 'Do it, Dad.'

I pat his shoulder. Mary looks at the floor.

'I'll do it,' says Dad.

On the way back to Dad and Mary's I keep patting Dad's shoulder when Mary isn't looking and I want desperately to call Pen and Buster. Back at the house I do, hiding at the bottom of the garden. Both Pen and Buster can't understand my subdued voice.

'But that's great news!'

'I know. I can't shout.'

Both guess.

'Bugger that,' says Pen. 'I'm going to ring him up now and say well done. That man! That liver of his! Bloody hell!'

'I'm a realist,' says Mary, in the kitchen later when Dad's asleep. 'We'll see,' she says.

'I know, but imagine what he might have said.'

'We'll see,' she says.

The next morning when I say goodbye, 'Enough money?' asks Dad.

'Plenty.'

'I love you, my son. Now stay out of hospitals.'

'You too,' I say.

And I have no idea when I climb into the taxi to the station as he waves goodbye on the doorstep, legs akimbo, hands on his hips, like a captain on the bridge of his ship, that the next time I see my dad he'll have three days to live.

CHAPTER 23

Draft Copy for Guidebook:
The city of Lincoln is famous for its fourteenth-century cathedral and its castle where ne'er-do-wells in the nineteenth century were hanged to death on weekends from its ramparts, huge family crowds gathering from miles around to drink ale, munch venison snacks and comment on the speed and efficacy of strangulation like they might do an Olly Murs X Factor solo today. The broader county of Lincolnshire has some lovely unspoilt towns, one of which isn't Skegness (the Fens' answer to Blackpool Pleasure Beach) and two of which include the birthplace of Margaret Thatcher, Grantham, and Stamford, the town we have to thank/curse/burn to the ground and slaughter the inhabitants of for the current proliferation of BBC costume dramas on telly. The corporation were set to quit screening them in the early 1990s but did one more for the road. Middlemarch, *much of it filmed in Stamford, sold to virtually every English-speaking country in the world. That said, the town is so scrumptiously pretty, clean and well kept that you half want to wrap the streets in greaseproof paper, sprinkle them with sugar and see what they'd taste like topped with almond shavings. Attractions nearby include Burghley House, used during filming of* The Da Vinci Code, *and*

the Grantham Museum, which focuses on its other famous one-time resident, Sir Isaac Newton, featuring several low-level child-friendly interactive exhibits that enable you and your wife the time and luxury of rewriting Newton's Laws of Motion as applied to a toddler, these being as follows:

Newton's First Law of (Toddler) Motion – If a toddler is standing still, to make it move you must apply a packet of chocolate buttons. Once the toddler is moving it will continue to move at the same speed and in a straight line unless another force acts upon it. This force is known as 'seeing a sibling with more chocolate buttons'.

Newton's Second Law of (Toddler) Motion – A moving toddler moves even faster when a packet of Mini Eggs acts upon it. The toddler accelerates in the direction of the Mini Eggs, the amount of acceleration depending on the exact number of eggs and their perceived chocolatey-ness.

Newton's Third Law of (Toddler) Motion – If a toddler is pushed or pulled it will push and pull to an equal extent in the opposite direction until somebody is in tears and all the Mini Eggs are scattered on the floor of the museum and the curator is staring at you and it is time to leave for Peterborough.

We ducked into Lincoln and cruised Rutland Water. We rode the Jellikins rollercoaster at Fantasy Island in Skegness. And we're now outside the National Parrot Sanctuary in Friskney, near Boston, on the western edge of the Wash.

'The parrot is apparently the first thing to go,' Dinah's saying into her mobile. 'They're a very good bellweather of the economy. Parrots cost four times as much as dogs. Their toys are four times as expensive, vet bills are the same. Last year they rehomed 335. This year it's already 490.'

It's something we've done a few times on the trip to make ends meet – sold stories to the nationals. Dinah's speaking to *The Daily Telegraph* news desk.

'Tell them about Derren Brown's parrots,' I remind her.

Dinah flaps her hand at me.

On a tour of the sanctuary, home to more than 1,400 rescued birds, owner Steve Nichols revealed how the recession had prompted an unprecedented number of parrot rescues. They weren't just coming in with poorly feet, damaged air sacks and cancer, but through the financial trouble of their owners. The magician Derren Brown's parrots were even here, although this was more because he was so busy and a trustee of the place.

I write on a page in my notebook: 'Derren Brown's parrots, Figaro and Mephisto. Rehomed. He obviously failed to control their minds.'

Dinah takes the notepad from me, reads it, smiles and hands it back.

Phoebe starts to say something. I put my finger to my lips.

'Oh, OK then,' she says, into her mobile. 'Not to worry.'

Dinah hangs up.

'Ner,' she says. 'They've got two age-of-austerity stories already for tomorrow.'

'You didn't tell him the Derren Brown joke.'

'He wasn't interested.'

'If you'd made the joke, though…'

'Trust me. If the parrots had done their own sleight of hand card tricks he wouldn't have been interested.'

'Maybe it's more tabloidy.'

'Let's give it up,' says Dinah.

'We just need a pun.'

Phoebe asks when we're going.

'Help us, pops. What do parrots make you think of?'

We go through the possibilities.

'Beaks.'

'Pieces of eight.'

'Who's a pretty boy then?'

'Pirates,' says Charlie.

'That's a good one, Charlie. Shiver me timbers – parrot keeping is on the wane.'

Dinah laughs. 'Shiver me timbers. That's awful, Ben.'

'Bright colours,' says Phoebe.

'Another good one.'

'What about something about the credit crunch and millet. Crunching millet.'

'Crunching millet! And you dared to criticise shiver me timbers!'

'OH, I KNOW. I KNOW!' shouts Phoebe. 'MUFFIN! Muffin from *3rd & Bird*. He's a parrot. He is, Dad.'

'Another good one, Phoebe.'

'What about the dead parrot sketch?'

'Parrot-keeping has ceased to be,' says Dinah.

'It is an ex-hobby. Parrot keeping is dead.'

'That's it.'

This time I call the *Daily Mirror* and after I mention Derren Brown's parrots I'm able to sell the story as a 100-word news-in-brief for £40.

We're staying in Peterborough, where I took my diploma in journalism more than twenty years ago on a floor above the Peterborough *Evening Telegraph* building. We're staying in two rooms above a pub, just off the main square near the Guildhall, and with the kids asleep, Dinah and I are watching TV in bed by ourselves when Dinah says, 'Ben, can I tell you something without you going mad? You know I told you when you were in hospital that I went to the Thackray Museum?'

She peers round to look at me.

'Well, that was a lie. I went shopping in Leeds.'

'Oh.'

'And the reason I haven't got any pictures of the Royal Armouries? It wasn't because I couldn't work out the automatic flash. I didn't go there either. And I also took the kids for a meal in the Corn Exchange I didn't tell you about.' She bites her lip. 'And to a movie. I didn't even take the blue folder out with me.'

She holds the duvet up over her face.

'Both folders were together?!'

'Yes.'

'I see.'

I turn back to look at the telly. She lowers the duvet and continues. 'You kept ringing me up. The reason I didn't answer was in case you made me go and visit somewhere.'

'And now you feel bad because I had a kidney stone that according to several websites is the only male pain equivalent to that of childbirth?'

She nods.

'Are you angry with me?'

She pulls a frightened face.

'We haven't had one day off since we left, Ben. Even in Center Parcs we went to that doll place. I just wanted one day off. Will you forgive me?'

'No.'

'If I let you listen to Billy Joel's greatest hits in the car tomorrow?'

Then something occurs to me.

'Hang on, is that why you switched your phone off that night?'

'I didn't switch it off.'

'OK, purposely didn't recharge it?'

She laughs. 'I knew if I visited you, you'd ask me what I'd done and I wouldn't be able to lie. Sorry.'

'So what did you do that night?'

'I had a takeaway Pizza Hut pizza and watched *What Katie Did Next* on ITV2.'

She holds her head, shakes it with shame and I laugh.

'So did you pay for the meal in the Corn Exchange or play the Frommer's card and get it complimentary after promising to consider them for a 200-word review?'

'We paid. Sorry.'

'One day without me, and you turn into a muggle.'

She laughs and I order her as a punishment to get up and fetch me the rest of the Kettle Chips from the cool box and I'm channel surfing, eating these later, slapping her hand whenever she tries to grab one, when we stumble on it. It's a news report about a cocaine factory in the Colombian jungle. There's a photo on the screen of the reporter whose words we're hearing. I don't recognise his face, partly as it's been twenty years and partly because he's shaved all his hair off. I recognise his voice, though.

'Bloody hell.'

I lean closer to the telly.

'It is. That's Karl.'

I read the caption at the bottom of the photo and I'm right. It's Karl Penhaul reporting for CNN.

'Who?' says Dinah.

'Karl Penhaul. I studied journalism with him. We were on the EMAP training course together. We shared a house for six months.' I turn it up. 'That's so bizarre. We lived down the road from here.'

Karl's talking via a satellite phone. He's in the jungle, embedded with a gun-toting gang of drug dealers who are in the middle of boiling up several kilos of cocaine. It's part of a series of special reports he's filming on cartel drug wars.

'And he works for CNN now?'

'He must do. How weird is that? We were actually based up the road from here in the EMAP training centre.' I point up the road towards the ET building. 'I can't believe it.'

The report ends with Karl whispering that the gang has been snorting coke for quite a while and that he thinks now it's time to make his excuses and leave. When the report ends, I'm still slightly shocked.

'Don't you think it's funny that we're in Peterborough now?'

'Yeah.'

'And I used to get better marks than him in every exam,' I tell Dinah.

'Did you, love?'

'In law, public administration and shorthand. We had to make up our own dummy *Peterborough Evening Telegraphs*. They were really big on news gathering. We had to go out one afternoon a week and come back with news stories. I always scooped him. I came back with some belters.'

'Well, he scooped you today,' says Dinah, laughing. 'He's undercover filming a cocaine factory…'

And now I realise what she means. 'And I sold a story about Derren Brown's parrots.'

Dinah looks across at me, spluttering with laughter.

'Ahhhh,' she says. 'Do you wish you were embedded with drug dealers in Colombia, my love, instead of eating Kettle Chips in your pyjamas in bed with your wife at nine-thirty?'

I used to give Karl a lift into college each morning. I picture us now in my Renault 9, parking down River Lane, arriving at the training centre. I remember the way Karl used to talk. The way he always gesticulated Kenny Everett-style with his thumb and forefinger, pointing them, when he spoke, like they were guns. I picture his wispy hair that he's now shaved off.

We start to watch something else.

'He's my Sarah Smith, isn't he?' I tell her later in the bathroom.

'You're not still on about him, are you?'

'I just think that was so weird.'

And in bed I say to Dinah: 'Did I ever tell you the story about me and Karl? How I fell out with him? It's quite funny. I was staying at his parents' house. I think it was in Hunstanton. Somewhere like that. It was the summer after the course finished and it was Julie's birthday the next day.'

'The Julie you went out with before me?'

'Yeah. The one from the course. I was really stupid. You know what I was like then and he was quite a strange guy, Karl, weirdly self-righteous even then. But always quite admirable, too. He always used to stick up for the gypsies, I remember. The *Evening Telegraph* often wrote stories about them. He had arguments with the lecturers about the tone of the coverage. He even became friends with the boss of the gypsies. I shouldn't have done it.'

'What did you do?'

'I stole a pink teddy bear from him. His parents were away. It was Sunday morning and I woke up in this attic room. It was the summer after the course had finished. It was full of teddy bears, this room. I needed a present for Julie. I was driving down to see her in Newhaven. I was already late.'

'You gave her his pink teddy?'

'There were hundreds in the room. I thought he'd laugh. He went mad. Julie had to post it back. I can remember him very calmly telling me with this real suppressed fury in his voice: "You will post that teddy bear back to me that you stole, first class, and if you do that I will consider not pressing charges."'

'He threatened the police?'

'It cost about twenty quid to post it back. The thing was three-feet high. I told Julie I'd won it at a fairground and it wasn't kite-marked properly, was some form of hazard. I can't remember what I said.'

'She was fairly gullible, then?'

'She was. And Karl never spoke to me again. I really liked him too.'

'What did Julie say when you asked for it back?'

'She was surprised. In fact, it was kind of the beginning of the end.'

'And after that you met me.'

'Yeah.'

'So if it wasn't for that pink bear maybe you'd still be with her.'

'Maybe.'

'Wow. And do you think it was the theft of that pink teddy that catapulted Karl into the macho, unforgiving world of war reporting?'

'I think it did.'

'What else can we attribute to the pink bear?'

'I believe he shaved his hair off the day I took it too. It was an act of contrition at the trust he'd shown in me, that I'd abused.'

'It's got a lot to answer for that pink bear.'

'It has.'

'And does he keep that shaved hair in a special box, the lid of which is engraved with one word, scratched out in his own blood, that word being "betrayal".'

'He does.'

'And does he very occasionally, whenever he feels dangerously close to trusting someone again, open that box, take out that hair, put it on his bald head, and stare at himself in the mirror and think of that bear and the day you took it?'

'He's probably doing it right now. Look,' I show her the page dedicated to Karl Penhaul on the CNN main website.

She reads it out: 'Karl Penhaul is a video correspondent for CNN based out of Bogotá, Colombia. Before this he was embedded with the 11th Attack Helicopter Regiment during the recent war in

Iraq. When the regiment was disbanded, he became an embedded journalist with the 82nd Airborne Division, reporting on Iraqi civilian casualties, US POWs and the push toward Baghdad. In the ongoing aftermath of the Iraq war, he has reported on the surges of violence and attacks on coalition troops as well as the newly instated government. Penhaul has reported on the war in Afghanistan, and covered the drug trade, kidnappings and guerrilla tactics in Colombia. He has also covered the Chilean miners' crisis, the Haiti earthquake and is currently working undercover.'

Dinah raises her eyebrows.

'Think of what he must have seen. The people he's met. He's lived through earthquakes, tsunamis, wars. He's seen it all first hand.'

'Are you jealous?'

'A bit.'

Dinah touches her head five times then drums her fingers on the headboard. 'Lots of urges today,' she says, craning her head to look into the bathroom, pulling it back a fraction then doing the same motion again.

I click on a YouTube video of Karl talking about his exploits on a special CNN programme called *Karl Penhaul Remembers Big Stories*. He's perched on a stool next to an anchorman in a suit. We watch it together. Karl tells the anchor that his reporting zeal was born out of a wanderlust he developed backpacking around South America.

'I bet he's not got kids though,' says Dinah.

'That's true.'

'And he's probably never survived a four-millimetre kidney stone, either.'

'Of course, he hasn't.'

'Let him keep his embittered box of hair,' says Dinah.

'And his shitty pink bear.'

'Come on loser, sleep now,' says Dinah.

She turns the light out and, in the dark, she says shuffling up to me: 'I'm glad you're not a war reporter.'

'Although I would have been a brilliant one.'

'Of course you would, love.'

CHAPTER 24

Draft Copy for Guidebook:

Bishy, barney-bee
When will your weddin' be?
If it be 'amara day,
Tairk your wings an' floi away

It isn't always easy to understand what a person from Norfolk is trying to say. If this happens the important thing is not to panic. If you panic he will panic and if he panics he will dig for peat. Over the centuries locals here have created 200 kilometres of navigable waterways (the Norfolk Broads) simply through panicking and digging for peat. If they dig for any more peat there'll be nothing left of Norfolk and the North Sea will wash in and flatten all in its path, so don't panic them, OK? Norfolk, home to the villages of Little Snoring, Great Snoring and Really Fucking Annoying Snoring, is often seen as a sleepy backwater where not much has happened since they invented mustard, although that's not the whole story. Great Yarmouth is hard to beat for belt and braces good times, while for more sophistication the North Norfolk villages –

including Burnham Thorpe, the home of Lord Nelson – are worth a visit. We had fun in Norfolk and to ensure you do too here's a helpful glossary of translated phrases:

'I'll do it presently.' – I'll do it when I have finished digging this peat.

'My booty.' – You're very pretty.

'Hoooooooooge!' – Quite large.

'Tha's a rum ol' doo, innit?' – Well I never, we have made another massive hole digging for peat again.

We're in the hotel pool at Norwich Sprowston Manor Marriott.

'OK, guys, now before we go we need to do something funny. Do you want to do something funny?'

''K,' says Charlie, his dimples sucking in as he smiles.

'What is it?' asks Phoebe, bobbing up and down in the water.

'Well, we're in a place called Norwich, where a TV series Mummy and Daddy both like is set. It is called *I'm Alan Partridge* and Alan Partridge used to live in a Travel Tavern in this city and he had a catchphrase. His catchphrase, which is like something you say over and over again so that it becomes synonymous with...'

Dinah makes a wind up motion.

'OK, what I want you to do, when I count down from ten, is shout ahhhhh-haaaaaa.'

''K,' says Charlie, gleefully.

'Can you do that?'

''K,' says Charlie.

'Just shout ahhhh-haaa. That's it?' says Phoebe.

'Yep.'

'That's not much fun, Daddy.'

'It will be. Trust me. Because we're going to do it *very* loudly. That's all of us together – even Mummy – who thinks she can get out of it by pretending to dislodge water from her ears. Mummy?'

Dinah takes her finger out of her ear, gives me a wary look and pushes off to swim another width.

'All of us are going ahhhh-hhaaaa,' says Phoebe. 'And you, Mummy. Mummy, and you!'

'Do we have to?' says Dinah, the other side of the pool.

'Daddy says so.'

'Even though everyone probably does it when they stay in a Norwich hotel, love?' says Dinah.

'Guys, if you do it really loudly you'll get extra rides later, OK? Are you ready guys?'

''K,' says Charlie.

'So there'll be no telling off for shouting. Only for not shouting loudly enough. Ten, nine, eight, seven, six, five, four, three, two, one...'

I point at Charlie.

Our collective AHHHHHHH-HAAAAAAAAAAAAAAAA! echoes round the pool, bringing the adult swimming lane to a standstill.

'Brilliant, guys.'

''Gain,' says Charlie. ''Gain.'

'No, that's it,' says Dinah.

'One more,' says Phoebe, holding up a finger. 'Please, Dad.'

''Gain,' says Charlie. ''Gain.'

'We'll get thrown out, Ben.'

'Let me see, there's a picture of a man diving in with a red line through it on the sign there by the foot splash. And there's a picture of someone running with a line through it. But hang on,' I look at Dinah. 'There's no picture of Alan Partridge with a red line through it, which means we CAN do it again.'

'Ya-ay!' shouts Charlie.

'Oh, please!' says Dinah.

'Just one more time. Right, kids. A really big one. Especially you, Charlie.'

''K,' says Charlie.

'And I don't think Mummy was very loud that time. Was she?'

'Mummy, loudly,' says Phoebe.

'And then we get out?' says Dinah.

'And then we get out and do the big plate thing at breakfast,' I tell her.

She laughs.

'OK, a massive one, guys. Ten, nine, eight, seven, six, five, four, three, two, one…'

And as we all shout 'AHHHHHHHHHH-HAAAAAA!' the pool guy slowly walks round. He bends to his haunches and looks at us questioningly.

'Alan Partridge,' I tell him.

'Right,' he says, and wanders back to his store cupboard. 'Alan Partridge,' I hear him wearily telling his colleague.

We've been scouting around East Anglia this last week or so. Norwich Castle couldn't have been more child friendly if it had been a bouncy one. In the horse town of Newmarket, the kids saw former Grand National winners licking mineral blocks at The National Stud on a guided tour, which Dinah was hilariously convinced was going to culminate in an inappropriate horse orgy. We've punted in Cambridge, visited Linton Zoological Gardens and, at the Air Space Area of the Imperial War Museum in Duxford, there were hands-on gizmos for kids to learn about lift, thrust and drag, all of which I was ironically forced to employ removing Charlie from the Morse code section at the end. We dipped down into Suffolk and, after this, spent a few days in the Essex countryside doing activities as diverse as walking around a disused nuclear bunker in Kelvedon Hatch and going on a John Constable walk in East Bergholt, before we looped back into Norfolk, where we are now.

We check out of the Marriott after breakfast, follow the A47 and hit our most easterly point of the entire trip entering Great Yarmouth. We park in a pay and display off the promenade and are given a netted sock of tokens for the pleasure beach by the stand-in manager. What usually happens at funfairs is you're bedazzled by the jingles and flashing lights, the revolving and zigzagging rides and don't know what to go on first. The first ride Phoebe can't go on is the Gallopers.

'She's eating ice cream. No food, I'm afraid.'

At the Fun House, open-toed sandals are forbidden.

'But they're Doodles.'

'Don't care what you call 'em.'

At the Caterpillar Rollercoaster neither of them meet the height requirement (1 metre) while at the Haunted House, although there's no height or age requirement, the man warns us it's too scary for Phoebe.

'Right, I see, and how do you know?'

'She's sucking her thumb,' he says.

'She always sucks her thumb. That doesn't mean she's scared.'

'Is it scary?' asks Phoebe, pulling a frightened face.

'Undermining me slightly there, pops?'

The man smiles.

'What are we going to do now?' I ask Dinah. 'We can't spend ten pounds' worth of tokens on the grab-a-bear machine, can we?'

Back at the Gallopers the lady lets Phoebe on a painted horse but asks Charlie's age.

'You only mentioned food last time.'

'He needs to be three.'

'He is three,' I lie.

'Can you prove it?' she asks.

'Can we prove it?'

I look at Dinah.

'I'm sorry we don't carry our three-year-old's birth certificate around with us, or his driving licence,' says Dinah.

'We haven't got a utility bill in his name either,' I say.

The lady shrugs, and takes tokens from someone else. We try to explain how hard it is to find a ride. She asks if Charlie can walk.

'He's only sitting in the pushchair because we've been walking around for an hour looking for a ride he can go on. Charlie, show the lady.'

But I forget the handlebars of the buggy are loaded down with our sandwiches. As I let go, the buggy topples over, shooting Charlie backwards.

''Gain,' he says, jumping back into the buggy.

'Charlie, this is not one of the rides.'

'Although it is the best one he's been on,' says Dinah. 'Come on Charlie, show the lady.'

But when Charlie finally gets up, he runs into the back of the leg of a man in front of him, falls over and cries. Our ticket about to expire at the pay and display, at the entrance gate we give away our remaining tokens to a couple walking in with two toddlers of their own.

'Thus perpetuating the agony,' says Dinah.

And we're nearly at the car when my mobile rings.

It's Buster.

'He's not having it,' he says.

'What?'

'He's not having the chemo.'

'What?'

'The chemo's off.'

'Why?'

'Gorhard says he can't have it. We're at the unit. Mary's here. There's a blockage. Something's wrong with his kidneys. He's having a scan later then we'll know more. We're wheeling him back to the Shelburne now.'

'How's he taking it?'

'He's shaking his head. He's gutted.'

'Will he be able to have it later?'

'We don't know. I'll call you later.'

'How's Mary?'

'Crying.'

'I'll ring Gorhard and call you back.'

Buster hangs up. Dinah straps the kids into the car. I call Gorhard. He's no longer at the Shelburne. I try Buster again, but he's now engaged, probably telling Pen. Mary's not answering and I don't really know what to do now so we stick to the plan and drive along the promenade to the Merrivale Model Village, our next attraction. It's a 1 to 20 scale replica of some generic olde worlde idyllic English village complete with a pint-sized cricket pitch, a miniature railway line and some tiny quite trendy looking antique shops that if Dinah was 2 inches high she tells me she'd quite probably like to browse in. We have a surreal half hour here wandering around trying to work out what I should do. There are buttons for the kids to press to activate model knights on the castle. I keep trying Dad but he's not answering the phone in his room at the unit and Mary's mobile's still switched off as she's still there and Buster's unavailable. I can't work out whether to go straight to the station, or wait for more news. In the meantime I check train times, keep calling Gorhard, and eventually manage to leave a message for his secretary. In the end we decide to abandon the Time and Tide Museum and drive on to our next hotel and make a decision there. We're staying at Fritton House, a few miles south of Great

Yarmouth on the banks of Fritton Lake. We check in and I'm lying on the bed, Dinah having taken the kids down to dinner, when Gorhard calls me back. I explain I'm visiting Dad in a couple of weeks' time but that I'm worried after what happened today.

Gorhard pauses for a second before he says, 'Your father has deteriorated significantly.' He explains that he couldn't give Dad chemotherapy in his condition. Instead he'll have a chest X-ray and a scan. It could be a swollen lymph node, though this is unlikely. More probable is it's 'part of your father's deteriorating health'. Gorhard says if this is the case and it's renal failure, 'And your father continues to decline at the same rate, well, he isn't going to die in the next couple of days. I haven't had the end-of-life conversation with your father yet. But I would hate for you to miss something important.'

I book my train ticket and call Dad as I stare out across Fritton Lake from the back of the hotel. Mary answers.

'I think I always knew,' she says.

Dad comes on. His voice is dissipated, like an echo.

'It's a kick in the teeth, Dad,' I say.

'Hey ho,' he says.

'It's a kick in the teeth,' I say again because I can't think of anything else to say.

'My son,' he says, 'I've got Mary here, Pen and Buster, and I hear you're coming home tomorrow.' His voice croaks. 'What could be better? Hugs and kisses.'

'I love you, Dad.'

'Love you, my son.'

And to stop myself crying I have to whisper the word 'bye'.

Gorhard calls later that night with the scan result. 'I'm afraid there was no obstruction. Your father asked if he had months to live. I had to tell him weeks. I'm telling you days. I'm very sorry to be the bearer of such bad news.'

CHAPTER 25

There's a dark blue Mercedes blocking the drive. A dark-haired man stands at the passenger door in a blue uniform and blue cap. It's John Cleese's driver. I knock on the door. Cleese, as my dad calls him, is in the living room, talking to Mary. Pen comes towards me and gives me a hug. I drop my bag and squeeze her. Mary's niece Katie is making lunch. Dad's asleep in the downstairs guestroom.

'Go in and see him,' says Pen.

I open the bedroom door. Buster's warned me that Dad's face has changed ('Become longer, you know.') But it's still a shock. He's asleep, his mouth open, the sides turned down. There are blotches on his face, a red patch of congealed blood in the crook of his right arm from the blood tests. His hands and legs are creamy, dough-like. I don't kiss him. I leave him asleep and back in the living room Cleese grips my hand and his eyes well up.

'It's just so sudden,' I say.

'So, so sudden,' he says.

Cleese has to be somewhere soon so Mary wakes Dad and he goes in. Afterwards, it's my turn. Dad's dehydrated from talking so much. He makes a strange motion with his lower jaw that I remember Mum making at the end – his tongue ferreting for moisture in front of his teeth. Every now and again his eyes half roll back in his head. I hold his hand.

'My lovely eldest son,' he says.

'My lovely dad,' I say.

I sit on a chair by the bed and he tells me to remove the covers. I pull them back.

'Read my T-shirt,' he says.

On it is a map of the London Underground. Underneath the red and blue logo it reads: 'I'm Going Underground'.

'Cleese fell about,' says Dad.

He'd put it on that morning and hadn't realised its significance until he looked in the mirror. I pull the covers up. We go over yesterday.

'They were mixing up the formula when the call came in from the lab.' Dad shakes his head. 'I wanted that chemo. Gorhard knew that. It was a brave decision saying no to me. The right decision.'

He makes the motion with his mouth again. I fetch him water.

'Fill it only to there,' says Dad, and he indicates a level, 'because...' It's so he can tip it without spilling any.

Mary comes back in with me.

'He's in the snooker room looking at all the pictures,' she says.

'Is he?' says Dad, and his eyes darken with interest.

'Bringing back memories. Cambridge Circus,' says Mary.

'Dear old John.'

When Dad falls asleep I listen to his breathing. It isn't laboured but slow. It has a rhythm like the tide. His belly rises, swollen now halfway down, as he inhales and his cheeks inflate and then, as he exhales, they deflate, making a splashing sound like the sound of a wave breaking. We take it in turns to sit with Dad, bring in books to read. We hold his hand occasionally or say the odd remark, 'More squash, Dad?' or 'Painkillers yet?' or 'Movicol, Dad?' Whenever he wakes he's in a half sleep, a sort of beatific daze – his eyes half rolled back in his head. His reaction to a voice or a squeak of a chair is that his eye on whichever side of the bed the sound has come from will widen and hunt for its source, fix on it for just a second, as if confirming a thought, then disappear back into the top of his head. After a while there seems something wrong about taking turns – a false piety in volunteering for it as if you're broadcasting your greater love for Dad, so instead, eventually, we just slip in and out of other people's turns, often it being the four of us in there together, heads down in our books, exchanging glances whenever Dad's breathing changes or if a thought about some matter of care comes to mind to prompt a whisper 'His lipsalve…'… 'Squash…'

When Dad's lucid he smiles in his unique way (the sides of his mouth turned down) and says in a gasp 'My lovely children' or, if Mary is in the room, 'Darling, you are my rock.' Alone with him in the late afternoon I ask Dad if there's anything he wants to tell me. Dad blinks slowly, 'Be honest with your children.'

'I gave you a lot of trouble,' I say. 'Your best advice to me: only listen to two sorts of people. Those who love you and those who've been there before.'

'A good yardstick,' says Dad.

'You've led a great life,' I tell him. 'You've had two wives, who you've loved and been loved by. You've got three children.'

His eyes fade.

'I've been very lucky.'

'You have so many friends who love you.'

'Dear old John,' he says.

He falls back to sleep. I stay. I can hear Pen, Mary, Buster and Katie eating lunch outside in the garden through the open window. I listen to Dad's breathing, watch his chest moving up and down like a rudimentary pair of bellows and I wonder who he'll be with when he dies.

The next day he doesn't get out of bed, doesn't brush his teeth. He keeps getting hot, then cold. He eats nothing but Movicols. He drinks less squash, struggles to suck it up through the curly straws we realise too late he's having trouble with. By the afternoon he stops talking. He uses a thumbs-up for yes, a flat hand movement to mean no, and a raised eyebrow for most other reactions. Dad's nerve endings become hypersensitive. Even a single bed sheet on his belly hurts so he flings it off. The phone rings off the hook with people wanting to visit. Every kind word sets Pen and Mary off but although my dad's dying I cannot cry. It makes me ashamed and lonely so sometimes when it's not my turn to be with him, I sit on a wooden bench at the foot of the garden listening to the rip and munch of cows eating grass in the field behind the wrought-iron fence.

Asleep, his hands flat against the bed either side of him, there's always a hanky in his hand now, curled up ready to dab at his sore lips. He flutters his fingers occasionally, a sign his circulation is failing, according to Mary. When it's my turn now I read Dad P. G. Wodehouse stories. Whenever I stop his eye finds me at once.

'I didn't think you were listening.'

He raises an eyebrow and his eyes roll back in his head and I carry on.

On the day before he dies Dad grows agitated. He winces, hand flops onto his head. When we shout, 'We love you, Dad,' his 'Love you' back is virtually indistinct from his exhale. His eyes move less. His hands and feet are cold, although his forehead's clammy. He lies in a swoon now, head up, one arm almost pointing to the heavens like a Michelangelo painting. Occasionally he shifts position. He places his hands on his chest, moves his head from left to right, puts his legs up, then down. Pen lies on the double bed beside him in a comma shape, mopping his brow. He holds her knee while Buster, Mary and I take it in turns holding his hands, although he doesn't squeeze back now. His most animated motion is the way he pushes his lips towards moisture. Like a cat rubbing its face to your hand he roves his lips across the surface of the sponge, occasionally putting the whole thing in his mouth to hungrily suck.

A watery rattle enters his throat and that afternoon the Macmillan nurse, Margaret, rigs up the morphine driver. The noise is so reminiscent of Mum dying – that little whirr as it feeds the drug – Pen, Buster and I all exchange looks. Within minutes Dad's unconscious. His breathing settles into a pattern. Mary recites a catechism and after Margaret tells us 'It won't be long now', Mary breaks down. 'Oh darling,' she says. 'Oh sweetheart.' Over and over again. 'Oh darling. Oh sweetheart.'

For the next nine and a half hours we try coaxing Dad over the edge. 'We're all here, Dad. We love you, Dad.' Mary calls him, 'The best boy in Buckinghamshire.' She says, 'I love you more than I did the day I married you, more than I did twenty minutes ago when I said I loved you. Oh darling, please let go now.' In a random way we take it in turns to hold him. A hand if you're lucky, although if you leave the room to go to the toilet you get a foot on your return or maybe an elbow. It's painful hearing Mary's anguished love. It's during her outbursts of affection that I have to hold my head down and pinch my nose to stop the tears. It's claustrophobically intense – pleased to be here as Dad would have wanted, at the same time I want to run as fast as I can in the opposite direction back to Dinah and the kids seeing seals at Blakeney Point, walking around the Sandringham estate in the sunshine. Around teatime I hear crows amongst the birds outside. But on and on it goes. In the room it smells of lavender now from the cream Pen is massaging Dad's feet with. Steve, the surgeon brother-in-law of Mary, comes round. He feels Dad's feet.

'Cold,' he says.

He rubs Dad's legs.

'He's going blue. He's barely alive, poor man. The body's closed down. Only his lungs and heart working now. There's no blood getting anywhere else.'

An hour later Steve says, 'He has a very strong heart. Nothing wrong with his heart.'

And then when he leaves, what breaks our spirit is what he says before going, 'It might be another twenty-four hours.'

Mary sleeps beside Dad downstairs and the rest of us go to bed. An hour and a half later Buster says my name at the door. I sit up tingling with sleep. Buster says, 'He's gone.'

Downstairs Pen's lying across the bed kissing Dad's forehead.

I ask if I can kiss Dad. She moves away. I kiss Dad's forehead. I hear a sound, a gurgle in his throat.

I say, 'Goodbye, Dad.'

Pen tries shutting his eyes but they won't close. Mary says a prayer, gives us each a sleeping pill and we return to bed.

CHAPTER 26

*D*raft Copy for Guidebook:
Stretching back to pre-Roman times, Colchester, England's oldest town, is home to a huge army barracks but has an even prouder claim to fame. While Liverpool has the Merseybeat and Manchester staged the 1990s rave scene, Colchester is home to the nursery rhyme. The legendary merry old soul, Old King Cole, was from Colchester, and 'Twinkle, Twinkle, Little Star' was written by Jane Taylor in the town's Dutch Quarter in 1806. Meanwhile, Humpty Dumpty wasn't an egg-shaped man with poor balance, but a large cannon used by the Royalists during the English Civil War (1642–1651) in the Siege of Colchester. The town, we've heard, is currently working on its difficult fourth nursery rhyme featuring, it is rumoured, a cat, a fiddle and some tooled up members of the 16 Air Assault Brigade.

I'm parked at the top of Ray's Hill in Cholesbury, looking down the driveway at the windmill. When my mum died, Dad, having retired the year before from the BBC, went a little loopy here before Mary rescued him. One of the projects he threw himself into was painting everything in the windmill either black or white.

He whitewashed all the internal walls. The beams he painted black. He painted the kitchen floor white, the windowsills black. He had the outside walls repainted white and the sails went from red and green to black and white. Buster and I used to joke that if we stayed still long enough he'd paint us black or white as well. This white paint is flaking off the windmill now. The drive's been re-gravelled since Dad sold up and the fish pond has been removed so cars can turn round. The kids are asleep in the back of the car after a mad dash around the Roald Dahl Museum and Story Centre in Great Missenden that I cut short to bomb over here. I'm sitting beside Dinah on a bollard that still has a scrape mark on it from when Mum got the camper van wedged up on it more than twenty years ago.

'I remember the exact sound the camper van made reversing down here. The rat-a-tat-tat of the wheels going over that drainage grill.'

'Me too,' says Dinah. She holds my hand. I think backwards, picture us all here – my family. 'Do you remember warning me about your Dad the first time I came here? You made me so nervous.'

'Did I?'

'I couldn't believe how much your parents swore. Both of them. My mum and dad never swear.'

'They loved swearing.'

'And the one-upmanship. You and Buster sparring to make your dad laugh. What was it they nicknamed you?' asks Dinah.

Sunday lunches were always particularly good fun if one of us was bringing a new partner round. If it was me, Dad and Buster always brought up the stamps I used to collect.

'Stanley Gibbons.'

Dinah laughs.

'That's so childish of your dad.'

'I know. One Christmas I didn't get the air rifle I was hoping for. The last present under the tree was an umbrella that I was sure was the gun. I remember we burned the wrapping paper in the metal bin just there,' I say pointing down the drive. 'I was in tears as Dad explained why I hadn't got one. "Because you will shoot people, my son."'

Dinah laughs.

'We used to get sightseers, ramblers. They'd knock on the front door in their wellies expecting to be given tours of the windmill. Mum used to hate it when her knickers were on the line.'

'Why don't you see if they'll let you have a look inside?'

'Do you think?'

'Why not?'

'What time we seeing Mary?'

'You've got time. Go on, while they're asleep.'

I walk down the drive. Standing on the front doorstep looking through the glass panels into the dining room and touching the horseshoe door knocker, I remember the noise it made when the door slammed and I can feel the old me slithering inside my body, the me I was when I lived here. By the phone there used to be a blown-up framed photo of Dad dressed as a high court judge with a wig on, a gavel in his hand. He was peering over a pair of half-moon glasses, looking very stern. It was from his days in the Cambridge Footlights. Dad used to tell us off underneath it. He joked that it got him into the role of disciplinarian. There's no reply when I knock so I walk down the side of the house. When we were kids we had no back garden. There was just a barbed wire fence there. The year Mum got sick Dad bought some land at the back, though. Mum always wanted a back garden to sunbathe in so Dad decided to make her one. It was to give her something to look forward to. After Mum died, this became another project of Dad's. I came home to help him finish it. Buster was in Germany then. Pen had kids to look after. We had a little system. On Friday lunchtime I'd call my dad. He'd be watching a war film with some of the regulars from the Full Moon he'd started to prop up the bar with. 'Are you all right Daddy-boy?' I'd ask.

'I am fine, my son,' he'd say. 'We're having a little party. Keith's here, Pete, and you remember Dave from Piggots End.' I'd hear voices in the background, Dad saying, 'Down the spiral staircase, and straight on', giving directions to his wine cellar, and then back to me he'd say 'My son, you must watch *The Cruel Sea*' (forgetting I'd watched it with him a dozen times). 'That scene between Ericson and Ferraby where he says, "It's the war, the bloody war." Ahhhh it's just… perfect. You coming over later?' By the time I pitched up, Dad would be fast asleep in his armchair, all his new so-called friends from the Full Moon long gone, and the windmill would be a tip. I'd help Dad tidy, watch him move from room to room with a black bin liner clearing up the empties, shaking his head in wonderment as he'd tell me, 'There are sixteen people I now know by name and who know me by name in that pub. I tell you it's not the church that's the centre of the community, it's the pub. You missed a great film this afternoon. Right, that's the nasty bit over with. Let's find my son a drink. What would a son of mine want? We have it all here. Whisky, gin, beer, wine…?'

We'd eat one of the meals Pen would've dropped around frozen and foil-wrapped and then we'd walk round to the Full Moon, a pub he'd never stepped foot in for the twenty previous years we'd lived in the windmill when Mum was alive. Here, Dad, stood at the bar with his new mates, would dominate the banter, buying rounds, cracking jokes, telling stories. 'Number One Son,' he called me, or 'My personal tramp' because I wore his hand-me-down clothes. 'My shirt, yes, and my shoes. My personal tramp, what can I get you? Isn't it great he wears my clothes?' I'd listen to them planning quiz nights, tricks on the landlord Geoff, telling tales about their wives. Then we'd walk home through the back field in the dark, taking it in turns to lift the barbed wire for each other, and back in the house he'd pour himself whisky and gingers I'd dilute when he wasn't looking, and then Dad, with his feet thrown over the arm of his chair, would talk to me about politics, history, Pen, Buster, my writing, everything except Mum. When he fell asleep I'd extinguish his cigarette, take the drink from his hand, lay him down on the sofa under a blanket and in bed I'd hear him talking in his sleep, dreaming Mum was still alive, 'Mason said she had a better day'… 'It's the steroids. She needs to eat, my son.'

The next morning, no matter what he'd drunk the night before, the first sound I'd hear would be his shovel. We bought an elaborate stone fountain one weekend, we dug out a pond and installed spotlighting on another. When the phone rang neither of us ever wanted to answer it. People came to the door with condolence cards and Dad shooed them away. 'We're fine, fine, bit busy. Thank you, thank you [taking the card]. Goodbye. Got to get to World's End nurseries. It closes at five.'

We became equals. Dad asked my advice.

'Is that straight?'

'Looks straight to me, Daddy-boy.'

In the kitchen: 'Is that pie off?'

'Looks all right to me, Daddy-boy.'

We became sensitive.

'You all right, my son?'

'I'm OK.'

'You all right, Daddy-boy?'

'I think so.'

Grass was laid, fences erected and creosoted, trellis nailed into walls, creepers trained, hanging baskets bought, gravel poured into sectioned-off squares. A corral was constructed in the right-hand corner of the garden and sometimes Dad would crook his finger, and I'd follow him. 'And here's where the nymph will go. Do you like that? I think what this garden needs is a nymph. That will be nice, I think. Mum's nymph.'

It was two months after Mum died on a Saturday morning. Dad rose late, didn't shave. He drank red wine in the corral with his back to the windmill. I left him alone, and it was late evening when he finally came inside. He strode in, his head held back drunkenly. In the middle of the room, his back to me, he said, 'I think today is the day I will cry.' And then his shoulders had heaved like a small child's and very quickly he'd turned, rushed towards me and buried his head into my shoulder so fast and unexpectedly I didn't have time to react before he broke away, and scurried up the stairs, again, like a child. The following Friday when I called Dad was busy. The Friday after this he seemed angry with me. And soon after that I went travelling and while I was away he met Mary.

The sails creak in the wind and cast shadows over the lawn. On a bench overlooking the rose bushes we planted Dad mounted a plaque – 'Roses, roses all the way'. It was what he promised Mum when he proposed to her. I sit on the bench and stare for a few minutes at these rose bushes my mum's ashes were scattered over before I return to the car.

Pen saw Dad first the morning after he died. 'Go and have a look, it makes you feel much better,' she told me, when I came downstairs. In the room Dad was lying propped up in bed. He looked totally different. Miraculously he now looked more alive, dead, than he had for several days alive. His sunken face had filled back out. His eyes looked not empty but full of gentle amusement, a sentiment perfectly reflected in his hint of a smile, the line of his lips slightly wonky. He looked so alive, so much his normal self, I half expected him to make a joke at my expense.

'I think it's lovely,' said Pen when I came out and it was, and somehow it got me through the day. It counterbalanced the suffering, because in that look Dad seemed pleased with where he'd ended up. It was what we kept saying to each other all morning, Mary, Pen, Buster and I. We wandered in and out of the room and spoke to Dad. It was lovely. Dad was smiling. Whatever you said, he just smiled.

Mary's nieces, Katie and Claire, arrived. We urged them to go in. 'Go on – it's amazing. It makes you feel so much better.'

And eventually they did but when they came out Katie said Dad's face had filled out because his bodily fluids had flowed back from his stomach. She looked concerned when I told her how much we were enjoying going in to see Dad because, 'There's a fly in there, sweetie,' she said.

I didn't understand.

She put her arm around me, 'It's a hot day, sweetie.'

The funeral directors picked Dad up in a jeep. We had to move the dining table to get the stretcher through. Up until this moment Dad's death felt removed somehow. It was akin almost to a king having died. A figurehead. Someone mighty whose absence left a giddying feeling of uncertainty. But on the doorstep, watching the jeep pull out of the drive with Katie, Claire and Mary clustered around looking on, it hit me: my dad was dead. Pen and Buster felt it too and the three of us collapsed into a scrum, squeezed our faces together to block out the rest of the world and cried so hard into each other's eyes we scared everyone else back inside. The strange thing happened after that. Back in the house Mary said, 'I've just seen a mouse in the garden. A cheeky little mouse just ran over my foot.' Mouse was Dad's nickname for my mum because she was as quiet as one. Pen, Buster and I stared at each other: that was why Dad was smiling, I decided. We had Mary now and he was with my mum again.

We're on the mezzanine level in the barn, sitting around the table that Mary has Dad's obituaries spread out across, listening to her tell the story about how she met and fell in love with Dad.

'I was hungover. I had just turned fifty the night before. I was sad about that because I was still on my own. And I really didn't feel like going out but it was at Terry and Helen's. If it had been anywhere else, I wouldn't have gone.

'And Helen had put me next to this man,' says Mary. 'He was wearing turquoise socks.'

I laugh.

'And yellow trousers.'

I look at Dinah. She smiles.

'And he was a lot older than me,' says Mary, staring at the ceiling. 'And he was round.' She looks back at us. 'He wouldn't mind me saying that. He had a little belly. He did, didn't he?'

I nod and glance across at the painting on the brick wall opposite of my dad and Mary. Dad's wearing a red jumper and is standing behind Mary, who's sitting down on a chair. The picture has perfectly captured Dad's smile, his easy joyfulness. It's how he looked before he got sick and lost the weight and his face changed.

'I have to tell you David Hatch, your dad, was the least likely man for me to fall in love with. The LEAST likely. So we're sat there and I said to him, 'I was very sorry to hear about your wife.' And he said, 'Thank you.' And we talked, and despite his turquoise socks and his yellow trousers, I rather liked him. I could see he was kind. And he made me laugh. And at the end of the night he asked if I would like to go to the proms one day. And I gave him my number.'

Mary motions to write down a number.

'And the next morning my friend Trish asked me what she always asked me whenever I'd been out. Was there anybody there you liked more than yourself? I said, actually I think there was.'

Mary bites her top lip and looks away. I have to do the same.

'"Will he phone?" she asked,' Mary says. 'I said, "I think he will." Well, he called me at nine o'clock.'

'That's so Dad.'

'Nine on the dot.' She nods. 'He said, "I don't think you look after yourself very well so I'm going to look after you. I'm taking you out for lunch." He took me to the Full Moon, next to the windmill, where he was very pleased to tell me everybody knew his name.'

I laugh. So does Dinah.

'Two dates later I received a letter from David. From your dad. In it he said he loved me.' Mary looks away again. She turns back to us. 'I couldn't believe it. I could NOT believe it. I barely knew him. But I also felt wonderful. In the TV room down there, for the first time in my life, I kicked my legs out and danced for joy.'

'You danced for joy?'

'For the first time in my life.'

'That's so sweet, Mary,' says Dinah.

'I kicked my legs out. I was so happy. And I've been so happy for the last ten years.'

I pat Mary's back on one side. Dinah does the same on the other. Mary recovers.

'And now we must look after each other,' she says.

'We must.'

'As he would have looked after us.'

I hug Mary. Dinah strokes her back.

'Because I'm your adopted mum now whether you like it or not.'

Charlie and Phoebe appear at the top of the stairs.

'And look, come here, my darlings, I have all these grandchildren now too.'

We stay for lunch and afterwards I walk up to St Mary's Church graveyard with Mary to see the wooden cross they've just put up for Dad, while Dinah takes the kids to the swings in the village. The graveyard is on a hill with views across the Chilterns. The cross, to be replaced with a stone one when the ground's settled, has Dad's motto on it. 'Love, life and laughter.'

Back in the house afterwards Mary is saying to me: 'I thought he'd like you to have it.' In my hand I have a brown leather box. Inside is Dad's Ebel watch.

'My wedding present to him,' she says. 'The second hand's a bit erratic. Your dad wore it in the bath. But you can send it off to Switzerland to be mended. Better it's worn.'

I put the watch on and shake it down my wrist, the way Dad used to do.

'Thank you, Mary.'

She goes upstairs and comes back with a sports bag.

'Bits and bobs. Just give to charity what you don't want.'

I open the bag. Inside are a dozen of Dad's shirts, a pair of black leather shoes and his striped kaftan. I slip it on and walk up and down doing Dad's walk.

'You got it,' says Mary, laughing.

We leave shortly afterwards.

'I'll come down and see you in September,' she says. 'take you out for a meal.'

'That will be lovely. And my postcards will continue,' I tell her.

She laughs. We strap the kids in. She hands them Smarties through the open windows. I watch Mary's face as I reverse down the drive until it is out of sight.

CHAPTER 27

Draft Copy for Guidebook:

Bristol, or Brissel as it is pronounced, is famous for the Clifton Suspension Bridge and as the birthplace of Archibald Leach (Cary Grant), as well as all the members of Bananarama. It's also where the Plimsoll line, Ribena, tarmac, Wallace and Gromit and Little Britain's Vicky Pollard are from. Its family attractions include Brunel's SS Great Britain and its pretty zoo gardens, where our kids enjoyed a lion talk and my wife revealed in the marine room that if she were to marry a fish, it would be the porcupine puffer fish 'for its beautiful blue eyes'. Nearby Bath was a popular retreat in Georgian times, and its beauty hasn't altered in 200 years, and probably never will with planners so mindful of it they've actually built a shopping centre here with an entire mock Georgian facade and car parking for up to 850 hansom cabs. This being home to the eighteenth-century arbiter of manners, Beau Nash, expect to be tutted at for eating with your elbows on the table. Worth a look are the Roman Baths and Pump Room, while at the Jane Austen Centre there's a film about the author, as well as an interesting Language of the Fan display where we learnt the following:

1) *Fan in left hand covering face below the eyes – I wish to be accompanied.*

2) *Carrying fan in right hand and open in front of face – Follow me.*

3) *Drawing closed fan across forehead – You have changed.*

4) *Fan open, held behind head – Do not forget me.*

And finally 5) *Fan in pieces – my toddler son has got to the display while my back was turned looking at a bonnet.*

For the record, if push came to shove – and I refuse to give my reasons – if I had to marry a fish myself I would choose a giant gourami fish.

We're at the top of Glastonbury Tor watching a column of Hare Krishnas processing up and down, while grey-pony-tailed hippies in floaty clothes wander about humming the lyrics to John Lennon's '#9 Dream'. From where we're sitting we can see across Somerset, Wiltshire and Devon. Behind us is the roofless St Michael's church, destroyed by an earthquake in 1275 and believed (by people probably with enormous beards and bells on their toes) to be the opening to a fairy kingdom, whilst to our left we can hear excitable chatter about ley lines from two men carrying books with wizardy-style lettering on the front.

'This is nice,' says Dinah.

'The view or the nutters?'

'Both.'

She holds my hand.

We've been researching the 'London and Around' chapter, staying at one-room Premier Inns and Travelodges, belting around on the sweaty Underground. Before that it was Kent and the last few days, Wiltshire and Somerset. It's been hard. My note-taking's been sloppy. I haven't bothered taking pictures. I've felt bored for the first time. We seem to be doing similar versions of things we've done before. Wookey Hole was our fourth cave complex. Canterbury our seventh cathedral. We've been to eight zoos, six aquariums. We've ridden nine sightseeing buses.

According to the legend, Jesus visited this 500-foot high mound nobody knows which civilisation constructed with his great-uncle, Joseph of Arimathea. He built Glastonbury's first wattle and daub church and after the crucifixion returned and buried the Holy Grail below where we're sitting.

'What you thinking?' asks Dinah.

'I'm thinking about what Mary said that time. That I tried hard not to like my dad.'

We're heading into Bristol and when Cheltenham Road becomes Gloucester Road I start to recognise the streets: Cromwell Road, Wolseley Road, Shadwell Road. We're visiting two uni friends of Dinah's, Gemma and Pete. They live at the bottom of Sommerville Road, which is coincidentally the road I lived on in 1986 when I was briefly at Bristol Poly. We're early and Dinah wants to give the kids a little more sleep so I shoot past Gemma and Pete's and carry on up the hill. I park outside number 67. Leaving Dinah in the car trying to snooze herself, I step outside to call my old school friend Gus. When I first left home I wasn't equipped for independence. That's the most favourable way of interpreting my behaviour. Not only did I cowardly go to the same poly as Gus, turning down a better place I had at Warwick University, we even took the same course – social science. We lived in the same house – Mrs Ward's at number 67 – and even shared a room here. Gus quit after nine weeks because he was missing his girlfriend, Liora. I clung on for a further week before I did the same.

'You're not,' he says, when I tell Gus where I am.

'I can see the front door from where I'm standing.'

'Mrs Waaards,' sing-songs Gus. We go through the story again. How pathetic we must have been, how everyone must have thought we were gay.

'Ben,' Gus says. 'It was even worse than that. We had the same poster over our beds.'

'That Laurel and Hardy one. Where they're sat on that bench.'

'With the white dog.'

'With the white dog.'

I laugh.

'What must people have thought of us?'

'Do you remember hiding our records?' Gus asks. 'That cool guy came round.'

'That's right, you made me hide my "Ghostbusters" single under my bed.'

'We hid them all under your bed, Ben. Steve Arrington, DeBarge. You had "The Inch Worm" by Danny Kaye.'

'I didn't.'

'You fucking did.'

'Nooo!'

'We weren't sure what to do with Dire Straits. We thought they might be OK,' he says.

'I do remember those girls coming round. Do you remember? We were such idiots. It was 9.30 in the evening. They liked us. They came upstairs to our bedroom...'

'And we were in our fucking pyjamas,' says Gus.

'And I showed off the way I ate Dairylea triangles by putting the whole triangle in my mouth with the foil still on and sucking out the cheese and then spitting out the foil. I made them have a go. People were taking drugs. I was experimenting with soft cheese.'

I look at the black, solid-looking front door and the black and white mosaic tiled path and something else comes back to me.

'Do you remember the dog?'

'Fucking hell. That dog!' says Gus.

'We were such wusses around that dog.'

'It *was* a Dobermann, Ben. Do you remember leaving the house?'
He starts to laugh.

'You'd run down the stairs first really fast before it could come
out of the kitchen and then you'd leave the front door open for
me,' says Gus. 'I'd come hacking down a minute or so later when
the coast was clear and slam the front door shut behind me.'

'And didn't we do something with the mashed potato?'

'We hid it in a drawer, Ben.'

I start to laugh again.

'Why did we do that?'

'It started with spaghetti bolognaise. You told Mrs Ward you
didn't like it so she made shepherd's pie. You didn't like that either
– you were fucking fussy, Ben. You were embarrassed after the
spaghetti so you hid the mashed potato in the drawer. I copied you.'

'Why did you copy me?'

'I don't fucking know.'

'How long did we go on hiding it?'

'Don't you remember what happened? One day we opened the
drawer and it was all gone.'

'All the potato?'

'She must have found it and taken it out.'

'She never said anything?'

'She never said anything.'

'How much potato was there?'

'A drawer full.'

'I wonder what she thought.'

'She must have thought we were wankers.'

'And did we get mashed potato again?'

'I can't remember.'

Something else comes back to me.

'Do you remember the most embarrassing thing?'

'The tutorial,' says Gus. There are only certain people that make me laugh until I cry. Gus is one of them.

'It's still the most shameful moment of my life,' I say with tears in my eyes.

'Me too,' he says, between the laughter.

The first morning on the campus at Coldharbour Lane during our first sociology tutorial Gus, who I was naturally sat beside, had to introduce himself to the group. Sat around a circular table Gus said he was from Chesham High School in Buckinghamshire. He was studying social science and had found digs with a Mrs Ward, who lived close to the St Paul's area of the city on Sommerville Road. Gus was thanked, the tutor had looked at me and with a dozen pairs of strangers eyes upon me, all I could say was, 'Basically, same here.'

When I stop laughing I feel so emptied of amusement I can't believe I'll ever be able to laugh again. Hanging up, I feel drained and serious now. A little edgy, too, and suddenly remorseful. I can see myself now not through my own eyes but through my dad's. Mary's words return: you tried hard not to like your dad.

The evening is full of strange, evocative resonances. I'm alone, Charlie lying across my arms in the darkness of Gemma and Pete's front room, feeding him the nightly 8 ounces of formula and I can hear laughter in the next room and smell the thick gravy Pete's preparing, when I hear the distant strain of a piano. It's leaking through the wall of the adjoining terrace house but it might as well be coming straight from my own heart. I think of my dad on Christmas morning playing his hymns. The sound of wine corks popping in the kitchen reminds me of that hungry rasp at the back of my throat at the expectation of Mum's turkey, of Pe

Buster and I mucking about, Dad telling us off for not helping but almost secretly laughing at mine and Buster's attempts to get out of laying the table by sneaking off for last-minute visits to the toilet. Even Pete and Gemma's sleek black cat on the landing as I scale the stairs to put Charlie to bed reminds me of our old family cat Boots. At dinner I keep levering my dad into conversations. Pete tells us about his DIY plans for the house and I crowbar in a story about Dad once making a table that fell apart. I don't do it on purpose. I start a sentence and only realise halfway through it's about my dad again, at which point it's too late to haul it back. The third time I do this Gemma, who's already said she was sorry to hear about my dad, asks, 'How's your step-mum, Ben? Mary, isn't it?'

Pete, staring at me with wide unblinking eyes, mentions the obit in *The Times*.

'I didn't know your dad was the first producer of *Just a Minute*.'

'Yeah. And *Week Ending*... and *The News Quiz*. They were going to axe *Just a Minute* after the first series but my dad threatened to resign if they did. So it survived. And he gave David Renwick his first writing job, you know – who wrote *One Foot in the Grave*?'

'Really?'

Even though I'm not absolutely sure about this, I plough on. 'Yeah, he was working for a local paper in Luton and Dad gave him his first writing job. And you know Inspector Frost? The way he walks – the stop start way he moves, that quick dramatic spin. David Jason got that walk from my dad. That's my dad's walk.'

'Really? How does your dad know...'

'And the board game Ratrace, my dad invented that.' I continue like a school kid in the playground boasting my dad's bigger than your dad. But I don't care because suddenly I feel like one of those Janissary warriors from the Ottoman Empire, the captured soldiers from rival religions converted in defeat to the Muslim faith who then become the most loyal fighters of the caliph.

'We were kids and it rained in this cottage we went to stay at. I was about two. He devised the game – sent the board off to Waddingtons. A few years later they nicked it. He hadn't copyrighted it. They even used the same title.'

I end up telling them about the day I almost got my mum's Peugeot 205 blown up in a controlled explosion in the underground car park at Broadcasting House. I'd memorised Dad's security access code and I left Mum's car in Dad's spot on the same day John Major came in to talk to Radio 4 about the IRA's attempt to blow up 10 Downing Street with a mortar rocket. Security was extra tight and my mum's licence plate was not on the approved staff list. It was only that Dad happened to be de facto head of the BBC that day as it was a weekend that the memo about the intended controlled explosion landed on his desk. I'd been shopping in Oxford Circus obliviously. The first I was aware of what had almost happened was when I returned home to Dad waiting for me on the doorstep. He communicated with me for a couple of weeks on BBC headed notepaper afterwards. 'When you have finished with the ice tray fill it up.'... 'When you borrow my car PUT SOME PETROL IN AFTERWARDS'... 'WHEN YOU'VE FINISHED WITH YOUR PLATE, WASH IT UP.'

'I think I've only just realised what an arsehole I was to him,' I say. And the room goes quiet.

Dinah looks across at me. 'Well,' she says, with a little cough. 'Anyway, what have you two been up to?'

They start to talk about their kids, their plans for the house and getting up to go to the toilet I bounce along walls. Wobblin about in the bathroom, I experience a strange inside-out-l sensation down my dick. I gulp with pain and hear an au clink. I look down and on a ridge in the toilet bowl there's a small black object surrounded by light red blood. The blood bleeds into the water and I bend down and fish it out. It's hard and jagged like a Chinese throwing star. I wash it and place it in a spare contact lens case I find by the sink. I start to feel slightly light-headed now, maybe it's the sight of all the blood, and have to sit down on the toilet to steady myself. When I do, I notice the tiles on the floor appear to merge into one super tile, the spaces between them vanishing. I have to grasp the toilet roll holder.

'The tiles have become one super tile,' I say to myself and I start to laugh as the room starts to spin.

Dinah knocks on the bathroom door.

'Are you laughing to yourself in there? Come on, we'd better go. We don't even know where the cottage is.'

I look at the tiles again. One particular tile catches my eye. A swirl of surface grout looks like an eye. It appears to be an eye in profile looking out sideways at me and the tassels on the bath mat look like teeth. It makes me think Picasso was right – a sideways eye is inappropriate lust. I feel pleased with myself for having such an erudite thought at such a weak moment but when I shout this out to Dinah she sounds concerned.

'What's happening in there? Let me in.'

I'm sitting on Gemma and Pete's bed. I have a damp towel on my head; another round my midriff. Dinah tips a glass of water to my lips. I swallow a couple of mouthfuls.

'You all right?'

I nod.

'Do you feel OK?'

I nod.

'What happened in there?'

'Don't know.'

'What's that in your hand?'

'This.'

'What?'

I hand it to her.

'My kidney stone!'

'What!' She unscrews the lid. 'That's your kidney stone?'

'I passed it.'

'You mean… Urghhhh! Ben it's in my contact lens case and that's been down your…'

'It's not your lens case. I found it.'

'Where?'

'In the bathroom.'

'You put it in Gemma's contact lens case!'

'It's good news. I don't have to go back to hospital.'

'I think we need to get you out of here.'

Dinah transfers the half-asleep kids into the car seats and I'm coming down the stairs myself, feeling slightly better, when I hear Gemma say: 'Not at all, Dine. Blimey, I'd be all over the place, wouldn't I, Pete? I needed a week off from work when my mum broke her leg.' Then she laughs at something Dinah says. 'No, don't worry. I think it's funny. I've got loads of them. But why does he want to keep it?'

We've assumed Simonsbath is near Bath, maybe because it has the word Bath in it, but punching it into the satnav, it's a shock to discover it's two hours away. It's 9 p.m. and we don't have the owner's number or a proper address for the cottage we're staying in, which in the blue folder is unhelpfully called, 'The Cottage, Simonsbath'. With the window open to sober me up, Dinah drives over the Brendon Hills, great steep climbs in second gear before slow precipitous descents. She belts through Exmoor National Park. It's the longest drive of the trip but they're fastest B-roads we've seen. I nod off. When I wake Dinah asks if I'm all right.

'No tiles merging.'

'No.'

She laughs.

'You were probably just exhausted. Any more blood?'

'No.'

'How are you feeling?'

'Better.'

'Go back to sleep.'

Simonsbath is a small blink-and-you-miss-it village of two hundred or so people close to the Somerset-Devon border. It's past eleven when we arrive and we've still no idea where the cottage is. The only lit building to ask for directions at is the Exmoor Forest Inn. If that fails, it looks like we're sleeping in the car. Dinah goes into the pub and comes back out a few moments later. The Cottage, it turns out, is right opposite us. We can see it from where we're parked. We cross the road – on the front door the owner's left us a note about where to find the keys. Downstairs the cottage is normal – a living room, a dining room and a small kitchen – but upstairs the doors to the two bedrooms and the bathroom are shoulder height. They're like something out of *Alice in Wonderland* and even Dinah at 5 foot dead has to duck to get through them. She puts Charlie to bed, changes into her nightie and is downstairs waiting for me on the sofa when I come down from settling Phoebe.

'Bed or telly?'

'Telly.'

'You sure? How are you feeling?'

'Much better.'

'You gave me a fright back there. I've never seen you that out
'

'What did Gemma and Pete say?'

'They were just concerned.'

'Sorry about the lens case.'

She laughs.

I take the lens case out of my pocket.

'I want to make a collage when we get home. Put all sorts of things in it from the trip to tell the story. The kids will love it – the press passes for Santa Pod, some of Phoebe's rabbit pictures, a page from the blue file. Photos and...'

'You're not putting that in there.'

I laugh.

'Why not?'

'Because it's disgusting, Ben.'

'Really?'

'Yes.'

We watch an old *Iron Chef* episode on a random cable TV station. It's sort of *Ready Steady Cook* meets *Ainsley's Meals in Minutes* gone mad. A bloated William Shatner in a ridiculous purple robe is the host.

'It's a battle of seasonings, skillets and fire,' he shouts. Twenty of the 'world's top chefs' fight cooking duels, the crowd going insane as ingredients like tomato, basil and coriander are read out, and Shatner, whose face is visibly sweating under his bulk, shouts, 'TURN THE HEAT UP.' As the meals are prepared, two commentators in an overhead studio with head-mikes comment in the chatty yet imperative way they do for NFL games. The chefs, dressed in national costumes or scary outfits like WWF wrestlers, say things like, 'I don't know, it's like my whole life has been leading up to this moment.'

After it's finished I fetch Dinah's water and we go upstairs a~ in the bedroom, Dinah says: 'The best couples complement ~ other. One offers something the other can't. You straighten c scattiness, and I stop you worrying about things like hypochondria and your dad.'

'We're like a jigsaw,' I say. 'Our two pieces fit well together.'

'But the jigsaw changes shape over the years,' says Dinah. 'Our edges alter over time, adjusting to the changing edges of the other person.'

'We're different people from the ones who first met,' I say. 'The secret is road trips and going out for meals. This is when we adjust our edges.'

'And watching William Shatner sweat,' she says.

'Road trips, meals out and watching William Shatner sweat; they're vital to us.'

'And I definitely can't put it in my collage?'

'You definitely can't put it in your collage.'

CHAPTER 28

St Enodoc Hotel lies across the estuary from Padstow in the Cornish town of Rock. Rock, once a rundown fishing village, is today nicknamed Kensington-by-Sea. The Rothschilds holiday here, as do the Sainsbury family. Hugh Grant comes and princes William and Harry have been known to land at the local helipad opposite the golf course to water-sport at Polzeath beach. In our sub-post office back home they sell Sunblest. At the one in Rock you can buy quails' eggs. The St Enodoc is a boutique hotel. You can tell this from the clear glass vase of bright green apples on the reception desk. The hotel playroom is full of scary posh children who say things like this: 'She's got our pram. It was Hermione's. It's called stealing and it's wrong and you can go to jail and we're going to tell our mother when she gets back from her pedicure.'

This week we've followed the rocky North Devon coast south into Cornwall. We've visited the Arthurian Centre in Camelford, the site of the sixth-century Camlann battlefield where King Arthur was mortally wounded, and where I discovered Hatch is a common Cornish surname and that more than likely I'm a Celt, a fact that's been allowing me irritatingly to refer to all Cornish people as 'we' and anything in the county as 'our'. As in, 'Dina, have you tried our clotted cream?' We've been to Gnomel at Watermouth Castle in Ilfracombe, a witchcraft museum in Boscastle and the kids have cast spells in Merlin's cave beneath Tintagel Castle.

Everyone in Padstow over the age of eleven looks like Prince Harry. They have the same ruddy complexion with that messy spiky crop on top, and wear three-quarter-length designer surfing shorts and brandy-striped rugby shirts worn collars up under some puffy gilet emblazoned with the name of a public school. The town's nickname is Padstein after celebrity chef Rick Stein and so far we've seen: Stein's Patisserie, Stein's Gift Shop, Stein's Deli, Rick Stein's Cafe, Rick Stein's The Seafood Restaurant, St Petroc's Bistro, and Stein's Fish and Chips. It's like he's some megalomaniac slowly taking over the world beginning with gastro outlets selling freshly caught fish in Padstow. Who knows, maybe in a few years' time he'll have shed his chef whites altogether and will be in some military-style tunic sat in an elaborate underground bunker system beneath Tintagel Castle threatening to release some perfectly prepared, and garnished with parsley, nuclear weapons on the unsuspecting world whilst menacingly stroking some very lightly cooked turbot.

Several kids, their legs thrown over the harbour wall, are armed with crabbing lines and buckets. Dinah heads off to look for a school uniform for Phoebe (she starts school the day after we're back) while I buy a net and walk down the concrete slipway to the water's edge with the children. The harbour is full of brightly coloured fishing boats. Seagulls screech overhead. I show Phoebe and Charlie how to fish, leaving the net in the water, waiting for the small brown fish to grow used to its presence and when they're an inch or two away, running the net towards them and jerking sharply upwards. It's something my dad taught me. Charlie, his haunches, is wearing a white hat and a slightly too baggy

Hawaiian shirt, which, with his rolled-up trousers and his chubby legs, from behind make him look like some short, eccentric, aged, wealthy American – a sort of J. Peabody III. He peers into the net with utter concentration to see what Phoebe's bagged. Occasionally he races up the ramp and, for no reason, suddenly does a two-footed jump. Sometimes he puts a fisted arm out and runs full speed – his superhero pose. 'To the rescue!' he shouts, in his deepest voice. There's an old man and his wife sitting on a bench in the sunshine a few feet above us, shopping bags at their feet, and I feel a tremendous pride when I notice they're unable to resist watching my kids.

Hotel staff have recommended St Minver fete so we spend the afternoon there. It's a traditional village affair with a modern twist. There's welly-wanging (Hunters, of course) and a soak-the-banker sponge throw, while Phoebe wins a cuddly toy on the human fruit machine, which consists of three teenage girls from Winchester public school sat in a line at a table going 'ya ya ya' and then each holding up a lemon, some cherries or a slice of melon.

The Orange Bomber is a Heath Robinson contraption made of wood designed to test cricketing skills. For 30p you get to throw two wooden balls at a metal plate. If you strike it, a magnet decouples, sending a basket of oranges toppling over. The aim is to catch the falling oranges. You have to throw and start to run at the same time to succeed and, although it looks easy, almost everyone fails. Large crowds form and there's something wonderfully English about the spectacle. Advice, encouragement and good-natured abuse are shouted from the sidelines.

'Hugh, you couldn't catch a cold. Give it up.'

'Underarm, Marcus.'

'The boy's in flip-flops. Take the flip-flops off, Fortescue.'

We have a two-bedroom suite with views across the Camel estuary. The thin tongue of tide is out and fishing boats are marooned on their keels. We're on our balcony eating a picnic dinner when there's a commotion outside. People are gathering on the terrace outside the main restaurant beneath our window, staring across the estuary.

'Come here, love, something's happening,' and as I shout this, out of the clear blue sky nine Red Arrows roar over the headland in tight formation. They race diagonally left to right, passing so close overhead that at one point I can see the red jacket of one of the pilots in the cockpit.

'Kids! Quick!'

I stand behind Phoebe. Dinah picks up Charlie. The planes return trailing red, white and blue smoke behind them.

'Wow!' shouts Phoebe.

'What *is* that?' points Charlie.

The planes soar high and part in two swathes over the estuary. They disappear and return, the two groups flying towards each other, upside down and low over the masts of the lopsided boats, before peeling away at the last moment with a sonic whoosh. They come together one more time, tip their wings and soar away.

Phoebe hops up and down. 'Where are they, Dad?'

'They've gone, sweetheart.'

'Awwwww. Are they coming back?'

'There must be an air show nearby. They've probably gone there. Do you know what they're called, guys? The Red Arrows. You were very lucky to see them.'

Charlie, his eyes still on stalks, runs around the room holding his arms out like wings.

'Did you know that was going to happen?' asks Dinah.

'No.'

' could have been anywhere.'

'I know.'

'But we were actually looking out of the window at exactly the right time.'

'On a sea-facing balcony.'

'Why were they doing that at the end? That funny thing with their wings.' Phoebe tilts her arms backwards and forwards.

'They were waving, saying goodbye.'

'Why?'

'Because that was the end of the show or maybe someone important is in town.' I wink at Dinah.

'What?'

I look at her knowingly. 'You've been craning your head round every time a helicopter lands all day, love.'

'I don't fancy Prince William, Ben. How many times? I was looking out for him out of curiosity. I'd have been the same if it was Theo Paphitis. Do you think I fancy him? You know what I'm like with celebrities.'

'Bollocks,' I tell her, and she laughs.

We're mucking about in the jacuzzi bath after the kids are in bed playing James Bond games. 'So long, Mr Bond,' Dinah's saying, leaning over and gradually turning up the jets to maximum and, still spasming in the bubbly froth pretending to be electrocuted, I ask her: 'What would you do, though? Imagine it. Prince William tries to get off with you.'

'I think I've missed my chance now, love.'

'Just imagine it, though. You're in the queue at Di's Dairy and Pantry and he comes in to buy some Stinking Bishop. He's leaving Kate. She's not down to earth enough for him. He wants you to come to a party on his yacht and tell him all about Widnes a' the ICI chemical works.'

Dinah laughs. 'That's ridiculous.'

'OK, not Widnes. He wants to talk about something else.'

'I wouldn't go. I don't fancy him.'

'Course you'd go.'

'I wouldn't.'

'I bet I can come up with a scenario where you would.'

'Go on then.'

'OK, you find out he's been tracking you down for years.'

She laughs.

'He's been tracking you down ever since you met him at the opening of that spinal thingy at Stoke Mandeville Hospital.'

'That was Princes Di.'

'Pretend it was him. He's liked you since then. He can't believe he's seen you again after all this time. You chat to him at the cheese counter in Di's Pantry. You like him, he still likes you. He buys his Stinking Bishop. Then he presses himself against you. You wouldn't be able to resist.'

'OK, firstly it's a ridiculous scenario because why would I be on my own in Di's Pantry? Where are you lot?'

'We've gone to Stein's Fish and Chips. You didn't fancy it. And it's before he knew Kate. Before his hair started receding as well. He kept the picture Richard Duggan took of you for the *Herald* story. He has it on him, in fact.'

'Even though it was actually Princess Di.'

'We're pretending it's him.'

'OK, why didn't I go for fish and chips with you lot?'

'It doesn't matter.'

'I'd go for Rick Stein's fish and chips with you lot.'

'Even if Prince William was pressing against you?'

'What's all this pressing?'

'He's pressing against you, love.'

re you getting some pervy thrill out of this?'

gh.

'OK, what bits is he pressing?'

'He's pressing everything, his torso, his royal groin.'

'I'd still go for fish and chips.'

'You wouldn't.'

'Rick Stein's fish and chips? I would.'

'OK, you've got a stomach ache. You didn't want fish and chips because you had a stomach ache. You're in Di's Pantry and Prince William tells you he's got an hour to live. One hour, that's all he's got and all he wants to do in that time is be with you *physically*.'

'But I don't fancy him.'

'He's the future king of England, love.'

'If he's got an hour to live, he'd be riddled with disease. I might catch it.'

'It's not contagious. It's a non-contagious disease. Actually, that's not the reason he's got an hour to live. He's going to blow up in an hour. It's not a disease. The CIA has implanted some device inside him, some anti-monarch device, that's going to go off in an hour. It doesn't detract from his attractiveness, and he wants you, and we're having fish and chips and you've got a stomach ache.'

'No, I'd be looking at my watch the whole time.'

'For fuck's sake, you know for sure that the CIA is going to take him away after an hour. They're taking him off somewhere. They're flying him to the North Sea, dropping him in the ocean by helicopter. They've given you assurances about this. You won't be there when he blows up. Come on, you'd go for it?'

'I think I'm starting to get a stomach ache, actually.'

'OK, I give up. If you can't be honest with yourself...'

'Are you actually cross with me?'

'You're not imagining it.'

'You *are* cross with me!'

I laugh.

'Would it make it better if I said I'd shag him?'

'Yes.'

'OK, I'd shag him. Happy?'

'I knew it!'

She laughs.

'Come on, let me show you what I got for Phoebe.'

Inside the apartment Dinah lays pieces of Phoebe's school uniform out on the floor of the living room and across the sofa and armchair.

'I think I did really well. Three back-to-school long-sleeve shirts for six pounds. That's good, isn't it?'

'It's very good.'

'Three gingham blouses for the autumn term. Aren't they cute? Imagine her in those.'

I hold my heart and sigh.

'I know. Me too,' she says.

'What are those ones?'

'Pinafore dresses for the winter. Hopefully they'll still fit her then. They were so cheap I thought I might as well get them. And look!'

She opens another bag.

'Socks, knickers, a few blue skirts and a gym kit. I even got a yellow and black tie.' She holds it up. 'Guess how much?'

'Altogether? A hundred pounds.'

'Fifty!'

'That is good.'

'And in Padstow as well. I thought it would be a lot more.'

She stands back to survey the clothes. I do the same. I imagine Phoebe in her uniform. I picture myself waving her goodbye at the school gate. Dinah does the same and sighs deeply. I put my arm round her and she says, 'I can't believe she's going to...' An index ger shoots up to her eye.

'now.'

'She's still so tiny.'
She folds into me.
'I know.'

Later that night, curled up on the sofa, listening to Radio 4, hoping to find a bit of comedy, it comes on. A tribute piece to Dad presented by Gloria Hunniford. It starts with a clip from *I'm Sorry, I'll Read That Again*, the radio series Dad starred in back in the 1960s. It's always quite strange to suddenly hear Dad's voice on air, but what's truly shocking this time is what Gloria Hunniford says afterwards: 'Sir David Hatch, who died at home two weeks ago after a short illness.' Even though I know he's dead it's still like a slap in the face. It's so startling a bald and naked fact that I have to catch my breath. Dad's just not contactable. That's how I've been coping. My dad isn't dead. I just haven't rung him in a while. There are tributes from BBC colleagues, clips from *Just a Minute* and *The News Quiz*. John Cleese tells the story about the Going Underground T-shirt. And it's a confusing feeling sat here in this random Cornish hotel, arranging scatter cushions across my bare feet because it's cold with the balcony door open, feeling a massive swelling of pride for my dad, who I want desperately to ring, but a fraction of a second later realise I can't because he's dead.

CHAPTER 29

Every August we visited my gran and my mum's sister Aunty Romey in Sidmouth, Devon. They lived in a two-bedroomed seaman's cottage on Newtown Road, a short walk from the seafront. Granny Martin was our favourite granny, and Aunty Romey, my favourite aunty and also the most consistent present giver at Christmas, even if she often selected wholly inappropriate gifts (for my eighth birthday I received a video history of Tapton Colliery; Buster, six, was given *National Trust Homes in Derbyshire*). Gran, my mum's mum, always wore a blue twinset. She had a picture of the Queen on her kitchen wall and the worst thing I ever heard her say about anybody was, 'That man!' And that was about Adolf Hitler. Aunty Romey, who'd never left home, completed the *Telegraph* crossword and painted watercolours of bluebell woods and Jacob's Ladder beach, which she exhibited and sold at the Sidmouth Festival. It was the highlight of our summer, the two weeks we spent with them. The house was so small, Buster and I slept in bunk beds in the potting shed next to the lawnmower and the bags of John Innis Number 3 compost. It smelt of creosote and soil but we woke to the sound of seagulls.

Every morning we went to Jacob's Ladder beach. Dad marched us miles along the stones beneath the red cliffs to find a secluded spot where we could 'spread out', and here we'd spend all day, the tartan picnic rug spread across the chalky stones, eating corned beef sandwiches, drinking Corona Cherryade, swimming, playing catch, boules and French cricket. The tingling sensation of putting a T-shirt over a salty, sunburnt back. The crunch of sand in a corned beef sandwich. The suck and ebb of the tide sounding brighter on cold mornings. Pen and Buster swam, Mum sunbathed in her yellow bikini and I listened to Radio 4's test match commentary, shouting out to Dad important developments from the ledge of stones that led down to the water: if somebody was out, when Boycott reached his 100.

The last weekend of the holiday we always went on day trips. To Paignton Zoo, Pecorama, Bicton Gardens, or we'd fly kites on Branscombe cliffs. The outings were memorable because Dad always incorporated competition into everything. It was never enough to fly a kite, or visit a zoo, we'd all be ranked on how well we'd flown our kite or be tested on what we'd seen. 'Not bad Benjy, but Pen was better when it got really windy. Buster-boy, I put you third. Now who can tell me how long the average male baboon lives for? It was on the sign.' One of our day trips was the donkey sanctuary. We always went to the donkey sanctuary.

'It is not just the number of donkeys,' I tell Dinah. 'Although there are more donkeys here than anywhere else in the world. It's the presentation. You wait. You're going to love this.'

The sanctuary, a couple of miles past Sidford, the next town along from Sidmouth, is home to all manner of donkeys. In the fields surrounding the main block there are donkeys with eye patches, limping donkeys, moulting donkeys. There are donkeys that are perfectly all right. There are donkeys who look all right but aren't all right. There are mentally scarred donkeys, happy donkeys, sad donkeys, worried donkeys. There are donkeys tha don't give a damn, donkeys that do. Donkeys with damaged ta donkeys with poorly ears. There are donkeys that have seen too much. Donkeys that have not seen enough.

I lead us through the fields of donkeys into a barn that has on its inside wall pictures of each resident donkey. The wall is like the galleries you get in reception areas of small businesses showing photos of their employees. Except, as well as their picture and name, there's also a brief biography of each donkey listing salient facts about their lives and, for instance, their ability to smell polo mints through coat pockets. Also, entertainingly, you're told who they hang out with at the sanctuary ('Nelly is big mates with Daisy and Teddy – they are quite a little clique.'). Dinah starts to chuckle. Phoebe stands on the bottom rung of a fence to stroke the wiry back of Clara T.

'See what I mean. You get to know the donkeys. To understand the donkeys.'

She moves on to Fred Morgan. Fred Morgan has settled in nicely with the other donkeys since his arrival in 2005, although he still doesn't like his ears being touched. Jenny Collins, meanwhile, came in 2007 and 'always enjoys a mince pie on Christmas Day'.

In the Haycroft restaurant afterwards, while the kids eat flapjacks, a debate ensues about the mindset of benefactors who leave everything to donkeys. It's inspired by the board outside the restaurant listing their names. There are dozens catalogued in the sorts of columns you get dedicated to the fallen on war memorials: Enids, Bettys and Maudes are honoured for leaving their life savings to donkeys they've often never seen. It's a sad fact more people donate to the donkey sanctuary than to the local RNLI.

'Do you think they're mad?' I ask Dinah.

'Of course they are.'

'All the Maudes and Bettys. All of them are mad.'

'You wouldn't do that,' says Dinah.

'No, I wouldn't.'

'And nor would I because it's verging on criminal.'

'I agree.'

'They've got more money than sense. I mean, how many people are employed here? Look around you, Ben.'

She swivels around, staring into the courtyard.

'They're painting doors that don't need painting, they're cleaning up the donkey shit before it hits the ground. It's bonkers.'

'It is and it isn't.'

'OK, explain, Mr Enigmatic.'

'You just don't understand the donkey.'

'What?'

'I understand the donkey.'

'You understand donkeys?'

'I do.'

'And what don't I understand about donkeys?'

'Their nature.'

'And that explains your point how?'

'There is something poignant about a donkey.'

'Poignant?'

'Something hangdog that appeals to our sympathy.'

'Give me an example.'

'Donkeys barely lift their heads. Unlike horses. Horses are cocky. Donkeys always look meekly at the ground. Have you ever been looked in the eye by a donkey? No. Because they wouldn't dare. A donkey is what Mary rode to Bethlehem on. They're so meek, they've become symbols of meekness. When a footballer is considered unskilled you call him a donkey. And when they bray the noise seems to come less from aggression like the mule and more from a deep pit of self-pity.'

'You should work on the sales team. The Maudes wo love you.'

'Old people recognise this feeling from being overlooked themselves in post office queues. They have communality with donkeys.'

'And this is why old people disinherit relatives and leave their cash to Eeyores?'

'Exactly.'

'What a load of shit!'

'Have you got a better explanation?'

'They're bonkers.'

We leave the restaurant and wander around a few fields before popping into the visitor centre, a glorified gift shop, where you can buy almost everything you'd need to conduct a dinner party with donkey sanctuary merchandise including place mats, plates, bowls, candles, mugs, tea towels and salt and pepper pots. We buy Phoebe a story by Elisabeth D. Svendsen called *The Story of Eeyore, The Naughtiest Donkey in the Sanctuary* that Dinah reads to the kids in the car. Based on a true story, it's about a naughty donkey that came to the sanctuary and upset a fire bucket and nipped a farrier before escaping into a paddock it wasn't supposed to be in. It isn't exactly *The Shawshank Redemption* but it keeps the peace on the drive back to Sidmouth.

An hour later we're on Jacob's Ladder beach. The sky's overcast and the beach is half empty. But then the summer's nearly over. It's September tomorrow. We change the kids out of their clothes, which no longer fit them, we've been away so long. Charlie's trousers all look like pedal pushers and Phoebe's tops all stop at least an inch short of her wrist. They're in their swimming things, the tide's out and I muck about with them on the same sand I played on as a kid. I draw a circle round Charlie in the sand and tell him, 'You're trapped.'

'Trap me,' he keeps saying, and then every time I do, Phoebe him, by rubbing out a segment of the ring with her foot. 'It's all right Charlie – you can get out now.' Later Phoebe wades out to her waist sucking her tummy in against the cold. Charlie chases the tide in and out. When Phoebe's eczema hurts in the sea salt she sits on Dinah's lap and Dinah rubs cream on her while Charlie and I make a dam. Rivulets of water at the foot of the stones make veins in the sand. We build a semi-circular wall here that I reinforce with the stones that Phoebe reaches round for from Dinah's lap. Occasionally there's a leak.

'Dad! Quick. Dad! There!' Phoebe shouts, as Charlie and I furiously staunch the breach.

Sometime later I hear Dinah's voice.

'Love,' she's shouting.

I look up.

Her eyes are shielded from the sun. She's smiling 'You *can* just sit here and do nothing, you know.'

I look round. The kids have lost interest in the dam. They're a few yards away drawing circles round each other with their feet in the sand.

'Got carried away there, didn't you?' says Dinah, as I sit down beside her. The blankness of the cloudy sky blends with the still sea making it almost impossible to tell where the horizon begins. We watch Phoebe marshal Charlie about.

'They've become best friends on this trip,' says Dinah.

'It's lovely.'

'Look, Daddy!' shouts Phoebe, showing off an elephant she's drawn in the sand.

'Very good, Phoebe.'

'Mummy!'

'It's brilliant,' says Dinah. 'I love his trunk.'

'And mine,' says Charlie.

'Yours is lovely too, Charlie.'

'Tell me then,' I say to Dinah, back in the car.

'Guess.'

'Five.'

She closes the map.

'Less. Four!'

That's the number of pages left to drive across before we reach Brighton.

CHAPTER 30

Draft Copy for Guidebook:
Separated from the mainland by the Solent, the diamond-shaped Isle of Wight is the smallest county in England and known for being three things: a) the best place to find dinosaur fossils in Europe; b) the worst place to go if you don't like sailing (the international sailing centre of Cowes is here); and c) perhaps the most insular area of England – tourists are known as grockles here and our car was referred to, within our earshot, by a man from Newport we had disagreed with at a junction on the A3020, as a 'grockle can' (as in 'Go on, piss off in your grockle can'). That said, there are many family-orientated places for grockles to visit in their cans including the Isle of Wight Zoo, where our normally timid daughter demonstrated on the penultimate day of this trip round England just how blasé she's become about the daily presence of exotic animals in her life by ordering me with a bored yawn as we approached Tammy the Bengal tiger, 'Make him roar, Daddy.' It was also here on a keeper talk we learnt about a tiger's flehmen response, which enables them, through drawing air across their Jacobson's organ in the roof of their mouths, to physically

taste a scent, something our son, we feel sure, utilises when we try to secretly open packets of cheese and onion crisps.

Yesterday we visited the Tank Museum in Wareham as well as the Teddy Bear Museum in Dorchester, the fictitious home of a human-sized teddy bear by the name of Mr Edward Bear. Inside Mr Bear's mocked-up home Charlie and Phoebe met, hugged and attempted to knock over several of Mr Edward Bear's life-sized bear relatives. There was a toy room, while downstairs there was a separate exhibition complementing the teddy bear museum. And what would be the ultimate bedfellow for a teddy bear museum? Why a museum, of course, dedicated to the famous terracotta warriors entombed with the ruthless Chinese megalomaniac first emperor, Qin Shi Huang Di, responsible for the deaths of more than a million people. Here we watched a film about the emperor, though we never saw the end of it because the hilariously rude reception woman returned it to the beginning for another couple who'd just entered, even though we were in the middle of watching it, 'because you should have done your research beforehand.' She was right, of course, we agreed back in the car – it was unprofessional of us to just roll up at an important teddy bear museum dedicated to a make-believe Mr Bear without having first thoroughly researched the attraction.

Now we're parked at South Haven Point on the coast of the Isle of Wight. The kids, watching *The Jungle Book*, are up to the bit where Baloo in a grass skirt is dancing to 'I Wan'na be Like You'. It's raining and we're waiting for it to subside to go hunting on the beach for 140-million-year-old iguanodon footprints.

'Guess what I'm imagining?'

'I don't know,' says Dinah.

'I'm imagining I'm on *Desert Island Discs* talking to Kirsty

Young. I've just chosen "I Wan'na be Like You" as my third record.'

She laughs.

'Kirsty Young's looking perplexed because "I Wan'na be Like You" doesn't go with my other record choices, which are mainly Haydn and Bach.'

Dinah laughs.

'Haydn and Bach!'

'I've *become* cultured. It's twenty years from now.'

'I see. And you're such a successful writer you're on the show?'

'Yes.'

She laughs. 'Am I still your wife, or do you have someone more cultured?'

'It's still you.'

'Good. And your favourite music is classical?'

'Yes.'

'So no Bruce Springsteen, then?'

'No.'

'"Uptown Girl" by Billy Joel?'

'You know I only like *some* Billy Joel records, Dinah.'

She laughs.

'Kirsty wants to know the significance of the record. I've been imagining telling her about the trip. The kids watching *The Jungle Book* the whole time.'

'Five months travelling with small children,' says Dinah, putting on a Kirsty Young voice. 'It must have been jolly hard.'

'It was, Kirsty.'

'And how did you wash, if you don't mind my asking?'

'We didn't a lot of the time, Kirsty.'

'That must have been hard. For your wife especially.'

'Not really, she's a bit of a skuzzy cow, Kirsty.'

Dinah laughs.

'Your next record, Sir Ben?' she asks.

'Billy Joel's "Piano Man",' I say.

'Not "Uptown Girl", Sir Ben?'

'No, Kirsty.'

'Because you only like certain Billy Joel records?'

'That's fucking right, Kirsty.'

After an unsuccessful foray on the beach looking for dinosaur footprints and fossils ('No, I think that one was left by my shoe, Phoebe'... 'No, Charlie, that's another pebble') we drive on to the Isle of Wight Zoo in Sandown. The zoo has the largest collection of tigers in the UK, along with jaguars, leopards and, in an inventive enclosure, two lions we see licking their paws on top of an upturned mocked-up zebra-striped jeep, the jokey inference being the rangers inside have been gored to death.

'Distasteful?' Dinah asks.

'I like it.'

'Really?'

'Yes. Although they should throw a bucket of offal in there, too.'

'The entrails of the rangers?'

'Exactly.'

For days now, home is all we've been discussing. I've been telling random strangers at the Beaulieu National Motor Museum in the New Forest, on the boat to Brownsea Island, at Corfe Castle, how many days we have left, how many thousands of miles we've driven, how many months we've been away. In Lyme Regis just seeing a car painted the same turquoise as the Brighton seafront railings made Dinah call me over: 'Look, what does that remind you of?' But now, with Brighton just over the horizon, strangely we're both pretending it's not happening. In fact, on the Fishbourne–Portsmouth ferry it's the first acknowledgment of the day that we'll be home tomorrow when Dinah rings a few friends to see who's around. Sally and Richard are away. Bee and Simon, Banny and Pips, Keely and Jeff, Vic and Dan, Laura and Steve – they've all made plans.

'No one around?' I ask Dinah.

'Did you imagine some tearful homecoming?'

'I did a bit.'

'Ahhhh, love,' she says.

In Portsmouth for our 434th and penultimate attraction of the trip, we're on the HMS *Victory* in the city's Historic Dockyard. It's the oldest commissioned warship in the world and still the official flagship of the British Navy. Charlie's asleep in the buggy so while Dinah watches him and calls the hire car company to arrange the drop-off tomorrow, I'm on the tour with Phoebe. It starts in the day cabin containing Nelson's original writing table. I listen to the commentary, taking notes, while Phoebe sits at my feet copying letters of the alphabet from a ripped out page in my notebook. Each time she finishes a page she hands it to me. As the guide tells us how young seamen knocked weevils out of their ship's biscuits and older sea dogs simply ate them in the dark, I hold up the requisite number of fingers to indicate how many letters Phoebe's copied correctly. She nods, and holds out her hand for more paper. We climb ladders, duck along low-ceilinged gun decks. On the top deck the guide tells us how Nelson was mortally wounded by a French musketeer at the Battle of Trafalgar and I notice Phoebe's leaning on the brass plaque marking the spot where he fell. It's engraved and flush to the deck. Years earlier it protruded. I remember because my mum fell over it when we visited this ship. Reading the plaque after she'd tripped up on it, what she said next became a family joke: 'No wonder Nelson fell. It's bloody lethal that is.' Time flattens gratifyingly out. I was here with my family. And now Phoebe, the day before she starts school, is here with me. Like the Red Arrows in Padstow, it feels like another goodbye.

Leaving Portsmouth, joining the A27, we see our first sign for Brighton. Forty miles, it says. I look at Dinah. We're supposed to be visiting Arundel Castle. It's in the blue folder.

'Tempting to carry on home,' I say.

'I know.'

'Shall we?'

Dinah smiles. 'OK.'

'Kids!' I look in the rear-view mirror. 'Guess what?'

'What?'

'We're going home!'

'Home!' says Phoebe.

'Yeah.'

'To our hotel?'

'What have we done to them?' Dinah laughs.

'No, home, Phoebe. The house where you have your own bedroom. Do you remember your own bedroom?'

She nods and smiles through the thumb she's sucking.

'We're going home, Charlie,' says Phoebe. 'You remember home where we have our own bedrooms?'

'Dinah, for one last time, *The Jungle Book* please.'

Dinah finds the film.

'But first.'

Dinah takes out her iPhone and syncs it to the car stereo. 'Homeward Bound' by Paul Simon comes on. It's a song we've played intermittently since Liverpool. We've played it so many times we have new lyrics the kids have learned.

'Ready guys?'

''K,' says Charlie.

'Phoebe?'

She nods.

'One last time then, guys.' I open my window. Dinah does the same.

And as Paul Simon sings about sitting in a railway station, with the ticket for his destination, we chorus, 'We're sitting in a hired Vauxhall Astra, got a ticket for the Dewa Roman Experience, Chester.'

Then I point at Phoebe in the back seat. 'On a tour of night stands, our blue folder and Johnson's wipes in hand,' she sings.

I swivel round and point at Dinah. 'And every stop is neatly planned for a guidebook writer and his four-man band,' she sings. I take my hands off the wheel and raise my arms. 'Altogether guys.'

And we're all singing now, practically shouting: 'We wish we were, homeward boooooounnnnnd. Home, where our thoughts escape us, home, where our music's playin'. Home, where the Saga mini-break, jelly-making pensioners with bath slip mats and brand new tea cosies lie waitin'...'

And I point at Charlie, who quietly says the final line, his eyes darting self-consciously round the car, as we all stare at him preparing to burst out laughing, '... silently for me.'

The whole way round, through all the hardships, the highs and lows, my dad's death, the bat attack, the car accident, my kidney stone, I've imagined this moment. I've pictured myself choked. I've seen Dinah and me crying. But now it's here I just feel hollow.

We drive the showbiz route into Hove, exiting the A27 on the London Road junction so we come in via Grand Parade, passing the Royal Pavilion and the lit up Palace Pier.

'Hello pier!' the kids shout through their windows.

Along the seafront I smell the sea and I can hear the seagul and the screams from the Super Booster ride at the end of pier. It's 6 p.m. and West Street is already thronged. We p

twinkling lights of The Grand and the Hilton Metropole. The burned out West Pier is a silhouette in the fading light. Over the top of it the murmurating starlings swirl in enormous geometric shapes, forming implausible giant rhombuses that melt into squares, cylinders and other mathematical shapes. We pass the crenulated line of beach huts along the esplanade, the pristine lawn of Hove Bowling Green. The setting sun bleeds shimmering gold into the darkening sea as I turn up our road. I crawl to a stop outside our house. The milometer records 6,234 miles. Added to those we did before the accident in our car the trip total is 8,023 miles.

The doormat's buried in post and the hall carpet is filthy. In the living room, one of the shutter louvres is splintered. There's a black scratch on the wooden floor. The kitchen flooring has lifted. It's bouncy underfoot. Upstairs in our bedroom the chandelier hangs from the wall, its bracket yanked off. The wooden bathroom floor smells rotten. The carpet in Charlie's bedroom is stained.

'What the hell were those pensioners doing?'

'I don't think they were pensioners, love,' says Dinah, back downstairs.

We unload the car and, taking the bathroom things up, I find a balloon with the letter L on it. It starts to make sense – the stiletto marks in the wooden floors, the heaps of bin bags full of wine bottles and beer cans in the back garden. We notice more damage – the broken shoe rack, a button missing on the oven. A dining room chair is missing a leg, an electric socket is hanging off the wall. Several plants are dead. The lawn grass is a foot high. Countless items of crockery and cutlery missing.

Phoebe's pleased, though. She can't believe the bin bags of her ⸜ks I keep opening up from the study on her bedroom floor.

is it my birthday?' she asks, after the fourth one.

'They're yours, sweetheart. We packed them before we went away.'

'Really?'

'Can't you remember?'

She shakes her head.

Charlie's reaction is different. He cries a lot, trips over boxes and there's no space to push the doll buggy he's remembered that he used to love before we went away.

I find the box containing our bedclothes. I unpack the kitchen and bathroom things. I'm sorting the living room, putting the photo albums back under the telly, when I drop one of the annuals. It falls open at a photo of Phoebe and me on the seafront. We're side by side, walking past the Brighton Sailing Club. Phoebe's behind the same buggy Charlie's pushing around the kitchen right now, while I'm steering the adult one Phoebe would normally be sitting in. She's almost exactly the same age Charlie is now and the caption underneath reads: 'For a year and a half I've been convincing Dinah this is work!'

When I was a full-time, stay-at-home dad I used to tell myself it would be easier when they started school. 'It's just four years,' Dinah would say, when I'd had a bad day. 'It'll go by in a flash.' Sometimes I wished the time away. And now it's gone, Phoebe's starting school in the morning and all I want is to turn the clock back.

Phoebe doesn't want to go to bed after her bath.

'Because I don't want to go to school in the morning. I want to stay at home with you.'

Every time I leave the room she cries for a cuddle. Twice I come upstairs and talk to her. I sit on the end of the bed. 'Give me a quiz, Daddy.'

'You've got school in the morning, pops. Try to go to sleep. W don't you think of the rabbit you'll get at the weekend?'

'But I'm itchy. Talk to me or I'll be itchy. One quiz question. Please.'

'It's late, sweetheart.'

She twists her shoulders in frustration and starts scratching madly. 'One question? Please, Daddy. Please. I'm so itchy.'

'Then that's it, OK?'

'OK.'

'OK, how far away is the moon? Is it a) five miles b) the same distance it is to Tesco or c) 230,000 miles.'

'Noooo,' her legs go rigid like 1,000 volts are passing through her, 'do the voice.'

'OK, OK, calm down. You'll wake Charlie.'

When I quiz Phoebe, for some reason, it's become established I have to do this in the German accent of an SS officer.

'OK, OK. Von quvestion. How far avay is ze moon? Is it a) five males or is it b) ze same distance it is to Tesco or is it c) 230,000 males. If you are wrong, you vill be punished severely.'

'Well, I think it's further away than Tesco,' she says. 'Because that's down the road. Err... is it C?'

'You must answer de quvestion or zere vill be punishments. I haf told you zis.'

'OK, C.'

'Zat is cor-rect.' I pull her covers up. 'Go to sleep zis instant or zere will be punishments that you vill not believe.'

'What punishments?' she says, smiling.

'Come on, pops, it's bedtime. If you want that rabbit at the weekend...'

'OK.'

She lies down, pops her thumb in, takes it out again.

'Daddy?'

'What now?'

'Why do I always suck this thumb?' she asks.

'I don't know.'

'I always suck this thumb because the other thumb,' and she pulls a face, 'doesn't taste very nice. I have a tasty thumb and a yucky thumb. Of course I would suck my tasty thumb. Night, night, Daddy. Turn the light off.'

The next morning Phoebe's lying in a comma shape across her bed, the duvet moulded tightly around her like a sleeping bag. I kiss her cheek. 'Morning, pops.'

She doesn't stir. I open the curtains and pull her thumb out. She smiles and sucks it back in without opening her eyes. I cross the box-lined hallway to Charlie's room. Under the covers, his face is a luminous white. There's a faint aroma of cheese. 'Morning, cabbagey boy.' I kiss his springy cheeks and walk back to Phoebe's bedroom.

'Two sleepy customers this morning,' I shout to Dinah.

Phoebe scratches her white blonde hair at the side by her ears and sits up. Her pyjamas are on the floor. She takes them off when she gets itchy in the night. I hold the bottoms up and she swings round, threads her legs in. I go to sit on the top step of the stairs.

'Train's about to go,' I shout.

Phoebe runs down the steps of the half landing, plonks herself on my lap.

'All aboard!' she shouts. 'All aboard, Charlie,' she shouts more loudly. I make a train whistle and Charlie emerges. He climbs on the other leg. As I descend the stairs on my bum, Charlie works his arms backwards and forwards like steam engine wheels. They dismount at the bottom. In the kitchen I sift through the boxes and find the porridge. I make their breakfasts and Phoebe's sandwiches.

Dinah works for a news wire website that has to be out by 11 a.m. She comes down in her nightie and starts work in the study, occasionally popping her head in to remind me of things: 'I've put her PE kit bag by the front door.'

I dress Charlie. I do the same to Phoebe, putting her shirt then tie on. 'Head back,' I say, tickling her chin with the fat end as I bring it up through the loop. In a small voice she says she doesn't want to go to school.

I keep my tone breezy. 'Everyone goes to school, sweetheart. You have to learn things.'

'I want to stay here.'

'If you didn't go, Mummy and Daddy would get into trouble.'

'Would you go to jail?'

'We might do.' I reach for her tights.

'I do tights,' she says.

After this it's her blue pinafore. I pull it over her head and she pops her arms through. I do it up and holding her on both sides of her head, the way my dad did when he was looking at me, I kiss her in the middle of her forehead.

'Shall I get Mummy to do your hair?'

'Because Daddy is rubbish at hair?'

'Yes.'

Dinah comes out of the study to put Phoebe's hair in bobbles. She reminds me to take the water bottle.

'To the door guys,' I call, after she's finished.

Dinah gives Phoebe a cuddle, tells her she'll have her favourite tea ready tonight – pasta with pesto sauce and a chocolate mousse for afters.

'And for me?' demands Charlie.

'Of course.'

'Y-ay.'

I drop Charlie first at his new nursery. I find his peg. I label his apple with a sticker with his name on it. I change him into his day pumps. I tell Mrs Randall I'll ring later to see how he's getting on. I give him a cuddle. He won't let go.

'Shall we find the trains?' says Mrs Randall, holding his hand.

Charlie nods.

He lets go of me. I turn to leave with Phoebe but Charlie breaks away from Mrs Randall. He wraps himself round my leg. Mrs Randall picks him up. He reaches for me with both arms. I take him from her. He koalas around me. I kiss his head and tell him what a brave boy he is. That he's having chocolate mousse later.

'I want,' he just shouts, his head back, 'to stay with you and Phoebe.'

'But Phoebe's going to school too.'

Mrs Randall prises him off me, fingertip by fingertip.

'Let's find the trains,' she says.

Charlie flings his head back and wails.

'We can wave to Daddy through the window.'

Mrs Randall carries him to the window. He's still reaching out for me as I leave the room. Walking down the stairs I hear Charlie shouting, 'Daddeeee! Daddeeee!'

'Charlie is only two,' says Phoebe, as we exit the front door. 'So he cries. I don't cry, do I?'

'No,' I say, and outside looking up at the window I see Mrs Randall holding Charlie. But he won't look at me. His face is buried in her shoulder.

Numbed, I drive to Phoebe's school off Church Road in Hove. I don't really hear what she's saying. I'm thinking about Charlie. I find a space. I turn the engine off. It's five minutes before the gate opens.

'Do you want a little chat?' I ask Phoebe.

I undo her belt. She climbs forward to sit beside me in the passenger seat.

'What shall we chat about?' she says.

'I don't know.'

'Not school.'

'OK.'

'I know, what about my new shoes?' she says.

In the heel of each of her black shoes there's a toy – a little doll in one and a plastic cat in the other. I bought them for her in Lymington. She takes off her shoe and lifts the red flap inside the heel and reaches into it and takes out the doll.

'I'll have the doll,' she says.

She takes off the other shoe and takes out the cat.

'You have her cat.'

She hands me the cat.

Through the windscreen I watch children file past holding the hands of their mothers. There are several very small ones in sparkling uniforms that must be in Phoebe's reception year. We play with the doll and the cat. Phoebe races the doll up the seat like it's a cliff face. It falls off and my cat helps it back up. When it's a couple of minutes to, Phoebe says very seriously, 'Daddy, I think we should put the toys back in my shoes in case we forget them.'

I hand her back the cat. She puts it and the doll back in her shoes. Phoebe fastens them.

'There,' she says.

'Are you ready, pops?'

'Not yet.'

She puts her thumb in, leans into me. I stroke her hair. We watch children going in. Phoebe makes remarks.

'I like her hat.'

'That's a big lunch box.'

Eventually she nods at the door.

'What?'

'I don't want to be late, Daddy.'

'Oh, yeah. Sorry.'

'Did you forget I was going to school?'

'Yes,' I lie.

I open the door and grab her stuff – her book bag, her sandwich box, the PE kit and her water bottle. She climbs out. We walk from the car park to the school entrance holding hands. With her cold tiny hand in mine, every time she says something cute I feel myself about to go.

'I wonder if there'll be a hopping club. I haven't told you about my old hopping club,' she says.

'No, you haven't. What is it?'

'Well, it's a club and we hop.'

'I see.'

'It was in my old nursery, Daddy. Jessie didn't want to play. She played with someone else but if she wanted to hop she could. In hoping club you don't have to do it all the time. You can do it if you want and not do it if you don't want to. It doesn't matter – you're still in hopping club.'

'It sounds great, hopping club.'

'It's just hopping club, Daddy.'

At the gate, amongst the scrum of goodbyes, I remind her she's got her favourite tea tonight.

'I know, Mummy told me already.'

She pulls an exasperated face.

'Give me a kiss, pops.'

I bend down and kiss the side of her face. I hand over her book bag, her lunch box, the PE kit and her water.

'Daddeeeee!' she says.

I bend down. She twists my head so she's talking in my ear.

'I can play with Mr Nobody,' she says, smiling.

I stand up.

'What do you mean?'

'If I can't find anyone to play with. I can play with Mr Nobody.'

'Good idea.'

'Daddeeee!'

I bend down again.

'Cuddle,' she whispers in my ear.

I cuddle her. I whisper in her ear. 'I love you.'

There are older children lined up the other side of the gate.

The teacher bends down, puts her hands on her knees, and asks Phoebe's name. Chewing the end of her water bottle self-consciously Phoebe whispers it. The teacher bends down again and cocks an ear. Phoebe says it again.

'Well, Phoebe, this is Ella,' says the teacher. 'She's in year six. She will take you to your classroom.'

Ella takes Phoebe's hand. The teacher smiles and holds her heart at me and Phoebe walks into the playground with Ella. I watch her go. I watch her until she's round the bend and out of sight. She doesn't look round once. I walk back to the car through the knot of children arriving. My little girl, my tiny little girl is in school. I drive home saying it over and over to myself: my tiny little girl is in school. In the house Dinah's waiting for me in the kitchen.

'Well?'

'She was great.'

'Charlie?'

'Not so good.'

'What about you?'

'Not so good.'

'Come here.'

And when Dinah hugs me I can't hold it in. Great fat tears bubble up and explode from my face. Dinah tries to pull me back. But I press my face further into her shoulder.

'You're picking them up at lunchtime!'

Phoebe's only doing half days for the first term. The same hours Charlie's starting at.

'I know. But…'

'She'll be bossing them around in no time,' says Dinah. 'Put that kettle on. Mary called by the way. She's coming this weekend. I've booked the Ginger Man restaurant.'

'Good.'

'I thought you'd be pleased.'

I put the kettle on. Dinah returns to the study and when I come in to give her the cup of tea, I say, 'Listen, I know it's too early and not a great time to suggest it but you know how long it takes to plan.'

'Oh God, what?' says Dinah.

'We'd do it differently. Less driving. Not so many one nights at places. And obviously we wouldn't have so long. But take the whole summer off again. What do you think? *Frommer's: France with Your Family*? Surely nothing can go as wrong next time.'

AUTHOR'S NOTE

The draft guidebook copy sections in this book were not ultimately used by Frommer's in this form. The guidebook was published as *Frommer's England with Your Family* (Wiley, 2010).

ACKNOWLEDGEMENTS

Thank you to Jennifer for suggesting I write this book, Mark Henshall for his support and encouragement, Anna for all her help and patience, and my two kids, Charlie and Phoebe, for going along with it all.

@BenHatch would like to thank:

@Allison_Rushby
@andrew_mueller
@baculator
@brendadhill
@Briggy44
@catherinecooper
@catherinemack
@crimeficreader
@destinylover09
@DollysDay
@FannyIngabout
@figgylover64
@frankellet

@goodasgearon
@HelenWilde1
@HellenBach
@isabelcostello
@jazzxchantoozie
@jennycolgan
@Joannechocolat
@Judyastley
@julie_cohen
@keris
@kirstylou29
@ladytubedriver
@LakesPR

@lisajewelluk
@lizfraser1
@LondonBessie
@LucyLawrie1
@M_Hensh
@MarieMann1
@MaryECostello
@mattwhyman
@MichaelConnor
@mikegayle
@NikkiiNola
@paul_steele
@petefork

@QuirkyGuide
@RaymondLeBlanc
@ReaLouiseWener
@SophyNorris
@Stephenfry
@SussexMummy
@T_in_DXB
@TeganChapman
@trishaashley
@vpeanuts
@wendyfreckles
@WriterDove
@writermels

and:

@_flamboyant_
@_Lauren_Walker_
@_marklin_
@_trashionista
@1_Lovelife
@101AmberGreen
@1969Steve
@1PeteDenton
@1shielariley
@1stNovelbyLynn
@2morrowknight
@3songsnoflash
@411homebiz
@4fifty1
@501places
@91Felicia
@AAMBOOKCLUB
@AaronQuinnBooks
@abbiekochmann
@AbbieSouthsea
@abbytur
@AbieLongstaff
@Abiwhere
@ABrosnancron
@ACarrollSmith
@ACharles_writer
@achuka
@adam_leigh
@adammarek
@AFoggyMama
@agnonia
@ahmpreston
@AlanReynolds2
@alansclayton
@alanshare
@alanya_turkey
@AlaskaMiles
@AlaskanNovelist
@alba_187
@albertfountain
@AlbumOfThoughts
@alchemyofscrawl
@alex_landoni
@alexbrownbooks
@AlexGeorge
@alexhammond
@ali_missharibo
@AliB68
@alice_parrant
@alicecuninghame
@AliHarrisWriter
@AliMcNamara

@aliphant27
@Alison_Bruce
@AlisonHoltBooks
@alivicki
@AllenHamen
@AllisonHagen
@allisonpearson
@allseeingaaiiii
@AlmostDrMoJo
@alpacamarketing
@AM_Preston
@AmandaLCowley
@amcconnellej
@AmeliaCarr
@AMHairiSimpson
@amonck
@amy606
@AmyJRomine
@andrea_desherb
@andreaalli
@andreagillies
@andreawrites
@andressilvaa
@Andrew_Johnson
@andrewkdawson
@AndrewMackayBP
@andrewmmadden
@andylimb
@andyUtrecht
@Andyy50
@angie_c_curtis
@aniaahlborn
@anna_smithson
@AnnaLefler
@annascottjots
@AnnCleeves
@AnneMCarpenter
@annesebba
@AnneWareham
@annholmwood
@Annie_Acorn
@annieothenshow
@annmart1
@AnnTran
@AnnWicker
@anthony_mcgowan
@AnthonyJArmitt
@AntoniaChitty
@AntonyARLewis
@AntSaysThis
@AnyaLipska
@ap0emaday

@apartyofseven
@araTHEwriter
@ardisfloro
@arealholiday
@aricochet
@ArniJensson
@ArtforLifeOrg
@ArtMason
@artofbackpackin
@artstarzz
@ashokbanker
@Aspersioncast
@Astrocom168
@aThumper
@authorheathsamp
@authorjentucker
@authorprofile
@AuthorRLynn
@AuthorSJDRUM
@AwhwardProse
@babbleburbs
@Baldychaz
@Baltasar_Wisdom
@banoffees_best
@barbarawaterst
@BarbHanAuthor
@BarnestornJohn
@bbbshaw
@beardazeus
@beatrixcoles
@beckonbalance
@becky_hitchens
@Becky_Shep
@BekiHobbs
@Belgerith
@Belinda_Pollard
@Belladax
@beltonwriter
@ben_cheethamUK
@Benjalou
@benjaminjudge
@benmathaicomedy
@BenMatvey
@benmind
@BenOttridge
@benpratershow
@benswoodard
@berniestrachan
@bernimcgill
@berylkingston
@bethany_ramos

@bev_carr
@BevHamilton
@bevheth
@bexycoleman
@bfbshatch
@bgbcomms
@bgwordsmith
@BigHippyChris
@bigmo75
@BigNormski1
@BigSpeckyB
@bikerhen
@BillieJoWoods
@birdeatsbaby
@bizarroguy
@BJoshee
@BKidsUK
@Black_Author
@BlastedHeathens
@bletchleypark
@blissgirl222
@BlogadsBookHive
@Bluestockingmum
@Boardman_Author
@bobbyc3
@BokaCola
@BonningtonTimes
@bonuschief
@Book_Dads
@BookBoutiqueUK
@bookettajane
@BookGroupAuthor
@BookInformation
@BookishMagpie
@BookNutter
@Books_of_Note
@booksarecool123
@BOOKSforWomen
@bookshop_becky
@Bookwalter
@bookwormink
@bordercollies
@BPuttroff
@BrainyTips
@BrammoCraig
@BranchMeredith
@BrandyRivers8
@brendadrake
@BrenVes
@BrianNCox
@brianpaylor
@BrianPBorcky

@bridelizabeth
@Brightonfeed
@BrightonVisitor
@BromleyEsq
@Broodon
@brooksybradshaw
@BroughtonLass
@buried_by_books
@BurtonBrown
@bxwretlind
@CA_Kendrick
@cafecoho
@calbion
@callytaylor
@calvin_wade
@Camilladresses
@cantabooks
@capesandcorsets
@CaptainBeany
@CarenKennedy
@careyparrish
@CariKamm
@CariPercy
@carlenesharpe
@carolinelam4
@CashLaramie
@CassidyJonesAdv
@Cat_Astrophe28
@catburrows
@CathanLeahy
@cathbore
@CatherineDreyer
@cathkingauthor
@cathryanhoward
@CathyThompsonSF
@catmacdonald
@CatrionaChild
@CatVon_K
@cazar58
@Cazbah88
@cazduffy
@cbEntertaining
@cbLifestyle
@ccjacksonbooks
@cdmeetens
@ceebee308
@CeliaAnderson1
@celias_thoughts
@celinewest
@cewyer
@Chadbourn
@charlenesarao
@charlespooter
@CharlieNitric
@CharlotteBetts1
@charlwrites
@ChelseaFine
@cherilaser
@Cherry2987
@ChiBoolClub
@chicaderock
@chilledoutb
@chloegreen21
@Chocgirl
@ChoosePrecision
@ChrisBellNZ
@ChrisConnel
chrisholm_alex
hrisLongmuir
issiemanby
sstovell
hebutcher

@ChristinaBooks
@Christinekorda
@ChristinesWords
@chriswakling
@Chuck3030
@chukkie58
@ciangobrien
@ClaireCookWrite
@clairejharper
@ClareWartnaby
@cliffjamester
@cliffjim
@clintsteiner
@clivehawk
@CloudRiders
@CloughbrackJane
@cmichaelsbooks
@co_Brighton
@coachpegr
@coachtiaperry
@coco_mum
@colegamble
@colin0117
@Comedyscreen
@conjensen
@ConniePhoebe
@contentqueen
@CoolStuffKorea
@coombemill
@copywriter_1
@Cornflowerbooks
@CosmicGrunge
@crankytwat
@Crazycanuckblog
@CRentzenbrink
@culturecurry
@CustardShortage
@Cynbagley
@D_L_Wells
@dagraystone
@DaiGoch
@daisychez
@dakotabanks
@DameCrusty
@Damian_Barr
@damianh43
@damianwcomms
@Dan_Dewitt
@danboyo896
@DancinTravelbug
@DanielaMarchesi
@danielaudet
@DanSmithAuthor
@DarleneQuinn
@DarrenCockle
@DatersEd
@DaveSargant
@davetherave1947
@David_Griffiths
@David_Spitro
@davidbainaa
@davidgatehouse
@DavidWilliams90
@DB_Henson
@dcPriya
@ddelamaide
@DebiAlper
@DeborahFrancis
@Debs_100
@debsylee
@DeeDeTarsio
@Deepu_DJ

@DEKarlson
@demurtales
@DeniseBayes
@DeonEstus
@Derek_Haines
@DerekBlass
@derekf03
@Desirel
@Diana_Townsend
@DianewasHR
@Dickinson_Matt
@dietjustice
@DimpleT123
@DinahLiversidge
@DionneLister
@discocat32
@DiverseTraveler
@DJConnellAuthor
@djtbuell
@dla1950
@DocNoir
@dodgybard
@dogtaniantastic
@donkeymouth
@Donnashc
@DonovanCreed
@DorothyDreyer
@DorothyHardie
@DorothyKoomson
@DottydeBono
@douglasackerman
@DouglasDiTore
@douglassteve
@drABurton
@DragoRigel
@dreamsofwriting
@DrEddyMD
@DrJeffersnBoggs
@DrKenBMoody
@dswalkerauthor
@duskyazure
@DW96
@Echo_McCool
@ecmarkety
@EddieClaytonUS
@EddInburgh
@edgetsready
@edhoganderby
@EditorEleanor
@EditorialHell
@edugel
@EILEENFORYA
@eileenkoch
@EJ_Mack
@ejacksonauthor
@EJWoolf
@ElizabethEmanue
@elizagreenbooks
@Elizjhaynes
@EllaGriffin1
@Ellayanor
@ElleAmberley
@ellebethmiller
@Ellen27
@EllenBookShep
@EllenGhyll
@ElleyWestbrook
@EllisButcher
@ellisesophie
@ElspethMurray
@elyseusineace
@Em30b430

@EmApocalytic
@EmerMcCourt
@emily_barr
@EmilyBenet
@emilyharvale
@EmlynReesWriter
@emma_darwin
@Emma_Silver
@EmmaB4
@EmmaBurstall
@EmmaDowd
@emmakaufmann
@EmmaKnott
@emmapublicwords
@emmawhyman
@emmboglen
@EmpireLore
@EndpaperTheatre
@EnriqueLawson
@ephraimchizzy
@ePrintedBooks
@epublishabook
@EriKaldor
@ErikAtwell
@ErikLynd
@erinhuckle
@ErinnaMettler
@ERMurray
@ErolLincolnUys
@essiefox
@EunoiaReview
@Ev_Bishop
@eva_hudson
@evanscj15
@evilmynx
@evrodream
@EWFF88
@ExamineWriting
@expatdiaries
@fabriziomartel
@FaeEnchantress
@FaithMortimer
@FamiliesChilter
@Farawayhammer
@fartabulous
@fatgreekodyssey
@FebThe5th
@female1960
@Fenlandgirll
@fi_q
@Fictian
@FidoMorgan
@finianblack
@Finikketi
@FionWrighthrow
@FitzHelen
@FKDoyle
@flashwriting
@flunkie42
@fostwrite
@franklandtalks
@FredCuellar
@fredhurr
@FreedomYoga
@freelancejoe
@fridamojito
@fruityteacake
@Fuddington
@fudgecrumpet
@FullertonsBooks
@fumanchuchat
@FundaysDotCo

@FXMC1957
@fxp123
@gabrielle_kimm
@Gaby_1217
@galena_g
@GallacherJoanne
@GaraguTravelers
@GarryandGreg
@Gary_C_King
@garyshield73
@gaylesworld
@geekcat
@geekofhearts
@gemma_m_storey
@geneharold
@GenePoolDiva
@Georg_Grey
@GeorgeEBlack
@Getoninwriting
@GFBArnett
@Ghunibee
@GibbyGibby1
@gill_wyatt
@gillybean64
@GillyFraser
@GinaDWriter
@gincansu
@girlbehind
@girlwithgumption
@GlennCoachTrip
@Gmankow
@Goals_Coach
@GodexGodot
@goodandbadjapan
@goodiespodcast
@GoodMenProject
@GoodMgmtIsNot
@goriami
@gorillaland
@got_angst
@GranceSaunders1
@GrantMGillespie
@grasso26
@greatbigbadger
@greatbritishpud
@GreatLittleMind
@greenwellys
@gregorysgirl86
@gregorystenson
@GSocialMediaPro
@gulliversbks
@GuyLongworth
@h_thompson
@habarosen
@habzamaphone
@HalcyonPost
@halesdaisy
@HannahWeb
@hanzzcobb
@HaplessDad
@harper_jenny
@HarrietFaithEva
@harrisonwriter
@HarryPatterson1
@Hatchigan
@hayleydiamond
@hazedavis
@HazelDeeSmith
@heathercornish
@heatherwastie
@HeathMullikin
@HeikkiHietala

@helen_kara
@Helen_R
@Helen_writes
@helenaeaton
@HelenaKBC
@HelenAyinde
@helenbarratt
@helengrantsays
@Helenhaynes
@helenlooise
@helenmariegrant
@helenochyra
@Helenography
@helensedgwick
@Hell4Heather
@HemmieMM
@henriettabird
@henrigyland
@HillySA
@Hiren173
@historymama1900
@HMCastor
@HolidayPlanner
@holliemsmith41
@hollycave
@HollyHatch1
@HomeStreetHomeY
@huangfrances
@HxCourierEditor
@iamburley
@IamCindyBush
@iamimmon
@Ian_MacGregger
@IanAspin
@IanGJones
@iatraveler
@IBeCaseyB
@ibooknet
@iChatMac
@IconnewsTV
@IconsEyes
@icybloke
@ideabasket
@IDontHateMyDate
@imstevewilson
@Indie_Elf
@InkMuse
@InMyLife
@insidebooks
@ionproductions
@ipondhop
@IriiLopes
@Isabelwriter
@IsbellaMacotte
@isithattime
@ismaetop
@IstoriaBooks
@itcheefeet
@itslinhere
@ixlbook
@JackieJoe52
@JackieRange
@jacoyork
@JadeyWood
@Jameethewriter
@James_Donohoe
@jamesmcknight
@Jamie_LD
@jamiefewery
@JandTree
@JaneRusbridge
@janes_blog

@janesteen
@janet_schneider
@JanetEdwardsDF
@janiecheck
@JaniceHorton
@JanitaChoo
@jannieb18
@janstar72
@JARigsby
@JarroldBooks
@JaseR75
@jasonclampet
@JasonJackMiller
@jasonpalinchef
@Jax2000
@jaxbees
@JayAhrends1228
@jayrjun
@jazobair
@jazzyjenn03
@jbmumofone
@jeandavisonTDT
@jeevanvasager
@jeffarazzi
@JellyHandSlap
@JemRoberts
@JenBlood
@JenHendren
@jeninstroud
@jenkarinwrites
@Jenn_Thorson
@jennaguy
@jenniesbevcom
@jenniewriter
@Jenny Francis23
@Jenny_Meszaros
@jennyalexander4
@Jennybryce
@jennywilldoit
@Jens_E_Huebner
@Jeremy_LinColn_
@Jessica_Culture
@JessicaJConnor
@JessicaNothey
@JessieMiller1
@Jey739
@JGKellerUK
@jhenrybenmore
@jillscribbles
@JillStevenson14
@JiminyPan
@JimStripe
@Jo_amusingart
@JoannaCannon
@JoanneC_2009
@JoChumas
@joemiota
@JoeMullally
@joeypinkney
@joflo37
@johannthors
@john_sealander
@JohnBetcher
@JohnDavisBooks
@JohnJAlbertine
@JohnLCBarnes
@johnmitchinson
@johnoc222
@JojiBeans
@jojomoyes
@JoleneCSC
@jomcarroll

@JoMurphey
@jonathandoylex
@JonathanGunson
@JonathanLHoward
@JonathanMeres
@JonathanTrew
@Jonessuzy
@jonesthescribe
@jonfmerz
@JonLeePButler
@jonpinnock
@jonreed
@JonYeomans1
@joreesnovelist
@JosaYoung
@JoshAllstott
@journoannie
@journojohnson
@JoWolfendale
@JoyceFaulkner
@Joycelynulo
@Jthompsonauthor
@judeet88
@JudithArnopp
@JudithHaire
@judithkinghorn
@JueShaw
@JulesCarey
@Julewilson
@JuliaCatherall
@juliajoanneb
@juliasamantha
@JuliaWordFire
@julichilliard
@Julie_Corbin
@juliekibler
@JulieLoomer
@juliemcgrory1
@Juliet_Moore
@julietgreenwood
@JulietteSobanet
@JulieYeudall
@jumblyMummy
@juniewal
@justfara
@justinbengry
@JustinBog
@justincassey
@JustinPollard
@jvonbargen
@jwironmonger
@kadelopa
@KaiMerriott
@Kanhakaren
@karenclarke123
@KarenGowen
@karenjeynes
@karenstivali
@KarlDetKenProDJ
@KateDagnall_
@katelordbrown
@KateSpencer2go
@KatherineOwen01
@KathFinney
@KathrynBooth
@kathy136
@kathyferber
@KatieLahani
@katyreganwrites
@KaypeeLondon
@kbabele
@KeithClark

@KeithSouter
@KElliott4real
@kemari
@kennhoss
@kentlife
@KeriLake
@KerriNTurner
@kevinkjh22
@kez007
@kfordk
@KidsFriendly
@kidtravel
@KimberlyWithNoE
@kimcormack
@kimmswriting
@KimTheBookWorm
@kindleauthors
@KiplingCaz
@KirkusMacGowan
@kirstendeanne
@KirstyCrawford
@KittyCostanza
@KittyGiggs
@kittywriter
@kizzy_bass
@kong_soeun
@koumantakis
@kramblings
@ktu35114
@l_millarwriter
@lablahblah
@labrow
@LaceKate
@LaChatNoir
@Lady_Byron01
@LaMoglie
@Lanky_Mcstubs
@LARGEjenny
@LariDonWriter
@LARSTRODSON
@Lasher_Lane
@latestdad
@Laura_E_James
@Laura_Wat
@laura1264
@LauraAustinNow
@LauraAWNTYM
@LauraCulshawArt
@laurajeanwrites
@LauraSherman
@LauraTyrrell
@LaureEve
@Lauren_2905
@LaurenGL
@laurster
@laydilejur
@lazycat1
@ldrlovepoems
@LeadToday
@Lee_Cobaj
@legallyanil
@leone_annabella
@Lesism
@LesleyCoburn
@LesleyHoldway
@lesrice45
@letgohealthy
@lethers
@LevertonWrites
@Libbypoetry
@LicenseToShine
@liddersmum

@lifetwicetasted
@Lillian4444
@limebat
@LimpingGod
@LindaCHoward
@LindaGreenisms
@lindamclay
@lindamcleod14
@LindseyHolland
@Lindyloocher
@Linguagroover
@lisadon11
@lisamarie20010
@literaryconsult
@Litopia
@littleredwriter
@Livbet
@lixygoose
@Liz_A_Marshall
@liz_fenwick
@lizfielding
@lizmacniven
@lizzie_lamb
@lizzieenfield
@LizzyStevens123
@ljbarton
@LKB418
@lloydpaige
@LM_Marlow
@lockwoodwriter
@Longcroft_Tales
@longjohnstuart3
@lookeastwest
@LooLooWriter
@lornableach
@lotsofcats100
@lotzofjoy
@LoudbirdPR
@LoudWomen
@Louise_Green
@LouiseDouglas3
@LouiseMarley
@Louiseorg
@LouiseVoss1
@LovelyThings3
@lovescocktails
@LPOBryan
@Luanne0
@LucindaTRose
@lucy_callag
@LUHi_89
@LukeRomyn
@lyddieeeeeee
@LyndaLehmann
@lyndz_ward
@LynetteBenton
@Lynn_Shepherd
@Lynnewin100
@lynskeybooks
@LyzaLedo
@m_vasquez
@M3VOY
@Mabesyboo
@maccamason
@mackbrownbooks
@madeleinecook
@Madeline_Ash
@madeline40
@MadLaketweet
@MadsMagnetic
@MagentaSkyUK
@maggiemou

@magscunningham
@MaithaAhmed
@majanovelist
@makedassister
@MamaJHearts
@ManBuysPresent
@mancbird30
@manchestermums
@MandaJJennings
@mandiekemp
@manfajyoung
@Manfymoomoo
@Manontopbook
@mara_mum
@marcbatez
@mariaAsmith
@mariadoc
@Maribeeb
@MarilynMountfor
@MarjacqScripts
@Marjerrison
@marjieN
@MarkAndrew88
@markbooks
@markchambers
@markknightauth
@marksporter
@MarksterTroster
@MarlenaFrank
@Marques_Lewis
@marshisms
@martineades
@martinipen
@martinlake14
@MartinLastrapes
@martinpalander
@Mary1luv
@maryinhb
@marypmalcolm
@masterkillercat
@matimage
@mattdunnwrites
@MattGCraig
@matthaig1
@matthewparisi
@matthwrites
@MattLeveller
@mattlynnwriter
@matttdillon
@MAWidner_Writer
@Maxanna1960
@maxkinnings
@mcrogerson
@MDeAbaitua
@mduffywriter
@meandmybigmouth
@Meentje63
@MeetMissy24
@MegjKingston
@Melanie_McC
@MelanieLewicka
@melanofinnocent
@MelChurcher
@Melcom1
@Melissafmiller
@melissahales
@MelodyIsWriting
@melrosemutt
@mepatterson
@merrybawz
@MichaelDola
@MichaelJSealy

@MichaelLogan
@MichaelRayD
@micheleandjel
@michellebetham
@michellejnorton
@michellepauli
@MickOweis
@midnitemurmurer
@mikecail
@mikeco158
@mikegothard
@MikeH55
@MikeJarman
@MikePannett
@mikeydonartin
@milehighpeople
@Milla64
@minibreakmummy
@MinistryOfMum
@MiriamWakerly
@mirunace
@missanyjenkins
@MissHaunted
@missielizzieb
@Missus_Cee
@MissyBiozzare
@Mistaken_Magic
@mistersedge
@MistyDietz
@mizzlizwhizz
@mohammedosam
@mollyflatt
@mollygreene
@mollymog2
@Monica_Devine
@Montberte
@mooglesac
@moonduster
@MorrisDance
@mouse_mallow
@Mousselmal
@Mr_Byrne
@Mr_Frodo_esq
@Mr_Matt_Reilly
@MrJamesKehoe
@mrjosephwynne
@mrpar70
@MrsCeeeCeee
@mrsdextrose
@MrsJackcabnory
@MrsMiddleham
@MrsPogleswood
@mrssc_scloset
@MrsTad
@MrsTee
@Ms_Annie_Cake
@msmac
@mt_nickerson
@mummylawyer
@mummyneeds
@mumphLT
@MurrayChristine
@MWheelaghan
@myetcetera
@mylesbevis
@MyNextRead
@MySOdotCom
@Mytwobunnykins
@Nadclo
@nankichawla
@nastybob
@nathaliemholmes

@NayamkaWard
@NCawood
@ncmpublishing
@ncottrill
@nealdoran
@NecoleStephens
@neiljones
@NeoRenfield
@nessatulip
@NettieWriter
@NeverMindBotox
@newcassie
@newspapernovel
@newsviewer
@NGillson
@niallfirth
@Niamh_Greene
@NiamhClune
@nicci_cameron
@niccicloke
@NicholasDrumm
@NickAhad
@NickMillward
@NickShamhart
@nickwastnage
@NicolaMegson
@NicoleDwrites
@nicolenenninger
@NiecyOKeeffe
@Nigel_Cook
@NikkiGoodman1
@niknokiniknack
@ninabellbooks
@NJohn5
@NLPSuccess
@NobuMBlanks
@noelle_clark
@NotLizJones
@NoToTheRight
@Notyetpublished
@Novelicious
@NovelKicks
@novelspot
@NoWayImCool
@NSGreatDictator
@NykiBlatchley
@olivecollins
@olsbasingtweets
@omartyree
@omerkarapinar
@onemorepage
@onevoicesmiling
@oneworld365
@OriginDisorder
@ostrich4
@pactarcanum
@pamelahyan
@Pamreader
@pAmsLoVe
@pandorabullet
@PandoraPoikilos
@papaetpiaf
@parkerbats
@patershaven
@PatNewcombe
@PattyDown
@paula_bowes
@Paula_K_Lewis
@paulanthonyspen
@PaulaRomances
@PAULinIDLE
@pdreadfuls21

@peewitsunshine
@PeggyBechko
@penelopeyoung
@PenPendragon
@petabeeuk
@Pete_Grimm
@petegable1
@petegable888
@PeterCarroll10
@PeterHobbs1
@peterjonesauth
@PeterLavers
@PetsChronicles
@Phantomimic
@pharr2
@philip_parry
@PhilipCJames
@PhilipFaiers
@PhilippaJane
@PhilTrenfield
@PhoebeRanderson
@pichetsinparis
@piercebooks
@Pinkfox56
@Pipbest
@PiperBayard
@platinummind
@playbythebook
@playliststory
@PoetryPleeze
@Polenth
@Polly_M_Gordon
@pollywilliams
@PomIAmWrites
@PooFaceMcGhee
@pops131
@PoshSalty
@positivesarah
@PoultonSmith
@pramjitnathan
@preselimags
@PrestonEhrler
@pricklychicken
@prjenni
@ProducerNicky
@prof_elemental
@ProNetworkBuild
@proscans
@Prune1167
@PT_Writer
@PublishingGuru
@publishingtalk
@pursuitvacation
@queenofparks
@Quintonius
@QuixoticKatie
@rachaelhale1
@rachaelphillips
@RachCarter
@RachLpoll
@radiogal126
@radiotabu
@rainbowlem
@rainedonparade
@RamaPatankar
@Ramikantari
@ramjeebhai
@raschatz
@Rbrutti
@Reader_Writer
@readinasitting
@ReadingDickens

@ReadWriteLuv
@rebeccaebrown
@rebirthplace
@Red_Books
@RedBookReview
@RedMojoMama
@RedMummy
@Reflectionsco
@reflexrox
@reggieridgway
@ResearchEmer
@RevSRobinson
@RGMckay
@RhysOJenkins
@ricardobell
@Richard_Hardie
@RichardAsplin
@richardsmind
@RichardWeigand
@ridgwaytim
@RinSimpson
@RjSaxon
@RLMDirect
@RNAdams2
@RobbieBonham
@robbskidmore
@RobCornellBooks
@robertjtownsend
@Roberto_Nacci
@RobertPRifkin
@RobertsoKing
@RobertWRossEsq
@RobinVDM
@robolollycop
@RobRonsson
@RobStevensbooks
@RocknrollaTrvl
@rockthumper
@Rodney_Willett
@RodolfoGrimaldi
@Ron_Leighton
@ronnietaxas
@roomedia
@Ros_Warren
@RosemaryGemmell
@RoseThePose
@RosieGoodwin
@rossmcgill
@rowancoleman
@roxannesmolen
@roystoncartoons
@Rputhran
@rroulliard
@RSMeintjes
@RubeusHagrid236
@rumdoodles
@runpetewrite
@RussWrites
@RustyMcGee
@rutterkinuk
@RyanSoros
@sacredwench
@sadknob
@sally_apokedak
@SallyAsher
@SallyFairyAnn
@sallywriter
@SallyZig
@salpritchard
@SamanthaZ
@sammillsauthor
@Samuel_Clemons

@sandeefee
@SandraCub
@sandrarpsmith
@SandrascSandra
@SanjidaOConnell
@sarah_hilary
@Sarah_Hopkins_
@sarah_tranter
@SarahAddyman
@sarahalexandral
@SarahEngland16
@Sarazon
@SarcyBStard
@SashaHeseltine
@SashaWagstaff
@SaucyGibbonNews
@SavvyGeekSpeak
@sbroadhurst
@scandanaviansec
@Scarberryfields
@scarlett_wilson
@ScarlettBailey
@scransom
@seandodson
@second_time_mum
@SeemaGill1
@seren313
@seumasgallacher
@SGibbsFiction
@sharilow
@SharleyWesley
@Sharonannmarie
@sharongosling
@SharonWoolich
@shatterhand55
@shauna
@shazjera
@shelleybob
@shelleysilas
@SherritheWriter
@shoppingjenny
@Shortlisted
@ShrewUntamed
@siansparkles
@silviaj888
@simeone135
@Simon_Lelic
@Simon_Theaker
@SimonJuden
@sinclairmacleod
@SingtonWilliams
@siobhanmckenna6
@sirra_girl
@sjcoltrane
@SJennison_Smith
@sjskinner
@skmamun05
@slagkill
@sleepysocs
@slippersm
@SMossWrites
@SNFairyTales
@SocialSavvyGeek
@SocialSpud
@SofiaFellini
@soil_botherer
@SolangeHando
@SoLiterary
@solomanInkwell
@sonialakshman
@sophiehannahCB1
@spacejock

@spayne128
@speakingsuppers
@spectoria1
@speedysnail
@spikeykay
@SplendidGregory
@SpockWriter
@SpookyMrsGreen
@Spoonfulofvodka
@Spring_bird
@Sqibby_Kate
@sssambrux
@stacinvestivgate
@starsamaritan
@StarSparkle_UK
@steamingindie
@stebax
@stefandemetriou
@stellduffy
@StephenAmidon
@stephenbooth
@stephenleather
@Stephjsmith77
@SteveCageauthor
@SteveGory
@stevemsocialmed
@StevenPrigge
@stevescoles
@SteveUmstead
@stevieacko
@StevieGodson
@steviemorrow
@SteVorley
@stillreading
@stillsoul
@StormySavannah
@storyofmum
@StPartridge
@stressymummy
@stuart42mac
@stuber
@suburbansparrow
@Sue_YourCat
@sue2point0
@suefortin1
@suehmuk
@Suejleonard
@suemidlock
@suemoorcroft
@Suerow
@SueWilkesauthor
@SufiJohn
@SumayyLee
@Sundaysblog
@sunnyg1r105
@supervixen1
@SusanemRoberts
@susangreenbooks
@SusanHartWriter
@SusanLeighNoble.
@susieporsz
@suzannahhills
@suzelibrarian
@suzyjoinson
@SwankieSister
@SwatiSharma_may
@swattyb
@SWGolding

@swiftstory
@Syepal
@tagwrites
@tailwags_treats
@Takethefamily
@TalesofaTwinMum
@talliroland
@tallulahrosebud
@TameBear
@TaraHyland
@tedcoine
@tedgioia
@TeresaStenson
@TerryAdlam
@tettig
@tglong
@THamiltonwriter
@ThamyDuff
@thatjuliacrouch
@Theadorris
@TheAgentPhil
@TheAngelaClarke
@TheAuthorClaire
@thebookwright
@TheBrightonBuzz
@Thebubblegunman
@thebullyears
@TheCultOfGenius
@TheGrinTweeter
@theidlepoor
@thejimjams
@thekuriousoranj
@theladyofpearls
@TheLostDiaries
@TheMattyCakes
@TheMusgraves
@thenewcurrent
@TheNewStatman
@TheNLVampire
@ThePondJumper
@thepurplediva
@thereviewgirl
@thetvdetective
@thewhitespike
@thezenblog
@ThisIsFleeting
@ThitiaOfficial
@ThomasHTaylor
@ThomasRayCrowel
@ThomasStott
@thompsonfrank
@thorlanesskog
@thwax
@tiberosestudio
@timepostoffice
@TimGreaton
@timmaughan
@Timothy_Hughes
@TimRelf
@TimVanSant
@tinaevaughn
@TinaGlasneck
@TinaRodwell
@tinkertoldmeto
@TodayImReading
@Toltecjohn
@tombennett71
@TomKerevan

@TomSmithGuitar
@tonisands
@tony_judge
@TonyAdamsBuilds
@TonyEvoyOne
@TonyHunterUK
@TonyJohansen
@tonyjohn47
@toodletinkbaby
@tortoiserock
@TotalNerdyBird
@TPG_Rising
@trajneedogsbody
@TransArtGuide
@TravelAhoy
@TravisAPenery
@trinza
@TrishaNicolson
@truesilveruk
@TRWriting
@Tsaksonakis
@tudor_geek
@TVbloke
@twilliams81
@twiterrock
@twokidsandamap
@TwtsFromHistory
@TyCobb_GS
@Ujjwal_krishna
@ukeditor
@UkSarahBarnard
@UlkuR
@UnfinishedCat
@UnleashedWriter
@VaChicklet
@VaJewel
@Valacier
@ValdetSelimaj
@Valhealy
@valuepointorg
@vanessav4
@Vendice_Partner
@Vicki_Lagnehag
@VickyLimbert
@VictoriaBennion
@victoriajane
@victoriaamary
@VictoriaTwead
@VincentZandri
@VinodMadhok
@violabjorn
@VivWatton
@VixBarry
@vmarks1984
@voulagrand
@VvSavage
@W_stonesThanet
@walshhhh
@walterm
@Waltroon
@WaterstoneDorch
@waterstones_cov
@Waterstones262
@WaterstonesAbLS
@WaterstonesEK
@WaterstonesHH
@WaterstonesOxf
@WaterstonesRose

@WaterstonesUoB
@WaterstonesUxbr
@waterstonhat
@Watsonaterr
@waveyourarms
@wearyhousewife
@WebbWeavers
@webomac
@WedgeSandalss
@WeeChrissieB
@welshmumwales
@wendylacapra
@wendyyoung
@whimsywriting
@Whizbuzz
@WillBevis
@WillHorton9
@WilliamPeeps
@Windsor_wstones
@wj_smith
@Wolverhampton1
@wombledavid
@womentoinspire
@wordeze
@WordsOfWisdom24
@wordsxo
@WorstWitch
@WrightForbucks
@WriteNowClark
@writer_at_play
@WriterDe
@WriterinFrance
@writerkcampbell
@writermacie
@WriterRowan
@Writers_Cafe
@Writers_Forum
@writersgifts
@WritersSocial
@Writeychap
@WritingEdgeMag
@writinggroove
@wrysprite
@wstone_holborn
@Wstones_Arndale
@wstoneslincoln
@wstonesSutton
@WstonesWitney
@wurdsmyth
@wyaspcraig
@xenomike
@Xequa
@xkizzi
@yellowjo
@yellowmoonuk
@yoddilove
@Youthlesswolf
@Yvette_Stewart
@ywsanchez
@zencherry
@zerotorockstar
@zipporahs
@zoebristol
@ZoeMillerAuthor
@zsonz
@ZyphireZ